Champagne is for Breakfast

Champagne is for Breakfast

GEORGE BAIN

new press

TORONTO

1972

ISBN 0-88770-161-2 (cloth)
ISBN 0-88770-162-0 (paper)

new press
Order Department
553 Richmond Street West
Toronto 133, Ontario

Design/Peter Maher
Typesetting by Academic Professional and Scholarly Publishing Services Ltd.
Manufactured in Canada

For Marion,
who collected the recipes,
did most of the typing,
and assisted, bottle by bottle,
in years of arduous research

Contents

Champagne is for Breakfast

Now look what I've decanted

—me

*L*ET THE ACKNOWLEDGED wine-enthusiast show his head and sure enough, sooner or later he will find himself eyeball to eyeball with someone who will thrust on him a glass of wine, confected by the thruster's brother-in-law in a plastic garbage-pail in the basement, and demand to be told on which face of what slope in which country the grapes for the wine-concentrate were grown.

I suppose that stamp-collectors, radio hams and cultivators of African violets also have their problems with the resolutely unknowing, and I am satisfied, beyond all temptation to try those other interests, that there are rewards in wine as a hobby far surpassing any that are to be gained from putting kinky-edged pieces of coloured paper in a book, establishing contact with Schenectady, or pressing one's thumbs into the moist, black soil.

Still, that kind of guy can be trying, especially when he insists that it is all snobbism anyway, and declares that if God intended us to drink anything else, why did he give us dandelions? (Or, why did God give us his brother-in-law, the one with the plastic garbage-pail?) But it is not simply to forestall the philistine that I hasten to put it down that I am not an expert. The fact is that while I can ignore an awkward truth with the best of them, there are certain truths that simply will not go away—and that is one of them. The following story is neither original nor new, not that I would be likely to let any such filmy abstractions as those stop me, but it may help to illustrate the point.

Once there was a small luncheon in London, given by the host for the purpose of showing off a couple of great wines, which were served with the labels masked. One of the guests was André Simon, the founder of the International Wine and Food Society, who died in 1970 at not quite ninety-four, cut down in the prime by a life-long preoccupation with food and drink. The wines were a 1929 Château Lafite, which was itself no mere stripling, and perhaps the last bottle extant, outside the cellars of the chateau itself, of Château Mouton-Rothschild 1899. The first presented no problem. Having tasted the second, Simon said that he could not identify it because there could be no more left of what it seemed to be. But it had all the characteristics (one imagines a pregnant pause, a last discerning sniff over the rim of the glass, the furrowed brow) of the great 1899 Mouton. Cigar. First time.

Now *that* is an expert, and there are not many of them around. In fact, there are very many who are entitled to be called expert who could not touch that sort of stunt. Perhaps it does not become me to be asking questions, as the party responsible for what follows between these covers, but still, how in hell does anyone do a thing like that? Consider. The luncheon, as I recall it, took place in the late 1950's. Allowing for the possibility that between 1899 and then, there were a few years in which Mouton-Rothschild made no wine which it put its name to, there might be forty-five or fifty vintages of Château Mouton-Rothschild in being, in at least a few bottles tucked away in someone's cellar. Of course when we say that, we leave out of consideration all the hundreds of other wines which the sample in that glass might have been. But even if we confine it to those forty-five or fifty Mouton-Rothschilds, it must be remembered that any one of them might be a little different from the last time it had been tasted—quite a little bit different if a long time had elapsed between tastings. Wine changes with time: it will be different in a waning old age from what it was at its prime, and it will be different again in its prime from what it was in awkward youth. Thus, to be able to pick that *one* out, even by saying what it could not be, it would first be necessary to have imprinted certain characteristics of it so firmly on one's memory as to be able to recognize them, enhanced or diminished from what they had been ten, twenty or thirty years earlier. It would be like making instant identification of an old school chum at eighty-one by remembering that as a kid of nine he had big ears.

Our memories for tastes and smells probably are the worst we have, largely because we have done so badly at defining the sensations of taste and smell even to ourselves. How do you describe an apple?

It is sweet or sour. How do you describe the difference between two apples, both of which are sweet? Well, the one was . . .um; well, it was sort of like, more apple-ish, you know what I mean? Now go ahead and describe the five greatest apples you have ever eaten. With the years.

All right, how do you? It is in part because we are so bad at communicating ideas about taste and smell that so much of what is written about wine sounds precious and phoney (as a good deal of it undoubtedly is). Even I, an admitted wine freak (freak, used in the modern idiom, is permissible, but we *do* feel bad at being described as winos), even I, blink a little on reading that a wine in some aspect is like a rabbit with which Aldous Huxley, in some unimaginable context, seems to have concerned himself: "Beautiful in its rounded, living sleekness, a white rabbit enchants the eye and hints, at the same time, of the warmth and silky contact of fur with flesh." Now that, admittedly, is sexy writing of a high order. I would even go so far as to say that a wine might have a rounded, living sleekness, but as to the warmth and silky contact of fur with flesh, I am not so sure—although I appreciate the effort.

The small point that I am trying to make is that to know, it is necessary to be able to describe, at least to oneself, and to be able to describe, it is necessary to be able to discern; and that the discerning of the characteristics of something so ephemeral as a whiff in the nostrils or a sensation to tongue and palate and the back of the throat, is damnably difficult. But it is true—and not just of wine—that insofar as the senses are concerned, we suffer not so much from an insufficiency of language as from a self-consciousness that will not permit us to find and use it. Thus "good," "very interesting," "quite nice," "um-not-bad". How is anyone ever going to remember um-not-bad?

So much for that diversion: what we were talking about was the difficulty in knowing wines, knowing them intimately enough and surely enough to be able to say confidently that this is so-and-so because. . . .

There are at least thirty-three countries in the world which produce more than one million gallons of wine a year each; Italy and France both produce more than one billion. That makes quite a pool to become familiar with. Let us settle on France. In France there are, let us say, seven main wine regions (we might as well say that; I have done so, arbitrarily, in this book), all of them producing wines which, even within the one colour, red, white or rosé, have different characteristics. Let us pick one of those regions—Bordeaux. There are, within Bordeaux, five main districts; we will confine ourselves to the most important of them, the Médoc. By now we have greatly narrowed our field. Within the Médoc, there is what is called a classification of the principal chateaux (it is out-of-date, having been made in 1855, and a new one today almost certainly would be longer), and in it there are sixty-one names. And every one of those chateaux makes wine every year.

Do the dimensions of the problem of becoming a Master of Wine (an actual title used in Britain) begin to dawn? Leaving aside such rarities as an 1899 Château Mouton-Rothschild or a 1929 Château Lafite, which will be found only in a private cellar (and not in many of these, obviously), there will be perhaps six or seven vintages of a given Médoc in play on the market at one time—not, of course, in Canada, where the liquor commissions' highest purpose is to get the bottles out of the cases and the cash into the till, but in more sophisticated jurisdictions. Remember that we are not dealing in constants, for wine (unlike liquor) matures in the bottle, and remember also that we are talking about only one small corner, although an important one, of the whole world of wine, and the whole matter of acquiring expertise becomes appalling.

Well it might. But the fact is that the professionals do not regularly go around performing such prodigies of card-index recall as that attributed to André Simon, and so long as pens and notebooks last, there is no reason why they should. They take notes, which is not a bad thing for the amateur to do as well, although I have to admit to being rather haphazard about it myself. But what is absolutely certain is that there is no reason why the splendid variety of wines that is—or ought to be—available should worry anyone but the experts. It is, rather, something to rejoice in; there are so many to try that a lifetime of diligent application would not nearly exhaust the field.

So where do I come in? I have disavowed any claim to the title of expert. However, if anyone wanted to call me a knowledgeable amateur, I would be willing to cast down my eyes, blush becomingly, scuff my toes, and give an absolutely life-like, if bogus, imitation of modesty. Some people build boats in their basements; some carve chair-legs out of unoffending pieces of wood on lathes; some are week-end painters; others sit cross-legged on mats and contemplate the infinite. My thing happens to be wine. In any case, because of a small disc problem, I do not sit comfortably cross-legged on mats, to contemplate the infinite or anything else; I have tried painting and have established beyond possibility of self-delusion that I have no talent for it; all our chairs have the prescribed number of legs; and with wine, it is not necessary to buy a life-vest, as sailors must do (although a nobleman of England, whose name I do not now recall, should perhaps have done so—he fell into his own butt of Madeira and drowned, poor sod).

Does all of that sound somehow negative and defensive? I am neither negative nor defensive about my hobby, really. I suppose, to be brief about it, I could say simply that I like the look, smell and taste of wine; I like the sorts of places in which it grows; I like the fact that it is a natural product of infinite variety; I like its having a long history; and I like the idea that some time, preferably a long time hence, I will uncork a bottle which will come up to some undefined standard of perfection, whereupon I will exclaim, "That's it"—and quietly and blissfully depart for that Great Wine Cellar in the Sky.

Q. *What is the provincial liquor commission?*

A. *About 100 per cent.*

$\mathcal{M}$AN SEEMS TO have been making and drinking wine since shortly after he climbed down out of the trees. The literature on the subject is thin on facts about how the discovery of fermentation was made, but the common assumption is that it came about by accident. Someone left an urnful of grapes for some days while he went about other business. The grapes crushed themselves of their own weight, as they will, the juice was released, fermentation took place, and . . . one hesitates, in the circumstances, to say, Bingo.

The householder returned, and being of a frugal nature drank the no-doubt gooky mess, and discovered that it had an agreeable effect on his tum and on his general disposition. The story, if it lacks documentation, at least has a winning plausibility. What *is* known is that the Egyptians were already making wine a full 5000 years ago; the Phoenicians and Greeks carried it to all parts of the Mediterranean, and the Romans planted vines practically everywhere they went, in the valleys of the Rhône, the Moselle and Rhine, and the Danube.

Wine got good notices in the Bible; there are innumerable references, most of them favourable. Jewish sages attributed curative properties to wine, calling it the greatest of all medicines. In fact, the medical profession itself has frequently spoken well of wine; one notable member, Louis Pasteur, said, "Wine can be considered with good reason as the most healthful and the most hygienic of all beverages." That, presumably, included milk, which his work helped raise to an esteem that eventually put it in every refrigerator in the Western world.

Wine today is a significant item in international trade. It is a part of the everday life of very many people in considerable parts of the world. It is also, on the other hand, surrounded in some rarefied circles with a mystique that is almost impenetrable to the layman. In Canada, it is assigned to that family which "includes every spirituous and malt liquor, and any and every combination of liquors and drinks that is intoxicating, and any mixed liquor capable of being used as a beverage, and part of which is spirituous or otherwise intoxicating". Given that doleful interpretation of wine's place, it has been considered by our law-makers fit to be trafficked in only by public authority, specifically, the authority of the provincial governments, which are in charge of such licensed lusts as Canadians are permitted, lust coming under the general heading of property and civil rights. It is one of the faults of the liquor commissions—of which I seem to be able to drum up quite a few when I put my mind to it—that having been conceived as a means of *controlling* the lust for drink, they have not been deeply imbued with the notion of service to those who would like to yield gracefully to that lust.

The provincial governments do very well out of the drink business; the buyer of *wine*, as I hope to be able to show, does very badly. I don't have to argue—in any event, I don't—that the sale of liquor, meaning spirits, needs to be taken out of public hands. The provincial liquor commissions, to my mind, are perfectly capable of marketing liquor, which is as standardized as canned peas. Take the bottles out of the case, write on the mark-up, put them up on the shelf and deal them off to the customers as they come in. Nothing could be simpler, and if public policy deems it desirable to control the sale of liquor in that way for what is conceived to be the common good, I would be the last—or no worse than the second-last—to say it No.

But wine is different in very many ways. First of all, it is not, except in a small number of situations, most of which ought not to be encouraged, a rigorously standard product. A good wine-merchant searches out a good product for his customers, sometimes in small quantities, and often with difficulty. "Small quantities" and "difficulty" are both anathema to public authority. What, for instance, is any one of the vastier liquor commissions going to do with fifty cases of anything? Fifty cases will only muck up the book-keeping, the annual catalogue, and the boards in the stores—and perhaps engender bad feeling (which it is bad politics to do) if Customer A, who is not only a wine lover but a supporter of the government, gets some, and Customer B, who is also a wine lover and supporter of the government, does not.

Moreover, fine wines, unlike spirits, are not the same from one year to another: a warm summer with just the right proportions of sun and rain will produce a different wine from one which is cold and unrelievedly wet. To this awkward fact, the answer of all the provincial liquor commissions except, in a limited way, that of Newfoundland, has been to pretend that no such differences exist, and for the rest, to adopt the marketing methods of the automobile industry—one model-year at a time. This innovation in the marketing of wine is unique to Canada, as may be illustrated by a few excerpts from wine catalogues in other places. Consider, for instance, this list from Averys of Bristol, an excellent, old established British firm with a particular reputation for offering fine red burgundies:

1969 Vintage

Beaune Toussaints
Vosne Romanée, Suchots
Beaune, Grèves
Chambolle-Musigny
Gevrey-Chambertin, Combottes
Pommard, Arvelets
Corton
Latricière-Chambertin
Mazis-Chambertin
Chambolle-Musigny, Amoureuses

There are five more, but even that does not give a complete picture of the list because those are only the French-bottled burgundies; Averys were also offering thirty-one 1969 burgundies that they had imported in barrel and bottled themselves in Bristol. So, there were forty-nine in all, of that one vintage. Following 1969 in the catalogue were fifteen of the 1967 vintage; fifteen of the 1966 (eight of their own bottling, seven French-bottled); seven of the 1964 vintage (all French-bottled); and following those, smaller numbers of wines of the 1961, 1959, 1955, 1953, 1952, 1947, 1945, 1926, 1923 and 1921 vintages. In total, seventeen vintages and one hundred and six wines. In contrast, the Liquor Control Board of Ontario, with its monopoly in a market of 7,000,000, was offering twenty wines from the same area, the Côte d'Or, a large proportion of them wines of decidedly meagre credentials, and not a vintage catalogued against the name of any one of them. The customer had to make his purchase and take what he was given.

Say that I have loaded the dice in choosing this firm for the comparison and I will have to admit that there may be a *soupçon* of truth in it; in fact, I have already acknowledged Averys' reputation, particularly for burgundies. But it is not one of a kind. There are others in Britain and in other places, that can be cited. For instance, in New York, D. Sokolin & Co., 178 Madison Avenue, was offering wines of forty-four good chateaux of Bordeaux in fifteen vintages, including all the best since 1947 (and a couple of the worst), at the same time that the Liquor Control Board of British Columbia listed a grand total of one (1) of comparable standing (year unstated). On top of that, the customer of D. Sokolin was offered the wines of forty-two chateaux in the 1970 vintage on a basis of pay-now-for-delivery-in-mid-1973. Thus he had before him a great variety, not only of producers, but of years, which means different states of maturity; this, in turn, means a variety of prices. While all generalizations are unfair, it *is* true of all the provincial commissions, differing only in degree, that they offer their customers none of these.

If it is argued that somehow it is the sad but inescapable fate of government commissions not to be able to do better by their clients in these regards, I would offer for consideration the Swedish state list of the wines of Bordeaux. It runs to 105 items, from the most modest regional growths to the most exalted chateaux, red wines and white, half-bottles, regular bottles and magnums, in fifteen vintages.

For the scant service that he receives, the Canadian wine-buyer gets no compensating economies. At the time when the British Columbia Board was selling its one claret of what is called a classified growth, Pontet-Canet, at $6.05 (the price went up later by ninety cents a bottle), D. Sokolin in New York listed four of at least equal standing, Château Giscours, Brane-Cantenac, Lynch-Bages and Belair, at between $39 and $49 for a case of twelve, or roughly between $3.25 and $4.40 a bottle.

The pricing policies of the Canadian provincial liquor commissions are, to put it in as restrained a way as possible, mysterious. In most cases, the commissions flatly refuse to reveal what those policies are. One province, New Brunswick, responds to inquiries about the proportions of the market held respectively by New Brunswick wines, other Canadian wines and imported wines, price mark-ups, discrimination in mark-up between foreign and domestic wines, and other related matters, with the one piece of information that there are two wineries in the province, and then the following two sentences: "All other information requested is not for publication. Further information may be obtained from the Canadian Wine Institute in Toronto." The institute is the trade association of the Canadian wine-producers. If a little more reticent than most, the New Brunswick Commission is not alone in refusing to divulge the mark-ups it applies; nor will it say whether it applies the same mark-ups to imported as to domestic wines. Most will not say. This is a curious attitude in view of the fact that profits from the operations of the liquor commissions flow directly into the consolidated revenue funds of the provinces and are therefore taxes. It is rare in most well-organized states nowadays to find that information about taxes is considered to be no business of the persons taxed.

The three largest provinces, Ontario, Quebec and British Columbia all acknowledge that the mark-ups they apply are different for wines produced within the province, within the country, and abroad. In the case of Quebec, the figures are not disclosed. The British Columbia and Ontario practices are similar. That of Ontario will serve to illustrate: the average mark-up on wines produced in Ontario is sixty per cent; on wines produced in other provinces, seventy-four per cent; on imports, one hundred and five per cent. These mark-up differentials afford the provincial wine industry in each case with a form of tariff protection which the provincial governments are questionably entitled to provide and which the industry is manifestly not entitled to claim. With the sole exception of the province of Quebec, the domestic industry enjoys by far the lion's share of the market, from a low ratio of fifty-five per cent (domestic), forty-five per cent (imported) in Newfoundland, to a high of ninety/ten, domestic to imported, in Saskatchewan.

In late June, 1972, John Simpson, reporting in the *Globe and Mail*'s Report on Business, said: "Perhaps the best measure of the success of the Canadian wine industry is that the production of grapes in the Niagara Peninsula, the major source of supply, will soon be insufficient to meet the demand for wine." This, he said, was the biggest problem facing J. H. Beatty, the then-new president of the Canadian Wine Institute. He also said that the industry was petitioning the provincial government to be released from the requirement that Ontario-made wines be produced entirely from grapes grown in the Province. And, finally, he said that the growth-rate of the industry in Ontario has been about nine per cent compounded annually.

One of the great success stories in Canadian business—it has been so written in several places—is that of the little firm called Domestic Wines and By-Products Ltd., formed by Pasquale Capozzi in the Okanagan Valley of British Columbia in 1931. Its first president was a young Kelowna hardware merchant called W.A.C. Bennett, who later went into politics. After a slow start, Calona Wines, as the firm became known, bloomed in the 1950's and 1960's. By 1968 when (as might be expected, this being a Canadian success story) control was sold for 9.6 million dollars to the US food products firm, Standard Brands, four or more of every ten bottles of wine sold in British Columbia were Calona wines. This, perhaps, is not surprising considering that the Liquor Control Board of British Columbia lists no fewer than sixty-one of them by name, including Calona Champagne, Calona Crackling, Mountain Red, Calona Apple-Up, Calona Royal Red, Calona Still Rosé, Calona Riesling, Calona Royal Port, Calona Cocktail Sherry and Calona Cherry Jack, Berry Jack, Black Jack and Double Jack. The sixty-one Calona wines listed make only three fewer than the combined total of those of France, Germany, Italy, Spain and Portugal, Europe's five leading producers.

The justification for the Ontario government to extend a handsome measure of protection to a provincial industry growing at the rate of nine per cent a year, compounded annually, is hard to find. The British Columbia government, both by discriminatory pricing and the relative non-listing of foreign wines, gives the same generous support to a provincial industry in which the leader already holds forty per cent of the market.

Not only are these provinces bilking their customers, bilking them of a proper freedom of choice, for a start; they are also on questionable ground, constitutionally. The regulation of trade and commerce lies solely within the authority of the federal Parliament, and the discriminatory mark-ups applied in these cases by the provinces constitute both an interference with trade within Canada and an intrusion upon Ottawa's right to regulate the importation of goods into the country. Some federal officials believe that a case could be made against the provinces, although they do not think it will ever prove politically opportune to try to do so. However, according to a rough strategy worked out for any new broadly-based tariff-cutting exercise that may be undertaken (arising out of the so-called Smithsonian agreement in Washington early in 1972), Ottawa will be after the provinces to drop their discriminatory pricing policies. Concessions on imports of wines (and liquors) can be traded for badly needed concessions for Canadian products in certain markets *if* the several provinces can be persuaded to give up protecting their native wine and liquor producers. It is an odd and embarrassing position for any national government to be in.

Where does the Canadian wine-buyer do best? By comparison with his counterpart in most of the larger cities of Great Britain and the United States, he does not do very well in any province, particularly as to choice, but also as to price. However, he does best for price in Alberta. Alberta is one of those provinces which do not divulge their mark-ups, but it is instructive, in light of Ontario's disclosed mark-up of sixty per cent on Ontario wines, that some Ontario wines can be bought more cheaply in Alberta than they can in their home province. Imported wines in all cases are cheaper in Alberta, in some cases, substantially cheaper. Alberta, Saskatchewan and Manitoba are the only provinces which say they do not discriminate against imported wines—Saskatchewan hedges by saying that "basically" there is no difference in the mark-up; it can be assumed that these are the only provinces which do not so discriminate. The regular Alberta list is totally unremarkable, but the Alberta Liquor Control Board (ALCB) also publishes a special-order list of wines held in insufficient quantities to be distributed to all stores, and this list customarily has contained some of the finest wines available in Canada. For example, it lists Montrachet, Marquis de Laguiche, 1969, Chambertin-Clos de Bèze, 1966, and Château l'Evangile, 1966, among the French; Rauenthaler Wulfen Riesling Spätlese, 1967, and Bernkasteler Matheis-Bildchen Auslese, 1967, among the German; and real vintage port, a rarity in Canada. (Since wines appear on Alberta's supplementary list because they are not available in quantity, there can be no guarantee that the several cited here are available now; my purpose is only to illustrate what the oilmen have had the opportunity to drink—and have drunk if they have had their wits about them.) These are fine, fine wines, which would do any wine-merchant's catalogue proud. The list, though, is short, and in the customary Canadian fashion there is no choice between one vintage and another; the commission sells what it has, and when that has gone, goes out and buys some more. The widest choice now available is in Ontario—not that it is ample, or even adequate—and to go with it, the worst prices. I often wonder what the Ontario vintners sell one-half so precious as the stuff they buy; the latter seems to be an extraordinary measure of solicitude for their well-being on the part of the Conservative government. What the currency of this trade is it would be hard to say, but if the wineries are not generous to the Tories at election times, they are guilty of the rankest ingratitude. The Ontario list has improved greatly in the past few years (which is more a measurement of how bad it was than how good it is), but it suffers from being too much subject to politics.

It used to be thought that the best wine-list in the country was presented by the Régie des Alcools du Québec (RAQ). This is no longer true. However, if not so long as the Ontario list any more, its prices are marginally less high. In addition, the RAQ does its customers the favour of publishing in its catalogue the vintage (singular) available of at least the more expensive wines that it has on hand at any one time; the customer does not have to go to the store, pay over his money, and then peer hopefully into his brown paper bag before seeing what beneficent authority has allowed him this time.

My vote for the best all-around wine list in the country goes to Newfoundland. (Loud sounds of mixed horror, hilarity and incredulity from the metropolises of Ontario, Quebec and British Columbia. St. John's more sophisticated than such pinnacles of civilization as we are? The man must be mad. In fact, I am not mad—not, at least, on that point.) The wine-section of the catalogue of the Newfoundland Liquor Commission is not long, but what is in it has been well chosen and is presented with some air of trying to meet the customers' legitimate wishes, rather than in the manner of a grudging accommodation to their insensate craving for what they ought not to have. Thus, under the heading, Clarets, one can find these few sample items:

Château Fourcas Dupré, Listrac, 1964	$4.30
Château Vieille Tour Larose, St. Emilion, 1966	$4.30
Château Durfort Vivens, Margaux, 1962	$7.00

Château Durfort Vivens, Margaux, 1966 (for keeping)	$7.00
Château Saint-Pierre-Sevaistre, St. Julien, 1966 (for keeping)	$5.90
Château Léoville-Las-Cases, St. Julien, 1967 (for keeping)	$6.60
Château Ducru-Beaucaillou, St. Julien, 1962	$7.75

There are other, less expensive clarets as well; a good, short list of burgundies, including a commendable Chappelle-Chambertin, 1966, at $8.60; and obviously thoughtful selections of wines of other parts of France, and Germany, Italy, Portugal and elsewhere. Altogether, a creditable list.

Considering their number, wealth and frequent pretensions to at least a veneer of sophistication, British Columbians accept an offering of fine wines that would be derisory in Ulan Bator. Manitoba's list is well-meaningly inadequate. And Saskatchewan, like Prince Edward Island, New Brunswick and, despite its stirrings, Nova Scotia, is simply uncaring of the wine lover.

But (for what comfort it may be worth), you still have me.

No, Agnes,
a Bordeaux
is not a house
of ill-repute

*T*HERE IS A very great quantity of wine drunk in this world. For instance in 1970, the most recent year for which there are figures available, five countries in western Europe—France, Italy, Spain, Portugal and West Germany—produced 4,110,260,000 gallons, or better than a billion gallons more than the estimate of the total number of people of all ages and descriptions on earth. When it is considered that behind those five countries there are very many other large producers (even Canada, which is not known as a wine country, produces eighteen million gallons a year now) and that a large part of the world's population has never heard of wine, cannot get it, or will not touch it on principle, it becomes apparent that those who do drink it, drink rather a lot of it.

By far the largest proportion of this wine is what the French call *rince bouche* (or even *rince cochon*), the English call plonk, and we call bingo. In other words, it is a liquid in any one of three styles, red, white and, occasionally, rosé, made of the fermented juice of grapes, and containing between nine and sixteen degrees of alcohol. And that is all. No one ever holds it up to the light to admire the colour, sniffs it to savour the bouquet, or tumbles it discreetly on the tongue, seeking out nuances of taste. Most of it is somewhat harsh, but it is pure to drink (in fact, it is a safe mild disinfectant), it aids the digestion, and it generally makes the drinker feel more contented.

Figures on wine production are full of surprises. For instance, although France and wine are almost synonymous, at least in the minds of wine enthusiasts, France nowadays is rarely the largest annual producer. It used to be, when the very large production of Algeria was lumped in, but now the honour of producing the

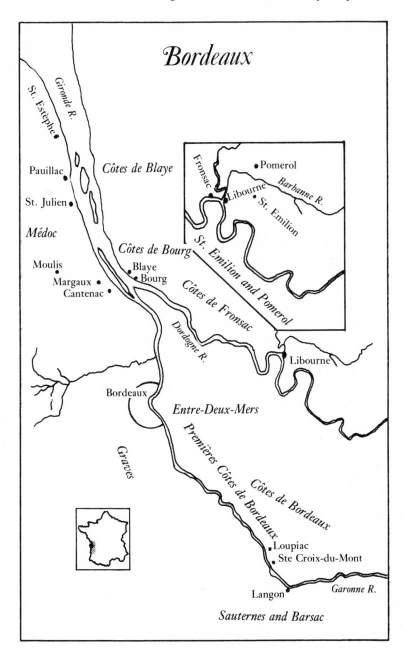

largest quantity most often goes to Italy. Where France remains first, and by a large margin, is as (of all unlikely things) an *importer* of wine. There are, however, other, more understandable realms in which France remains first. One is in the production of *fine* wines, and another is in having the largest single area of fine-wine production in the world. That is the region enfolding the seaport city of Bordeaux, in the southwest of France, from which, in an average year, comes about eighty million gallons of wine, or enough, if it were asses' milk, to bathe the whole population of Toronto (singly) several times over. (Sometimes the output is half again as much, but then the population of Toronto is not constant either, in bathing, or in anything else.)

Wine has been produced around Bordeaux for most of the past 2000 years. Certainly this was a wine-growing region in the first century. And because of accidents of geography and politics, a considerable part of what it has produced has always come our way—which is to say, west. In the beginning at least, this was more a matter of transportation than of taste. Bordeaux is that rare thing, a wine region that is (or very nearly) on the sea. Consequently, at a time when inland transportation was rudimentary or nonexistent, Bordeaux already had built up a trade with coastal western Europe, and particularly with Britain. Then there was the happy, if belated, discovery of an unacceptable degree of consanguinity in the marriage of Eleanor of Aquitaine to Louis VII (Louis the Young) of France; an annulment followed, and subsequently Eleanor married Henry (the about-to-be Henry II) of England, bringing the whole of viticultural Bordeaux, and much more besides, as dowry. That was in 1152.

The region remained English for 300 years, during which time the wine trade was consolidated, much too much so for it to be shaken even by the defeat of General John Talbot (whose name is commemorated in Château Talbot in the Médoc) at the battle of Castillon in 1453. The site of the battle is just a few miles east down the road from St. Emilion; the locals are always happy to direct an Anglo-Saxon to it, sometimes even unasked.

During the period of Britain's long ascendancy, the wine trade with France generally, but particularly with Bordeaux, which remained the principal supplier, had its ups-and-downs according to the state of relations between Britain and France. The "downs," however, never enjoyed widespread public popularity at either end of the demand-supply axis. When by the Methuen Treaty of 1703, the government of England sought to turn trade away from France and towards Portugal, it succeeded in creating a nation of port drinkers without stamping out the thirst for claret, the generic name for the red wines of Bordeaux. (As for the Scots, union or no union—it came about four years later, in 1707—they went on importing claret, and to hell with the excise. But then the Scots have always been awkward in matters of regulation on drink.) In 1813, when Britons at home were (supposedly) denying themselves all sorts of good things in their zeal to do down Boney, the Duke of Wellington, preparing for his final thrust in the Peninsular War, did not allow exaggerated considerations of loyalty or duty to stand in the way of the amenities. For his own table, he ordered from Dublin forty-five dozen of the best claret—540 bottles for the arithmetically slow—and twelve dozen of champagne. (Napoleon, on the other hand, was a devotee of burgundy.)

Long before that, of course, the demand for claret had leapt the Atlantic. Although the American colonists rejected much of what they had brought with them from England, including the monarchy, they kept the language and the taste in wines, both of which from time to time since have been matters of some regret on the part of those in their erstwhile homeland. In 1787, the United States Ambassador to France, Thomas Jefferson, was to be found noting that he had shipped to a relative (lucky relative) six dozen of "the very best Bordeaux wine...of the vineyard of Obrion". That would be Château Haut-Brion, which, incidentally, has been owned for some years now by the family of John F. Kennedy's Secretary of the Treasury, Douglas Dillon. Haut-Brion represents only one of a number of US entrepreneurial incursions into the Bordeaux region. In addition to that, US buyers have become the most aggressive seekers after fine clarets, particularly the biggest of the big names of the classified chateaux of the Médoc. But then demand everywhere has been going up, including places—Japan is one—where a market hardly existed at all only a few years ago. This (a discreet cough behind the hand here) has not been without its effect on prices.

The wine region to which the general title, Bordeaux, applies, consists of six main sub-divisions: the Médoc; Graves; Sauternes and Barsac; St. Emilion and Pomerol; the Côtes de Bourg, Blaye and Fronsac; and Entre-Deux-Mers. To place these, it is necessary to sketch in some geography.

The city of Bordeaux is on the Garonne River, which, some distance *downstream* of the city, is joined by the Dordogne; the two then flow to the sea as the Gironde. Entre-Deux-Mers, to dispose first of a large area but one of lesser importance, is that vaguely triangular piece of land lying between the Garonne and the Dordogne. Sauternes and Barsac lie alongside the Garonne, upstream (inland) of the city. Graves crowds in upon the city itself, up to its southern and western suburbs, and, in places, well into them. The Médoc begins a few miles downstream, towards the Atlantic, and extends along the west side of the Garonne and, after the junction, the Gironde.

Cross now the triangle of Entre-Deux-Mers and continue to the far (east) bank of the Dordogne River: St. Emilion and Pomerol are to be found occupying a position roughly corresponding to that of Sauternes and Barsac, which is to say, inland of the city of Bordeaux. The Côtes de Fronsac are roughly opposite Bordeaux itself, and the Côtes de Bourg and Côtes de Blaye, after about the town of Bourg, face the Médoc across the broad expanse of the Gironde.

In the centre of all this sits Bordeaux, with its busy docks; a short distance away, on the Quai des Chartrons, are the quarters of the wine-merchants, who give rise to much of the port's traffic. Bordeaux is a gracious rather than a dramatic city; its principal monument is its 1300-seat Grand Théâtre, from which details are supposed to have been pinched even for the Opéra in Paris. No distance from the theatre is the centre of the *Conseil Interprofessionnel du Vin de Bordeaux*, where, if you play your cards right, you will be offered a glass of wine, or even two. In the past, Bordeaux has had a reputation for fine food; there no longer is a broad basis for that reputation. Within the city proper, there are two restaurants to which the *Guide Michelin* gives one star, and a short distance out of town, at Péssac, in Graves, there is a third. Of these, the Dubern, in the city centre, is novel in that the approach to it is through a grocery store—and through *such* a grocery store; anyone might be tempted to stop and make his own buffet meal. The restaurant, on the second floor, is reached by stairs at the back of the shop.

Bordeaux produces both red and white wines. In fact—another of those surprising wine statistics—a good deal more of white is produced than of red, notwithstanding the fact that Bordeaux generally is thought of as a red-wine district. Excepting the great sweet wines of Sauternes—and Château d'Yquem has its admirers who say, simply and flatly, that it is the finest natural sweet wine on earth—it is on its red wines that the fame of Bordeaux primarily rests. These include such names as Château Lafite (or Château Lafite-Rothschild; either is correct, but with one *f* and one *t*, please), the most celebrated of them all. Wine has been made at Château Lafite since at least the thirteenth century; the name has been famous outside its own region and its own country since at least the seventeenth, and what comes from Château Lafite now has achieved such an extravagant fame, with price to match, that it is fated to wind up inside only Greek ship-owners, Texas oilmen, royalty and the likes of Liz and Richard.

The term claret is simply what the English tongue has done to the French word, *clairet*, which in its original usage described a clear, light-red wine, a red wine which was light in colour mainly because white grapes were mixed with the red in the making of it. Claret remains light in colour—lighter, in any event, than that sort of polished-rosewood depth of colour that some of the burgundies attain—but not because white grapes are still used. The principal grape varieties are the Cabernet-Sauvignon, the Cabernet-Franc, the Merlot and the Malbec; different districts and in fact different chateaux use different proportions of each to gain their own effects.

Claret is a long-lasting wine; it is not ready to drink the moment it is made. A relatively inexpensive bottle of Beaujolais—and Beaujolais is not as cheap as it used to be either—may taste just fine eight months after the grapes were picked, fresh, fruity, to be taken in grateful mouthfuls. At the same age, most clarets will be still sixteen months from being *in* the bottle, far less out of it again. Even at the age of three or four years, a good claret of a good year may still be so hard, so astringent, as to leave the tongue curled up like one of those paper things that small kids blow out at parties, with a whistle in them and a feather on the end. The claret will not cost any the less on that account. Given time, that same bottle will develop qualities of taste, bouquet and texture which the Beaujolais could not aspire to on its palmiest day. But it does take time, and usually, the greater the wine, the longer the time. One thing that this underlines, of course, is the fact that the most luminous name or the highest price on the wine list will not always give the most enjoyment. As between a 1969 claret of great lineage (not to mention a price that would cause your banker to turn pale), and that unassuming bottle of 1969 Beaujolais, you would do as well with the latter, unless of course it happened to be your particular folly to buy labels. (There are people who do.)

What causes one wine to be ready to drink in six months and on the way downhill in two years, whereas another may not be at its best for ten years and then last for fifty? In part, it is the variety of the grape used, but more importantly, the way in which the wine is made. With the great bulk of the world's wine, of course, the whole issue is totally irrelevant; if it is in front of the customer, either in bottle or by the glass from the cask, it is ready—as ready as it will ever be. There have always been oceans of wine made for everyday drinking over the bar or at the kitchen table, and the market exists, as good as ever. But there also has been a general enlargement of the market for better wines, and with that have come some changes, most notably in the demand for early-maturing wines. It used to be the case that most of the demand for fine wines existed in the stately homes, where bottles were put down by the dozen, and by the *dozens* of dozen, not necessarily even for the benefit of the layer-downer, but in many instances for the benefit of his lucky heirs. No more. Or at least hardly ever. There are new stately homes, obviously, but people do not stay in them from one generation to the next. And of course a lot of the sort of people who used to occupy stately homes, with vast cellars and butlers, now live in stately apartments, with necessarily small cellars, or no cellars, and butlers, if at all, sent in from the temporary-help agency around the corner. On top of that, very many people who do not live in either stately homes *or* stately apartments and do not have the cash to tie up in a cellarful of wine, are still affluent enough to afford at least the occasional good bottle of wine, which they want to drink no later than next weekend.

All these circumstances weigh in favour of wines which are at their best early. Victorian England thought highly of the red wine of Hermitage on the Rhône, which an eminent authority of the day described as "the manliest of wines". Hermitage itself presumably is not much changed but its popularity has declined because it is a wine that takes time to reach that manly best. On the other hand, Beaujolais, which nowadays is a name to conjure with on the wine-lists of half the world, in relatively recent times was still known only to those who made its acquaintance among the carafe wines of restaurants in France. The changing circumstances of the market have also caused winegrowers everywhere at least to think about altering their methods of vinifying, or making, their wine. The wines of Burgundy, for instance, in many cases nowadays are made with an eye to their maturing earlier than used to be the case—and experts have been led to argue whether this is not done at some cost to their ultimate excellence.

In Bordeaux, where the finest wines have always been made in anticipation of their enjoying a long life, the question of satisfying the demand for immediately-drinkable wines has been approached with caution. The wine trade, which does not lack a well-developed commercial instinct, has been making adjustments to the new demand in at least the more plebeian grades. But it does not stop there. Different grapes have different properties and the claret made with a very high proportion of Cabernet-Sauvignon and a small proportion of Merlot will be initially less appealing than another in which the order is, say, reversed. The length of time wine spends in oaken casks in wine-making sheds or cellars has an effect, for the wine derives tannin, a preserving agent, from the wood. Whereas at one time, the great clarets were not bottled until after three years in barrel, they are more generally bottled now after two years, and in some cases, after only eighteen months.

But what particularly affects that initial hardness, which is characterized by the astringency already referred to, is, first, whether some, all, or none of the stalks are left on when the grapes go into the fermentation vats, and, second, how long the skins are left in contact with the juice or must. The stalks and skins contain tannin which is dissolved into the juice—then in the process of being transformed into wine—as soon as alcohol is produced. It is mainly the tannin which is responsible for the astringency of young wine and on the other hand, for its prospective longevity. (Here it might be noted that the colouring matter in most wine grapes is not in their juice but in the inner skins. Since this colouring matter, too, is not soluble in unfermented juice, but only in alcohol, it is possible to make white wines from black grapes—as is done in Champagne, for instance—by removing the skins before the alcohol has begun to form. If the skins are allowed to remain a short time, the result is rosé. The same facts of course account for the fact that white wines in general have less staying power than red wines; being in contact with the skins for only a short time, they contain less tannin.) In Bordeaux, the usual practice is to remove the stalks before the grapes go into the fermenting vats, but the skins are left in contact with the must for two, and in some cases, three weeks. (In Burgundy, nowadays, the common period is about one week. Not so many years ago, it was twice that time, or longer.)

Allowing for the fact that the wine of a poor vintage may reach its modest peak in a short time and that of a great one may take years—in other words, that conditions affect all rules—the sort of general rule that is given for clarets is that those of St. Emilion and Pomerol should be allowed seven to nine years, those of the Médoc and Graves, two or three years more. However, to return to the caveat, it would have to be noted that although the clarets of 1963 pretty well have been forgotten by now, the professionals say that those of 1961, which was the best year since the late 1940's, are only now *beginning* to be ready to drink and that they will go on improving for years more. In other words, if you have some 1963's, drink them; they have nowhere to go but down. If you have some 1961's, keep them; they will be better yet.

There are several points in all of this, having to do with vintage charts, glamorous names and value for money. One of those points, again, is that to lay out $30 to $35 for a bottle of 1970 Château Mouton-Rothschild as soon as it appeared on the wine-list of your favorite Tase-Tee Burger would be worse than a crime; it would be foolish. Better to come back in ten years. However, because a lot of expensive wine binned away in the cellar puts no caviar on the restaurant-owner's *own* table, and because there are very many people who will buy anything so long as it is expensive enough (as a candid wine-waiter once said to me), great quantities of potentially great wines, and especially clarets, are drunk each year before they have a chance even to approach what they might become. Too bad all around. It is not a bad rule with Bordeaux red wines that faced with two of very recent date, the cheaper is preferable. It is another that it is unwise to dismiss out of hand supposed bad vintages; the so-called off-year may be a better buy as between two which are of recent date, *if the price is right*.

In a survey some time ago of what was going on outside the jurisdiction of the People's Dispensaries in Canada, I discovered that Max (The Hat) Zimmerman, the proprietor of Zimmerman's, the World's Largest Cut Rate Liquor Store, in Chicago, had on sale Château Giscours, a claret of impeccable credentials, at $2.49 a bottle, or $26.95 the case. At the same time in New York, at D. Sokolin & Co., already referred to, wine from that same distinguished chateau was to be had for $39 the case, or $24, or $84—or $35 if you wanted to put up your money then to take delivery of a case of the 1970 wine in mid-1973. And there, summed up in the lists of two hard-marketing wine merchants in two highly competitive areas, is the story of what a good, or a not-so-good, or a not-really-very-good-at-all, vintage means, or ought to mean, to the wine buyer. The Château Giscours and the other clarets of equally good background that Max the Hat was offering at his Great Money Saving Bonanza Sale were all wines of 1968, 1965 and 1963, none of them years which are going to be inscribed among the great vintages of all time in the annals of Bordeaux. The various prices for Château Giscours at D. Sokolin in New York reflected the different values attached to different years—the most expensive, at $84 a case, being for the celebrated 1961 vintage. That, as the more alert will have observed, works out to $7 a bottle, case price. If any liquor control board in Canada had had in stock to *offer* at any time in the past couple of years a chateau-bottled claret already of that age and of a great vintage, leaving aside the fantasy of its offering it at that price, songs would have been written in its name.

It is the peculiar conceit of the devout adherent to claret (which constitutes a sort of religion for him), to believe that every wine enthusiast would be the same if only he or she had the refinement of sensibility. Subtle, they will say, is the word for claret, subtle and delicate and a little austere, and with each element of colour, taste and bouquet in perfect harmony. If that is a little precious for your taste, another way to define the difference between, say, a great burgundy and a great claret might be to say that the difference is as between "Wow!", and "mmm!" with a rising inflection. The appreciation is not less, but the claret evokes the more thoughtful expression of it—mmm!—and is capable of evoking it with just about anything that a red wine will go with.

Two days before his play, *The Critic*, was to open at Drury Lane theatre, which he managed, Richard Brinsley Sheridan still had not finished the last scene. He was inclined to that sort of thing. So, thoughtful friends locked him in his room with two bottles of claret and a plateful of anchovy sandwiches. This is a combination of food and wine the felicity of which seems to have struck few people but Sheridan's friends. Perhaps the salty anchovy sandwiches were intended to stimulate the playwright's thirst for the wine, although the lack of a thirst was never one of Sheridan's failings. But a hot roasted chicken . . . that would have been a different matter; or a leg of lamb; or, especially if the claret were St. Emilion (which sometimes has been called the burgundy of Bordeaux), beef, or duck or partridge; or a wedge of cheddar with biscuits, for that matter. Most accommodating are the red wines of Bordeaux.

Moreover, there is a Bordeaux wine for every course, if you happen to be in a mood to favour one wine region with your undivided patronage. There is for a start that very large volume of white wine to be accounted for, and from it something may be found to go with the fish at the beginning, and something else to go with the dessert at the end. (In fact, taking only minor geographical liberties, it is possible to find both an aperitif, Pineau des Charentes, for before the meal itself, and the ultimate brandy, Cognac, for after. Both of these originate not far outside the Bordeaux region, immediately to the north. No one need be deterred from trying the Pineau des Charentes by the fact that I think it tastes like nothing on earth.) To concentrate first on the beginning of the meal, there are the white wines of Graves, which are agreeable, and often very good value for the money. A notch lower on the scale of quality, but also drier, if that happens to be your particular form of mania, and less expensive, which probably happens to be everybody's, there are those of Entre-Deux-Mers. For dessert, there are the wonderful sweet white wines of Cérons, Barsac and Sauternes; those of the latter two are particularly fine. For right in the middle, with whatever is going there, there is the red wine of Bordeaux.

The wines of Bordeaux, red and white, and both dry and sweet in the white wines, are represented in most of the lists in the People's Dispensaries in all ten provinces. Thus far, it is hurrah all the way. However, some of what is offered there is elemental stuff. A wine called simply, bordeaux, will be a blend of wines gathered up from everywhere over the whole wide area; considering that there are roughly 300,000 acres under cultivation in vines, it will be readily understood that a good deal of what is produced, even in the world's largest fine-wine district, offers very little hint of what the longstanding and widespread popularity of claret rests on. But then, here and there, there are examples of the very best in clarets, as we will find in looking at the principal divisions into which the Bordeaux, as a wine kingdom, falls, beginning with the most famous of them, the Médoc, and with Graves, where the roots of the region lie—deep in the sort of gravel that builders use for making concrete.

The wines of each district of the Bordeaux region, principally those of the Médoc, Graves, St. Emilion and Pomerol, have their own characteristics, which the lay drinker can spend happy years trying to master; even if he fails, he winds up ahead of the game. But they also have a family resemblance, and if there are some dishes that all the red wines of Bordeaux can be said to go better with than others, perhaps they are with, say, a leg of lamb, or a roast chicken. Here is a lamb dish from the south of France, miles from Bordeaux, which does not demand a great wine: it would be well accompanied by something bearing simply the appellation of the region as a whole or one of its component districts—or any other red wine for that matter.

Daube Avignonnaise

5 lb. leg of lamb	larding pork
split pig's foot	1 tsp. thyme
garlic cloves	pinch of rosemary
3 large onions, sliced	2 sprigs of parsley
3 carrots, sliced	1 large piece of orange rind
1 bay leaf	red wine

Have the leg of lamb boned and tied. Reserve the bones. Cut the meat into good-sized pieces about 1″ thick, and in each piece insert a strip of larding pork, rolled in thyme and chopped parsley, and a sliver of garlic. Place the meat in a deep bowl with the split pig's foot and a few pieces of pork skin, if available. Add 3 garlic cloves, the sliced onion and carrots, the herbs and the orange rind. Add wine barely to cover and marinate overnight.

BROTH

Make a broth with the bones from the lamb leg, 1 veal knuckle, an onion stuck with 2 cloves, 1 tsp. salt, a sprig of parsley and 5 cups of water. Bring to the boil; then simmer for 2 hours. Strain and set aside.

Remove meat from the marinade, dry well and sprinkle with salt. Strain the marinade and reserve it.

Assemble the following ingredients:

5 tbsp. olive oil	1 tsp. thyme
1 cup coarsely-chopped lean bacon	1 bay leaf
2 crushed garlic cloves	pepper
3 onions, sliced	

In a braising pan heat the olive oil; add the bacon and cook for 2 minutes. Add the onion and garlic and *sauté* until golden. Add the lamb, pig's foot, pork skin, herbs and reserved marinade. Bring to a boil, and boil for about 25 minutes to reduce the liquid. Add enough of the reserved broth barely to cover the meat. Cover tightly. Cook for 2 hours in a 300° oven, then reduce heat to 250° and continue cooking for 1 hour. Remove the lamb and the pig's foot, skim off the fat and reduce the sauce by boiling for 2 minutes over high heat. Add meat from the pig's foot to the sauce; arrange the lamb in a deep serving dish and pour the sauce over it.

Serve with hot noodles or rice. Serves 6 to 8.

*The paths
of glory
lead but to the
Graves*

$\mathcal{A}$T THE COMMAND of Napoleon III, who wanted a showing of the great wines of Bordeaux for the Exposition Universelle that was to take place in Paris in 1855, a jury of Bordeaux wine-brokers sat down and classified the wine chateaux around them (the local Chamber of Commerce having skillfully manoeuvred out of the unwelcome task). What eventually they produced was a table broken down into five divisions, the whole thing calculated according to some laborious reading of the prices that buyers had been in the habit of paying for the wines of the various chateaux over a great many years. The logic was that if buyers consistently paid more for the wines of Château A than they did for those of Châteaux B and C, then Château A deserved a higher place in this viticultural *Almanach de Gotha* than did the others. It seems clear, however, that this was the devious way employed by the *courtiers*, as they are still called, to avoid the inescapable embarrassments that would arise if they themselves were to make the placements according to the test of eye, nose and palate. A calculation of average prices was one thing; a series of value judgements would have been quite another. In any case, the jurists can not have dreamed how permanent a work it was that they were creating; the thing is with us yet.

What makes this the more remarkable (but on second thought, perhaps not) is that the thing was imperfect even in the beginning. For instance, Château Mouton-Rothschild, which had been bought by the intensely proud Baron Nathaniel Rothschild two years earlier, was deemed not *quite* up to being placed in absolutely the first category—a fact which drove the Baron wild enough to adopt the motto under which the chateau has more than flourished ever since: "Premier ne puis. Second ne daigne. Mouton suis!" The spirit of this may be translated from the original baronial as "To hell with you lot."

Whatever justification there may have been for the judges' equivocation over Mouton-Rothschild in 1855, why they felt compelled to confine their *Premiers Grands Crus* (First Great Growths) to four, has not been explained—there has long since ceased to be any. Its wines as often as not now command prices equal to, or better than, those of the four which were put above it in 1855. But Mouton still remains officially only at the top of the Second Growths, from which position it carries on an intense rivalry with the four *Premiers Grands Crus*, and especially with Château Lafite-Rothschild, which is next door, and owned (as it has been since 1868) by another branch of the family.

But more than just having done Mouton-Rothschild in the eye, the distinguished *Syndicat des Courtiers de Bordeaux* performed less than well in that they did not cast a very wide net in looking for candidates for honours. St. Emilion and Pomerol were ignored by the panel as if they did not exist, perhaps because the wines of those parts were temporarily out of fashion, but also perhaps—and the suspicion *has* tended to linger—because the Bordeaux men were unable to bring a wholly dispassionate and professional judgement to bear on the merits of what was shipped through another *entrepôt*, namely, Libourne, on the Dordogne. Nor did they attempt to classify the chateaux of Graves on their own doorstep, except to lift Château Haut-Brion bodily out of its own district and install it, alone of all the chateaux of Graves, among the Médocs. In mitigation of this apparent narrowness, it must be pointed out that they *did* put it among the First Great Growths, along with Châteaux Lafite, Latour and Margaux, and that the wines of Graves, except for Château Haut-Brion, *do* appear to have been in a state of decline at the time. Nevertheless, Graves otherwise remained unclassified.

And yet the *Syndicat* made a classification of the chateaux of Sauternes and Barsac, the makers of the sweet white wines. Château d'Yquem was accorded not only the honour of being put in the first category, but of being put there alone, as the sole *Premier Grand Cru*. Those in the second slice were called simple workaday *Premiers Crus*.

And that, for a very long time, was that. It is only in relatively recent times that the classifying of the chateaux of the other main districts of the Bordeaux region has got as nearly complete as it has, and it is not complete yet. Even now there continues to be no classification, not an *accepted* classification, which lumps the whole lot into one, as sense demands. In so far as the Médoc is concerned, the original work of the 1855 jurists remains unamended.

It would be remarkable if any list made in 1855 and purporting to serve as a guide to relative values should remain perfectly good today. Obviously, there are certain immutable factors: a piece of property which had just the right soil, drainage and exposure to the sun in 1855, does not have them any the less today. Also, there is the fact that the properties involved are so valuable—especially today—that no owner lacks incentive to make the most of what he has. Nevertheless, changes occur. In the more than 100 years that have intervened, some chateaux have made themselves poorer, and their neighbours richer, by selling off portions of themselves. Some, which may have been suffering from bad management at the time of the classification of 1855, now deserve higher places than they were given then, and others, which may have enjoyed singularly inspired management at the time but were not able to maintain it, perhaps deserve lower. And then of course there are the many which, deservedly or not, did not make it at all in 1855 and would like in.

In any case, talk about amending the classification, or scrapping it and starting over, has been going on in a formal way since at least 1959. Nothing has come of it, perhaps because the pressure from those outside waiting to get in has not been as compelling as the pressure from those on the inside afraid of being pushed down a peg or two, or, perish the thought, pushed out altogether. (Where pressure to do something does not exceed by at least fifty per cent the pressure *against* doing that thing, nothing will happen. Teachers of political science may cite this, with or without credit, as the first law of politics.) The 1855 classification of the chateaux of the Médoc (plus Château Haut-Brion) obviously has been good for the sixty-one chateaux which are represented in it, and particularly for the four which were made First Great Growths. (Anyone can memorize four names and a handful of dates—or, more easily, one or two dates to avoid—and given enough money, presto, an instant connoisseur is born.) The advantages to the chateaux which were left out are less obvious, but it is probable that the presence of the classification has tended to elevate the prices of wines of the Médoc generally and to enhance its prestige. In any case, the prestige is undeniable.

The ordinary wine-buyer does well to look at the whole enterprise with a cool eye. The classification can be a useful guide, in the sense that it gives the same sort of testimony as a pedigree, but it is unwise to make a fetish of it. It does not follow at all—as anyone knows who has seen the results of blind tastings made by professional tasters—that because one of the First Great Growths of a given year is selling at two or three times the price of a Third Growth, it is two or three times the wine. The factor mentioned a moment ago, that of the expense-account trade and the label-buyers, enters here. Nor does it follow that because sixty-odd chateaux of the Médoc were put into five classes in 1855, all of those which were *not* included produce only *vins ordinaires* suitable for drinking by hairy-chested truck-drivers in Paris bistros at nine in the morning. That is hardly more true than to say that if a list were made of the sixty-one richest men in the world, all of those left out would be paupers. There are, for the diligent student bent on proving the point, 198 so-called Superior Bourgeois Growths outside the classification—and that is only for a start. (Some of the best known of these, including all that are listed in Canada, will be found in the appendices.)

The Médoc chateaux, classified and unclassified alike, are located north and slightly west of the city of Bordeaux, the first of them not ten miles from the city limits. There is a broad avenue leading out of the city, on which the traveller, having failed to turn on to the poorly marked road leading to all this vinous treasure, soon finds himself, hurtling across the bridge over the Garonne, hell-bent for Angoulême and Paris. Once recovered from this mistake, he can have a shot at finding the D. 2 to Pauillac from the other direction. (Somehow, ten or twelve years ago it was easier.)

The Médoc lies along the eastern or inland side of a peninsula which is bounded on the near side by the Garonne and the Gironde rivers, and on the far side by the Atlantic. The vineyards are not on the river bank, not, in any event, the best of them, for that is low-lying, alluvial soil which produces abundant crops but inferior wine. They lie, instead, on the higher ground behind. It is an oddity of wine grapes, illustrated endlessly, that they thrive best in what would seem to the lay eye to be unpromising ground. It has been said that wine, like people, benefits from a measure of adversity. Here the fields are generously salted with stone fragments the size of quarters, so much so that some of the fields from a distance glint whitely in the sun. Behind the narrow strip which encompasses all the main vineyards lies a great tract of the sort of sandy, piney country that a Canadian associates with summer cottages, and through which one drives expecting, around every next turn, to come fact-to-face with the water, until eventually, there it is—the Atlantic. It is along the sandy beaches here that Bordeaux summers.

The chateaux of the Médoc, and of the Bordeaux region generally, are not chateaux in the sense of the historical show-places of the Loire. They are homes and working establishments. Having said that, it is necessary to add that some of them, such as Château Beychevelle, which is the sort of place to which Prince Charming carried off the Fair Maiden to live happily ever after; Château Margaux, looking like an errant White House behind its iron picket-fence; Château Mouton-Rothschild, with its long, long driveway between sculpted trees... these, and very many more besides, are as true chateaux as ever were. The occupants of *these* houses plainly are not that familiar figure of folk-tales, the humble peasant *vigneron*, out in his blue smock tending his own few rows of vines. In Bordeaux, vineyard properties are relatively large (150 acres is not an uncommon size, and Château Pontet-Canet runs to 190, although not all, obviously, are so large) and they are run as businesses.

Consider as an example Château Giscours, twenty-four kilometres (fifteen miles approximately) from Bordeaux in the commune of Labarde. (Labarde is next door to Margaux and its wines generally are sold under that better-known appellation.) Château Giscours, a Third Growth in the 1855 classification, has about 160 acres under vines, although the property itself is 20 acres larger. Besides the wine-growing acres, it encompasses a large private park in which are to be found a small lake and stream, masses of rhododendrons, and a gigantic magnolia tree. The house might be described as Georgian with a French accent. It is of a pinkish cast under a grey slate roof, three storeys high in the middle section, two in the wings. It sits, not off by itself in splendor in the park, but flanked by the buildings in which the wine is made—buildings erected in what is described as the classic Médoc style, with low-pitched roofs clad in darkened orange tiles, scrolled supports under the eaves, and arched doorways. This is the arrangement here: the stately homes of the Médoc are to be found side-by-side with their reason for being. The owner of Château Giscours since 1952, when he came to the Médoc from Algeria, is Nicholas Tari. When he took over, the reputation of the wines of Château Giscours was down. He began by grubbing out large numbers of old and inferior vines, and then replanting. The wooden fermenting vats were taken out (there was some tut-tutting locally about *that*) and replaced with concrete vats, which are easier to clean. In 1970, Mr. Tari experimented with a helicopter for spraying the vines. The following summer was dismally wet in June and it was more than ever imperative to spray against the vine diseases which flourish in the damp, but Mr. Tari was back to spraying with high-wheeled tractor-vehicles which ride astride the vines, spraying arms outstretched. The helicopters were fast, but they were also expensive and they tended to miss the ends of the rows when they made their turns.

(Early 1971 was a time for lamentation and despair in the whole Bordeaux region. Not only was the weather wet and cold; hail storms struck the vineyards when they were in bloom. In the Médoc, vineyard owners estimated that their production would be down by half from the admittedly very large output of 1970, and still they counted themselves lucky at having escaped more lightly than their colleagues in St. Emilion. Later, things picked up, and although in volume 1971 was a small year, it was not a bad one for quality.)

Perhaps because it is produced by natural processes (the action of the natural yeasts upon the sugar in the grapes causes a conversion to take place which results in the twelve or thirteen degrees of alcohol that most table wines contain) more romance attaches to wine than to any other of the various forms of alcoholic drink to which man has been wedded for thousands of years. It is hard to become romantic about a copper brewing kettle or a Coffey patent still. But wine requires no great plant and no really elaborate equipment. In the beginning, as has been suggested, it probably occurred spontaneously. Thus it remains related more closely than any other drink to the ground that it was grown on—and knowing the ground, even vicariously, is part of the joy of knowing about wine.

The Médoc has not the scenic grandeur of the steep-walled Rhône Valley, or of the Rhine and Moselle in Germany; nor has it any town which is a patch on St. Emilion, not far away on the Dordogne. For wine-country, it is flattish. The ground rises from the river, and never thereafter does it manage more than a discreet undulation before disappearing into the piney scrub of that summer-cottagey country, the Landes.

Efficient—not particularly a romantic word—is perhaps the one that would occur most readily to the first-time viewer of this countryside. Efficient, and then neat. Still, there can be beauty in efficiency and neatness. The owners of the Médoc chateaux keep their stone fences in good repair, for instance; and very often at the ends of the rows of vines closest to the roads, they plant rose-bushes. Religious monuments abound. The chateaux themselves in many cases are imposing. Some are architectural jewels set in green parks or severely formal gardens (in some cases, both exist). Almost all are at least pleasant country-houses. On a property such as Château Lafite, the open spaces between the rows, measured, it would appear, to within thousandths of an inch, have so scoured a look as to suggest that if ever a ragged blade of dandelion leaf dared to show itself, it would faint dead away to discover into what a void its temerity had launched it. Your gravelled driveway should do so well.

The Médoc wine road runs northwest, through or by such communes as Macau, Cantenac, Margaux, Moulis, Listrac, St. Julien, Pauillac and St. Estèphe—all familiar names to wine enthusiasts. Beyond St. Estèphe, although we are still in wine country, the best lies behind. By far the greatest of the communes along the D. 2, on which the great names are strung like pearls on a string, are Pauillac, St. Julien, St. Estèphe, Margaux and Cantenac. Together, they claim fifty-three of the sixty-one chateaux included in the 1855 classification. Pauillac has eighteen of them, and of those eighteen, three are from the very top of the tree, Châteaux Lafite, Latour and Mouton-Rothschild.

The town of Pauillac is itself a pleasant little place, directly on the Gironde. Facing the quais, there is a comfortable small hotel, the France et Angleterre, where for under eight dollars a night you can get a double room with a balcony from which to watch the freighters pass to and from Bordeaux, many of them, no doubt, in the wine trade. In summer, the yachtsmen come in from Angleterre itself to absorb the local culture by the glass. The France et Angleterre does not have an extensive list of the local wines—very often the wine districts do not, for the bottles they produce are destined for tables in London and New York—but one can more than make do with the likes of a Château Lynch-Bages, or even, in a pinch, the good Pauillac wine, marketed under the name of La Rose de Pauillac and made at the growers' co-operative in town.

Also visible, at night, from the balcony outside your room in the France et Angelterre is a plume of orange flame, off in the direction of St. Estèphe. The flame is a matter of some local concern. It is the flame of vent-gases from the new Shell-Berre refinery, and the question that is asked is "Why here?", here in an area where respect for the vines is such that road gangs will not resurface asphalt roads when signs are posted reading: "La vigne est en fleurs." The fact seems to be—the story has a familiar ring—that local interests, pursuing what usually is referred to as economic growth, or progress, prevailed over the vineyard people who were worried about pollution. Relations were not subsequently eased by an incident which occurred during the period of the harvest at Château Latour in 1970. Acrid smoke from a municipal dump, which was said to have contained refinery waste as well as the more ordinary municipal refuse, floated over Château Latour's manicured acres and tainted a part of the crop. The effect was greatly to reinforce fears throughout the area that smoke containing refinery hydrocarbons can ruin wine even while the grapes remain on the vine. An association to safeguard the great vineyards was founded with the purpose of persuading the French government that as between petrochemicals and the grape, at least in the Haut-Médoc, there can be no question as to which comes first. Wine lovers everywhere can only say "Amen" to that.

It is a doleful note on which to retrace our steps the length of the Médoc (fifty miles at the most, less in its prime portion) and seek out the district of Graves. Graves begins just below Mérignac, the airport for Bordeaux, due west of the city, and covers the rest of the compass over to the Garonne, at this point running southeast. It is a much put-upon district, hemmed in more and more by the encroaching city; some of its finest vineyards exist as green islands in the midst of the sprawling buildings, just as do municipal parks, and it is cut up more and more by highways.

The environs of French cities, wine or no wine, are no more free of smog than those of North America. Given the fact that a highly-specialist argument once raged in England about whether a difference in taste could be detected between wines whose grapes were grown in manured fields and those whose grapes were not— presumably one would need to know the taste of manure—it is awful to contemplate what the effect of the urban sprawl into Graves may have upon highly-tuned palates in the future. (It is always possible, of course, that the general effluvia will render future palates insensitive to any taste less delicate than garlic salami, and noses unresponsive to scents more fleeting than boiled roofing tar.)

For the moment, notwithstanding the chipping away at the acreage of Graves (the same thing has happened in Burgundy, just above Beaune, where the Lyon-Paris Autoroute slashes across one-time vineyards), there does not seem to be ground for such gloomy forebodings. The greatest vineyard of Graves, Château Haut-Brion, is also one of those closest to the city, and Haut-Brion remains alive and splendidly well.

This, perhaps, is the place to say something about a widespread misconception about Graves. Château Haut-Brion produces a small amount of excellent white wine, but its greatness is, and always has been, founded upon its red wine and this has been the case with the whole of Graves. And yet, because almost every wine-merchant and every restaurant from time immemorial has included in its list a usually pleasant, but not very remarkable, slightly-less-than-dry white wine called Graves, white very frequently is taken to be the dominant colour of the district. Not so—not so, in any case, qualitatively. Leaving aside what may be labelled with the general name, Graves, which may be from ordinary to good, this district produces some fine white wines, of which the only example to be found in Canada is Château Olivier. The best of all, as with the reds, is Château Haut-Brion, but none has come my way, here or elsewhere.

The name, Graves, derives from gravel. Why vines should respond well to having to sink their roots through it, in some places through thirty feet of it, can only be that there is in them a masochistic strain. In any case they do, and they have been doing so for a very long time, because this is the oldest wine-growing portion of the whole Bordeaux region. The professionals distinguish between the best red wines of Graves and their peers in the Médoc by saying that the former are perhaps even a little harder when young, but become fuller when mature and more silken. The amateur who can make the distinction—I am not one of them—is entitled to some self-congratulation. (He may also allow himself a sly smile as he practises dutifully with a view to arriving at that degree of discernment. If he can marshal the bottles with which to widen his field of study to include prime examples of the wines of St. Emilion and Pomerol, he can be forgiven what might otherwise be regarded as mad little chuckles of indecent self-satisfaction.)

Proposition: Last Christmas, your uncle—the one with the money—sent you a case of Château Lafite, or Château Haut-Brion, or Château Calon-Ségur, or Château Pontet-Canet, or Château Pichon-Longueville-Comtesse de Lalande, or one of the other great wines of Médoc or Graves which are to be found in Canada. Now he is coming to dinner. Your task: to produce something that will do the wine so proud that next Christmas he will send two cases. . . . If nothing immediately comes to mind, you might try the following:

Roast Lamb en Croûte

6 lb. leg of lamb, boned
1 tsp. salt
¼ tsp. pepper
¼ tsp. crushed rosemary
2 garlic cloves, crushed

Combine the salt, pepper, rosemary and garlic cloves, and rub well into the lamb. Reshape the leg and tie with string. Roast in a very hot oven, 450° for 20 minutes. Reduce heat to 350° and roast for 40 minutes longer. Remove to a dish and allow to cool; remove the string.

DUXELLES

Finely chop ½ lb. mushrooms and place them—a handful at a time—in a tea towel; twist and extract as much juice as possible. Then *sauté* the dry mushrooms in 2 tbsp. butter and 1 tbsp. oil, along with ¼ cup finely minced onion and 2 shallots. Season with salt and pepper and cook until the butter and oil have been absorbed or have evaporated.

BRIOCHE DOUGH

Sprinkle 3 envelopes active dry yeast and ½ tsp. sugar over ¾ cup lukewarm milk. Let this yeast mixture stand in a warm place for 10 minutes, or until it starts to swell.

Put 3 cups flour in a bowl with 3 tsp. salt, 10 large egg-yolks and ½ cup softened butter, cut into pieces. Add the yeast mixture and mix to form a soft dough. Turn out on a floured board and knead in about another cup flour, a little at a time. Knead the dough for 10 to 15 minutes or until it is smooth and no longer sticky. Place in a lightly greased bowl, turning the dough to grease the top. Cover the bowl and let the dough rise in a warm place for 1½ to 2 hours or until it has doubled in size.

Punch dough down, turn out on a floured board, and knead for 2 to 3 minutes. Return to bowl and let rise until it has doubled in bulk again. Punch down and roll out to form a rectangle ¼″ thick. Arrange 4 thin slices of cooked ham in the centre; spread a layer of the duxelles on the ham. Lay the lamb, fat side down, over the duxelles and then coat the top of the lamb with the remaining duxelles. Cover this with 2 or 3 slices of cooked ham. Bring up one of the long sides of the dough over the lamb. It should cover a little more than half the width of the top. Beat 1 egg yolk with 2 tbsp. cream and brush the edge of the dough with some of it. Bring up the other side of the dough so that it overlaps the first by ¾ of an inch. Cut off any excess dough and brush the top edges of the narrow sides of the dough with the egg wash. Bring up the 2 ends to extend over the top by ¾ of an inch. Cut off any excess and lift the pastry-enclosed lamb onto a jelly roll pan, seam side down.

Brush completely with egg wash and decorate with pastry cut-outs made from the trimmings. Brush these with the remaining egg wash and then bake the lamb in a 400° oven for 20 minutes. Reduce heat to 350° and continue baking for 40 minutes more. Transfer to a heated platter and garnish with watercress. Serves 8.

And introducing that great new singing duo—St. Emilion and Pomerol

*T*HERE IS A clock in the church steeple in the village of St. Emilion which strokes the hours, po-nong, po-nong, po-nong, up to ten po-nongs at night, when, mercifully, it is cut off until six o'clock in the morning. At that time, presumably, the vineyard workers spring from their cots with glad cries for the dawn and prepare to trudge once more out to the fields; in St. Emilion this may make no long trudge, since some of the fields extend into the very town itself.

It is not necessary to be a passionate devotee of clocks that go po-nong, po-nong, or even to be able to tell red wine from red ink, to fall in love with St. Emilion. This is one of the loveliest wine towns of all France. There are not, in truth, a lot of wine towns which match above ground the charm they hold, bottled, in their cellars: Sancerre, stuck on its butte high above the Loire, certainly; Riquewihr, in Alsace, looking like a provincial capital in Ruritania, circa 1675; Châteauneuf-du-Pape, although everyone might not agree; and Beaune, the wine capital of Burgundy. But then Beaune is larger.

St. Emilion is something altogether its own, a gentle old town of pale cream-coloured, weathered stone, sitting at the top of a slope, surrounded by fields of vines. It is obligatory in saying anything at all about St. Emilion (as anyone knows who has canvassed the literature) to note the similarity between the name of Château Ausone, one of the district's principal viticultural ornaments, and the name of Ausonius, the Roman poet, teacher and consul who was born at Bordeaux and, after some wanderings, died there. The romantic notion is that old Ausonius not only had a villa at the site of the present Château Ausone, but perhaps even planted its vineyard. Although I have seen some persuasive evidence against

44

the claim, who am I to argue? What is Ausonius to me, or I to Ausonius?

In any case, there *were* vineyards here in his day, which was in the fourth century; and the *Syndicat d'Initiative de St. Emilion* will tell you that then, and over the intervening centuries, the wines of St. Emilion have graced the tables and won the praises of so mixed a bag as "the Caesars of Rome. Emperors and kings. The poet and consul Ausonius, Philippe le Bel, Edward VIII, Henri d'Albret, the Cardinal of Sourdis, Louis XIII, Louis XIV and thousands of no less prominent figures...." We know from other sources that Louis XIV, the Sun King, was aged twelve at the time he delivered his encomium to the wines of St. Emilion, an age at which his kingly tastes cannot have been fully developed, even for wine. And we are left to judge whether it adds anything to the force of the *Syndicat*'s list of distinguished patrons to know that in 1527 Henri d'Albret married Margaret of Angoulême and thereby added Armagnac to his territories (incidentally, of course). Certainly a glass of Armagnac to finish a meal which had been lavishly sustained by a good wine of St. Emilion would have a lot to recommend it. But we were talking about the town.

St. Emilion is filled with ancient architectural treasures, many of them churchly, for St. Emilion has a churchly tradition. Its name, incidentally, comes from that of a wandering holy man, one Aemilianus, who came this way in the eighth century and whose hermit's cell (actual or not) may be examined by travellers today. In the fourteenth century, St. Emilion became both the seat of a cardinal and a stopping-off place for pilgrims on their way to the shrine of Saint James the Apostle in Spain. Those events, in the language of our time, gave a strong boost to the local economy. In the centre of St. Emilion is the Place du Clocher, and off to one side of it is an ancient church. Here, if you happen to be in town on the day of a *kermesse*, it will be possible to fish, with a ring at the end of a piece of line, for bottles of Château Ausone, Château Cheval-Blanc, Clos Fourtet, Château Figeac, Château Pavie and others of the commune's Great Growths. These are better prizes than are usually to be won in church fishponds, which in my experience (none of it recent) have not been notably well stocked in high-class potables—or any other kind of potables, for that matter.

Also in the square is a good, small restaurant called Chez Germaine, with a formidable list of the local wines, and kitty-corner across from it, a wine-merchant's shop where more of the same may be bought by the bottle, the case, or the truck load, to be shipped home, your kindly chief liquor commissioner willing. There is, as well, the attractive and comfortable Hostellerie de Plaisance, a great bargain in hotels, where a good double room—there are only nine rooms in all—is still to be had for under ten dollars a night. The dining-room does a roaring local business, always a good sign; the people who lately put the lovely, dark, round wine of their district into the bottles may be seen taking it out again, glass by glass, as a complement to lusty five-course Sunday lunches. The balcony outside almost any room in the Plaisance is as good a place as there is to see in one swoop a large part of the panorama of the hilly town: roofs clad in darkened orange tiles of the same interlocking design used by the Romans, climbing one close rank above another; beyond, the remains of the old town walls; and pressing in on all sides, the regimented vineyards.

Off to what otherwise would be the open side of the square, a tower rises out of the pavement as if the architect or his builder in a fit of carelessness had forgotten to put a church under it. But the church is there all right. It is cut into the solid rock beneath the square and is entered from a street, which may be seen from the Place du Clocher, a nasty jump below. This remarkable church, which makes spelunkers of all who enter it, was carved out of the rock, columns and all, in the eleventh century. Other caves dug at ancient dates around St. Emilion are put nowadays to utilitarian lay uses.

Obviously, then, there are reasons for visiting St. Emilion other than its wines—or even, for macaroon-fanciers, its macaroons, which are a local speciality. But we are here for the wines. The wines of St. Emilion, oddly, are known and not known. Everyone who has ever scanned a wine list is familiar with the name of St. Emilion. There is a lot of St. Emilion wine. Its lustier flavour, together with the fact that most often it is not so astringent in youth as the wines of the Médoc, make it popular. Perhaps, also, the fact that St. Emilion has to reach a level of eleven degrees of alcohol to satisfy the minimum requirement of its *Appellation contrôlée*,* whereas a Médoc need reach only ten, has something to do with it. The extra one degree of alcohol helps to give the St. Emilion more body.

*See page 68

Still, at a more intimate level than that of the district name, St. Emilion wines are less well known than those of the Médoc. The names of all but Château Ausone and Château Cheval-Blanc (and perhaps not even excepting those) are less widely recognized than a good many of the classified chateaux of the Médoc.

There are several guesses that can be made as to the reason for this relative unfamiliarity going back even to 1855 when the *courtiers* of Bordeaux so pointedly snubbed St. Emilion and Pomerol. The Médoc classification that they produced then, smacking of tidy business practices and general order, has no doubt inspired a lot of public confidence ever since, in the wines of the Médoc generally, and of the classified chateaux in particular. That is not to say that there is any reason in law or logic why it *should* have, but confidence by no means relies exclusively on either or both of those.

Only since the middle 1950's has St. Emilion had an official classification in which the terms *Premiers Grands Crus* and *Grands Crus* have had meaning. Before that, St. Emilion had gone along in a carefree way with a sort of do-it-yourself classification. This enabled just about every vineyard in sight that was not manifestly inferior to have some sort of title as a Great Growth. Such a set-up was not conducive to confidence. The classification now has a most progressive feature. In theory, whether or not it ever happens, it provides for a chateau to be dropped if it lets its standards down. This is in striking contrast to the Médoc classification, which, as we have seen, has been less susceptible to amendment than the British North America Act. The new St. Emilion classification is composed of twelve *Premiers Grands Crus*, divided into an "A" group of two (Ausone and Cheval-Blanc) and a ten-member "B" group; and seventy-two *Grands Crus*. One of the seventy-two, and a good example of a small, centuries-old chateau of the district, is Château Soutard, a short distance northeast of the town. The proprietor is the Comtesse Michelle des Ligneris, but Château Soutard is operated by her son Jacques and his wife.

It is common in the Bordeaux region that house and *chais* or winemaking and wine-storage sheds exist as a unit, the house face-on to the drive, the buildings to the sides, so that there is a courtyard between. This is the case at Château Soutard. Pass through the house, and from the back, the view is northeast to the small River Barbanne, which once was a border between French and English troops, and beyond it, to the communes of Montagne-St. Emilion,

St. Georges-St. Emilion, Lussac-St. Emilion, Puisseguin-St. Emilion and Parsac-St. Emilion, all of which consider it worthwhile for commercial reasons to annex the more famous name to their own. (The Quebec commission for some years has stocked a wine of St. Georges-St. Emilion.) This area, it seems, once was covered by a sea, and when the water retreated there were left, especially on the high ground, as Jacques des Ligneris points out, large deposits of shells. Under a shallow layer of soil lies a layer of soft, porous-looking limestone; the roots of the vines go down into it.

The varieties of grapes used here are not much different from those in the Médoc, although the Cabernet is the Cabernet Franc rather than the Cabernet Sauvignon. The proportion of Merlot to Cabernet, however, is much higher, so that in fact the Merlot is dominant. This grape produces a softer wine, at the cost (or so it is said) of lasting power. Perhaps. But like most generalizations, there are plentiful exceptions, of which I can cite a notable one. Jacques des Ligneris took from the barrel a sample of his 1970 wine, then scarcely eight months old and green to the taste; he followed it with another, this one bottled, of course, from 1964, which in St. Emilion was an extremely good year, much better than in the Médoc; and he followed that with a bottle about whose age he invited a guess. It was evident even while it was being poured that it was of some age for there were bricky tints in the colour; it had taken on the colour of tiles, as the local term goes. The year was 1943. The wine that year was made while German troops still occupied the chateau—and bottled, incidentally, in pale green, almost clear, bottles, because whatever pigment it is that goes into making bottles green had gone to war (no doubt in whatever arm it is of the military that enlisted the green of the Lucky Strike packages in the United States).

If the wines of St. Emilion mature early and fade correspondingly, this one had not heard. Twenty-eight years had done nothing but bring it to a peak from which Jacques des Ligneris thought it would not fade for very nearly as many more. The taste was rich and faintly spicy, and in the bouquet, which came up in waves, there were overtones of pine cones, freshly-turned ground, and marzipan (and sort *that* out on your olefactory nerve). Out of the dim cool of the *chais*, top down on the car, we floated off into the sunshine in a state of ethereal bliss; it was not yet quite noon.

Since we have been speaking of the bouquet (although it is neither more nor less appropriate to a discussion of a St. Emilion wine than to any other), this might be the point at which to say something about getting the most from that facet of a wine's character. It is not, or it is not necessarily, an affectation to swirl the glass in the fingers so that the contents coat the sides—although it *would* be a little pretentious with a glass of certified plonk. The effect of the swirling is to enlarge the area of the wine's contact with the air so that evaporation takes place and the bouquet is released. In addition, of course, it allows you to view the consistency of the wine and to see if it has that viscosity which will cause it to form tears, as they are called, when the glass is put upright again. It is fairly safe to say before tasting it that if a wine washes promptly down the sides of the glass, leaving no trace of tears (or legs, another term), it will be thin and watery in the mouth.

The *chais* at Château Soutard were built in the early 1800's; the walls are of stone, more than a foot and a half thick, and the timbers are pretty much as they came, the main stems of trees with the bark removed. But into the old buildings, to replace the great oaken fermenting vats that were used everywhere until a few years ago, concrete vats have been introduced and two, even newer stainless-steel tanks. From the vats the new wines still go into wooden barrels, where they remain, racked off several times into other wooden barrels, for a year and a half or more after the *vendange*, or harvest. They are then ready to be bottled. During all that time the barrels are topped up about twice a week to keep the air out. Air is no friend of wine until an hour or so before it is ready to be drunk, and then it will improve it.

Vineyards wholly surround the town of St. Emilion; in fact, they come into it. Across a small square, the doorway of an ancient church faces the gates of Clos Fourtet, one of the twelve *Premiers Grands Crus*. The chateaux of ten of these twelve, in fact, are within walking distance of the town, mostly on the steep slope to the south of it in the direction of the Dordogne River. (They are not, however, riverside vineyards, for the Dordogne remains far enough off to be out of sight.) Some others of the best of the St. Emilion vineyards —including Château Cheval-Blanc, which nowadays is considered the best of all—are to be found on flatter ground, northwest of St. Emilion itself, hard up against the Pomerol border. The town which serves this part is the river port of Libourne, which is several times larger than St. Emilion but has no other readily discernible distinction. Libourne is an ancient town and is a very old centre of the wine trade, but time has not conferred on it any of the charm of St. Emilion.

There is nothing in the landscape or in the look of the soil, at least nothing to the lay eye, to tell the wine tourist when he has passed from St. Emilion into Pomerol. The vineyards run together—Château Pétrus, the acknowledged leader of Pomerol, is no distance from Château Cheval-Blanc in St. Emilion. In fact they share the same soil, now gravelly, the same ground, now more or less flat, and the same caprices of the weather. In 1956 the vineyards in Pomerol and this part of St. Emilion were devastated by winter frosts, whereas the St. Emilion vineyards, in what proved to be a less exposed position on the south-facing slopes below the town itself, escaped.

Perhaps because the district is small, the wines of Pomerol have been relatively little known. This has certainly been the case in Canada, where until very recently hardly an example was to be found. District wines labelled simply Médoc, or St. Emilion or Graves have always been staples on wine merchants' lists everywhere. But not Pomerol. That is not to say that district wines of Pomerol are not marketed; in fact, rated price-to-quality, they are probably better buys than the sometimes nondescript Médocs and St. Emilions. But we have not seen much of them. Nor are the chateaux of Pomerol particularly well-known, not even Château Pétrus, notwithstanding the fact that the professionals rate it—and prices consistently paid reflect that judgement—the peer of such as Lafite, Latour, Margaux, Haut-Brion and Mouton-Rothschild. Unless some few cases of Château Pétrus are privately imported, none reaches these shores.

It is the characteristic of all the red wines of Bordeaux, especially when they are young, but even in their suavest maturity, to have an astringent quality, like clear tea—may I be forgiven the mundane comparison—and for the same reason, because of the tannin, of which they contain rather more than most wines. Theirs is an austere beauty, the great proponents of claret like to say, as compared with the blowzier attractions of the great burgundies. Perhaps so. But it will gratify amateurs to know—at least, it does me—that professional tasters have been known at blind tastings to mistake a St. Emilion for a light burgundy, or vice versa (in these cases they have not been told that the wines they were being faced with were not all of one region or the other). The wines of St. Emilion, then, may be taken to have an austere blowziness, an out-going reticence, and a full leanness—and all sorts of other interesting, if conflicting, attributes. It might do to say that they are somehow more concentrated, winier wines than most of their Bordeaux compatriots, and that the wines of Pomerol fall somewhere between them and the Médocs, being soft, full, fragrant, and warm both in colour and taste, but still not downright extrovert in the manner of burgundies.

Excepting that the simple district name of St. Emilion is omnipresent, the wines of St. Emilion and Pomerol are not very well represented in Canada. But there has been some improvement. Of the *Premiers Grands Crus* of St. Emilion, Château Belair has been available on the special-order list in Alberta, and at a spectacularly good price—a Canadian best buy as it were. Alberta also has listed one of the recognized outstanding growths of Pomerol, Château l'Evangile, again on special order. As noted earlier, however, it cannot be guaranteed that these always will be found in stock. Château Petit-Village, a Pomerol wine of high reputation, has been available, at a price, in Ontario, as has another of more modest fame, Château Plince (at less than half the price). Two *Grands Crus Classés* of St. Emilion to be had in Ontario, both over-priced, have been Château l'Angélus and Château Franc-Mayne. The greatest number of St. Emilion wines listed in Canada has been in the province of Quebec, foremost among them, Château Trottevieille, a *Premier Grand Cru*; followed by Château Franc-Mayne and Château Grand-Pontet, both *Grands Crus*; Château Cheval-Noir, a minor chateau, and Château Montlabert, the credentials of which are altogether obscure. And that, excepting various shippers' wines under the general *Appellation Contrôlée* St. Emilion—and not a word against them—fairly well exhausts the catalogue of what there has been to find of the wines of that district and its small sister, Pomerol, from sea to sea.

Before leaving the east side of the Dordogne and Gironde, we should insert a note about some district names which undoubtedly are going to become much more familiar, given the rapid increase in the world demand for claret. Northwest of Libourne, which is to say, following the river down to the sea, there is a district which sometimes is called Fronsac, and at other times Canon-Fronsac (it has a score of vineyards, each with the name Canon attached, fore or aft, to its own), and at still other times the Fronsadais. Call it what you like, it is a district with a growing reputation. The wines suffer from being rough when young, and given man's all-embracing, world-wide impatience, this is perhaps a lot to suffer from, but allowed a little time in bottle, these wines develop very nicely. And they remain relatively inexpensive. Beyond Fronsac lie the Côtes de Bourg and the Côtes de Blaye, which it is not at all reckless to predict are going to come into much greater prominence as demand makes it more and more worth-while for growers to strive to raise their standards.

But to return to the better-established wines of St. Emilion and Pomerol: these are hearty, warm, flavourful wines, of a sort to go with hearty, warm, flavourful foods. The Hostellerie de Plaisance, in St. Emilion, suggests that the very thing to go along with a good bottle of the wine of the area is duck with green peppercorns. This is how it is made at the hotel:

Canard de Chalans au Poivre Vert
(Duck with Green Peppercorns)

1 duck—about 3½ lbs.
2 handfuls of mushrooms
1 oz. duck *foie gras*, raw or cooked
5 or 6 bread cubes fried in butter
pinch of salt
1 tbsp. green peppercorns
chopped shallots
butter
a little Madeira and cognac

Clean the duck; remove the wish-bone in order to facilitate the carving and rub the inside lightly with salt. Reserve the liver.

STUFFING

Cook the chopped mushrooms in butter, then add the duck's liver, chopped and lightly salted; brown the mixture for a few seconds with a pinch of chopped shallots. Remove from heat to a platter (the liver should be left rare), add the green peppercorns (which have been washed in cold water), *foie gras* and bread cubes. Mix lightly and stuff the duck. Truss it and place in a very hot oven for 18 minutes, salting it lightly. Transfer the duck to a platter, placing it breast down so that the blood runs into the breasts.

SAUCE

butter
chopped shallots
thyme
bay leaves
a sage leaf, fresh or dry
St. Emilion old wine
pan drippings
thickening

Crush the neck, pinions and gizzard of the duck into pieces. Brown them in butter with chopped shallots, thyme, bay leaves and a sage leaf. Drain off the fat, return the mixture to the browning pan, and moisten with 1 cup of St. Emilion old wine and the same amount of pan drippings, with a little thickening added. Cook and reduce for 15 minutes, skimming off fat, until 1 to 1¼ cups of sauce remain. A coffee-spoon of Madeira, a dash of cognac and a coffee-spoon of butter complete the sauce.

TRIMMING

Remove the 2 legs and remove the excess fat from them, also the skin if it is black. Rub mustard lightly on both sides of the legs and finish cooking in a frying pan in hot butter.

Remove the 2 breasts and put them on a platter. Then return the carcass to the oven for 5 minutes in order to get rid of any traces of blood. Take the duck from the oven and cut the breast bone with a large pair of scissors. Moisten the dressing inside with 2 or 3 spoonfuls of sauce.

Cut each breast into strips (6 or 8) and arrange them across the duck and stand the legs up on each side.

GARNISH

Serve with a big golden apple, peeled, cut in two and baked in the oven, well glazed with some of the sauce and then sprinkled with a little young Calvados. Serve the rest of the sauce separately.*

*Recipe created at Restaurant des Vannes, Liverdun, by M. Bousquenaud, now chef, Hostellerie de Plaisance, St. Emilion.

One born to love you, sweet —Browning (and I)

*S*OMEHOW THE NOTION has got around that Dry is Beautiful, that the ultimate mark of knowledge and sophistication is to ask for it "dry". Probably the idea comes from the martini, where it does not make much sense either. What most people mean when they specify a very, very, very dry martini, is one made with even more than the usual number of parts of (dry) gin in relation to parts of (also dry) French vermouth. Reverse the proportions of gin and vermouth and the drink will not taste the same; it certainly will be less volatile because the gin is the higher potency ingredient, but it will still be dry.

The budding new fad wine, as indicated by figures on exports (mainly to the United States) which have doubled in two years, is Muscadet, or more specifically, Muscadet de Sèvre-et-Maine, a white wine from near the city of Nantes, on the Loire. Needless to say, it is a very dry wine, dry as a bone. (I would even go further and call it tart, but then I am not a great fan of ultra-dry wines.) Undoubtedly, part of the explanation for its rush of popularity is the widespread illusion that to have anything dry is to have it right—and to have it drier is to have it righter.

This of course is rubbish, cult-worship, mumbo-jumbo. Now, then, is the time to get up a movement to strike back at the indiscriminate Dry-is-Beautiful notion wherever it raises its head. It would be as true to say (bearing in mind that all blanket judgements are untrustworthy) that Dry is a Mouth Puckering Wine with Public Relations, or, Dry is Acid Indigestion. Dry, in short, is zero. The only useful rule for wine, of course, is the rule of everyone to his own taste. Still, without departing from that, it should be possible to raise a shy voice to say that there is no inherent merit in dryness;

it has nothing to do with quality, or with anything except the absence of sweetness.

And yet we are beset with this drymania. In some corner of the land every night, some big-spender is flashing his diamond stick-pin and saying to the wine waiter with a lordly wave of the hand: "I'll leave the wine to you, Fred . . . just so long as it's dry." And he's talking about *red* wine. In most parts of the known world it would take all the waiter's ingenuity, plus a considerable streak of sadism, for him to produce a *non*-dry red table wine. Almost all red table wines worth mentioning, and a considerably larger number that are not, can only be described as dry. Even so, there are nuances of difference between, say, a fine burgundy and a fine claret: the peculiar richness of the burgundy may give it a slightly sweetish cast, at least compared with the more austere bordeaux. Does that put burgundy beyond the pale? It is to laugh.

But the real pity of the dry cult is that it has turned so many people away from sweet wines even before they have tried them. In some circles, to express an actual liking for sweet wines is to invite the sort of sideways look that I believe Russell Baker once said was directed at the person who dared to write funny pieces for *The New York Times* or to turn up at a New York policemen's ball in suede shoes. A great pity. Some of the most glorious white wines in the world are sweet.

The German wines, wines of the Rhine and the Moselle, are only really dry in years when there is not enough sun or not enough days of it during the growing season. In good years they are always not quite dry, and in the great years, when the sun-filled days last long into the autumn and gentle mists envelop the vines at night, the German winemakers produce, with painstaking care, the wines that command fabulous prices and go into connoisseurs' cellars to be cherished for years. The terms *spätlese, auslese, beerenauslese* and *trockenbeerenauslese* on a German wine label tell when and how the grapes were picked. To know the terms is to have some idea of the degree of sweetness there will be in the wines so described; it goes up by those four steps, as does the price, dramatically.

What sweet wines need is the right company in which to shine. (Since I have never been fortunate enough to find myself alone in the same room with a bottle of wine of *trockenbeerenauslese* quality, which is not only hideously expensive but rare, I can only speak from hearsay, but the company it is supposed to shine in best is its own; in other words, it will be savoured best by itself rather than with any food, including dessert, which a sweet wine usually accompanies.) Tokay Aszu, the great sweet wine of Hungary, would be a decided mistake with roast beef and Yorkshire pudding, but try it with fruit. Sauternes with lobster may not strike everyone as one of the great gastronomic marriages of all time—it does not me—but there are French gastronomes who insist that they make an ideal match. As for Sauternes at the end of the meal though, there can be no argument.

In general, it can be said that the sweet wines are dessert wines; they go with something sweet, or with fruit. And here a pause is necessary to sort out a matter of nomenclature. The term "dessert wine" is used in Canada and the United States to denote what is called elsewhere a fortified wine, one to which brandy has been added. Port, sherry, Madeira and Marsala are all *fortified* wines. The great German sweet wines, the Hungarian Tokay Aszu, and the wine we are principally concerned with here—Sauternes—are all *natural* sweet wines; these are the wines properly called dessert wines because they are wines to be drunk with dessert. Certainly sherry is not one, nor port, for though it comes at the end of the meal, it comes after the food.

Perhaps two things, apart from the pure fad aspect of drymania, have helped to build the prejudice against sweet wines: (1) the idea that anything which is sweet must be fattening; and (2) the notion that anything which is sweet must be cloying.

About the first, there does not seem to be any way—short of lying—of getting around the fact that sweet wines are sweet because they contain a relatively large amount of unconverted natural grape sugar. They are as rich as butter and, therefore, presumably fattening. However, points that are worth considering are the following: (1) What is there that is good that isn't, at least a little? (2) If the host happens to be pouring Château d'Yquem, he is not, unless he happens to be Aristotle Onassis, going to be forcing on you more than your metabolism can handle (especially if you are willing to assist it with a brisk walk). (3) If dessert is unavoidable, why not live a little?

As to any allegation that a sweet wine inescapably will be cloying, that needs only to be put to the test to be disproved. Look at it this way. Chocolate fudge we describe as sweet, but so do we a ripe peach. They are by no means sweet in the same way. What makes the difference, and saves the peach from being suffocatingly sweet, is its fruit acid. The same with sweet wine. The great sweet wines, of which Sauternes is undoubtedly the most widely-known, flow almost as thick as maple syrup and are of a yellow-gold colour, darkening to old gold with age, shades which are luscious in themselves. But neither in the bouquet nor in the taste is there a trace of anything that could be called sickly sweet. The word that fits the case is, rich.

The Sauternes district lies just outside the city of Bordeaux to the southeast. To reach it, the wine tourist leaves the city on the N.113 and if he is wise, drives to Langon, where there is a small restaurant called the Oliver, to which the *Guide Michelin* gives one star. The original Oliver of the restaurant Oliver in Langon was the late Louis, once chef at the Savoy Hotel in London and father of Raymond Oliver, author, television performer, and, hardly least, proprietor of Grand Véfour, one of the twelve restaurants in all France to which have been given three stars. When the more relevant information is added that the Oliver in Langon is also an excellent place to eat, and is attached to a plain, but good, small hotel where a room looking out on the market square can be had for a few dollars, the logic of choosing Langon as a base-of-operations in Sauternes and Barsac (the two are indistinguishable to the naked eye, as their wines are to most taste buds) must be established beyond all possibility of cavil.

In Langon, all of the vineyards of Sauternes and Barsac lie just to our west—among them such chateaux as Rayne-Vigneau, the wines of which are to be found in Quebec stores; Châteaux Filhot and Coutet, which are stocked by the Newfoundland commission; and the magnificent Château d'Yquem, listed in Ontario, Alberta and Nova Scotia (at shocking, but not uniformly shocking, prices).

It used to be the case that one could say with absolute assurance that the only good Sauternes was a sweet, sweet, sweet Sauternes, and that the only suitable response to the waiter who came snivelling along with the suggestion that he could produce a nice bottle of *dry* Sauternes to go admirably with the sole, would be to tell him to get lost. However, in recent years, driven partly by the world-wide passion for dry wines and the consequent turning away from sweet, some of the Sauternes-Barsac vineyards have begun to turn out dry wines as well. Château d'Yquem does this under the name of Château Ygrec—the label has a large *Y* on it—but this, to the best of my knowledge, has never come into Canada. It is worth noting that the Château Filhot listed in Newfoundland is listed as a dry wine. Unfortunately, while the sweet wines of the district are unsurpassed, the dry wines are not nearly so distinguished.

The superlative sweet wine of Château d'Yquem is produced in surroundings that can only be described as also superlative. The entire property—house, wine-making and wine-storing sheds, the expanse of 200-plus acres of beautifully coiffed vines, gravelled walks, flower-beds, lawns—looks more like one of the smaller showplace chateaux on the Loire than any busy, efficient and highly successful business enterprise has a right to do.

Each fall, with great patience (a quality, incidentally, which is inseparable from the making of great natural sweet wines), a relatively small quantity is made here of a golden wine that drips down the sides of a glass in globules after it has been swirled. Château d'Yquem is widely accepted as the richest in bouquet and in flavour of all the sweet wines. It is made from grapes painstakingly snipped from bunches which any housewife at a glance would unhesitatingly chuck into the garbage can. It is the peculiarity of the luscious wines of the world—and it is as true of the *trockenbeerenauslese* of Germany and the Tokay of Hungary—that they come from grapes which by lay definition would be considered bad. The grapes, in fact, are left on the vines until they have become overripe and have been attacked by a form of mould which the French call the noble rot. In very much simplified form, what happens is this: The mould causes water from inside the fruit to be brought to the surface, where it is dissipated, leaving the remaining juice much concentrated. (By a heat-drying process, rather than by the action of the noble rot, the same thing happens to a raisin; it shrivels and becomes sweeter than it ever was as a fully-fleshed grape.)

The overripe fruit is picked not bunch by bunch, but berry by berry, workers going over and over the rows until they have got them all, each, ideally, at its optimum point of overripeness. This plainly is a dicey operation for the grower, who needs not only patience but cool nerves, because the picking goes on late into the autumn, when there is a danger of extensive loss in the event of a sharp turn in the weather. It also makes for a costly wine, partly because of the labour required, but more importantly, because the juice that is in the grapes, while extremely high in sugar, is also much reduced in quantity. It is, in fact, a highly concentrated sort of grape nectar that goes, after pressing, into the casks of Sauternes and Barsac to make each year's wines.

Obviously, if an unlimited amount of sugar could be converted into alcohol, these would become wines exactly like any others except that their alcoholic strength would be much higher. They are, in fact, strong in alcohol. But with all wines the fermentation process stops when one of two things happens. Either all the sugar is fermented out, in which case the yeast's work is done; or the alcoholic content reaches such a point—at about fifteen to seventeen degrees—that the yeasts are bludgeoned into quiescence. Since in the latter case, unconverted sugar remains in the very sweet juices or must, of the nobly rotted grapes, the resulting wine is sweet—the sugar is carried over into the finished wine. The wine is also high in glycerine, which gives it its viscous quality, and in other elements which lend to the blooming bouquet and rich, rich taste.

(The procedures in the making of the sweet German wines are very much the same. In the making of the Tokay of Hungary, the same late picking of selected overripe berries again constitutes the very basis of the making of the wine, but the practices that follow thereafter are different. In looking at the label of a bottle of Tokay Aszu—aszu, incidentally, means the same thing as the French talk about when they speak of *pourriture noble*, or the noble rot—the buyer will find it designated three, or four or five *puttonos*, or *puttonyos*, indicative of the degree of sweetness. Tokay Aszu, in each case three *puttonos*, is to be found in the stores of Newfoundland, Quebec, Ontario, Manitoba, Alberta and British Columbia. Given the fact that in Hungary there is only one exporter, the state, it is to be wondered why the price should be lower, by more than one dollar, in Alberta than in Quebec.)

Listings of Sauternes or Barsac, or both—that is to say, the commune wines of Sauternes or Barsac—are to be found in all provinces except New Brunswick, Prince Edward Island and Saskatchewan. Incidentally, it is worth noting, because it crops up very often, that the designation Haut Sauternes has no official meaning; it may be used by an individual shipper to indicate that the wine is of a slightly better quality, but whether it is or not is a matter strictly between him and his conscience.

A wine described simply as Sauternes (or Haut Sauternes) or

Barsac obviously will be a less sweet and velvety-textured wine than a Sauternes of one of the classified chateaux; it also will be a good deal less expensive. Leaving aside Newfoundland's *dry* Château Filhot, the traditional chateau-bottled Sauternes which are available in Canada are Château Coutet à Barsac (Newfoundland), Château Rayne-Vigneau (Quebec), and Château d'Yquem (Nova Scotia, Ontario and Alberta).

And the dessert that Sauternes is a goes-with? The field is wide open, with the exception of anything with a strong chocolate flavour. For some reason chocolate is a killer for wine, as, among fruits, so is the orange. If plain old everyday fruit does not strike an appealing chord, you might try this:

Poire Dijon

1 cup *confiture de cassis* (black-currant jam with whole berries)
1 cup *cassis de Bourgogne* (black-currant liqueur)
6 canned pear halves
vanilla ice cream
3 oz. sliced almonds, toasted

Combine the black-currant jam with ½ cup of the *cassis*. Have ready 6 sherbet glasses. Spoon 2 tbsp. of the black-currant mixture into each glass. Now place a half pear in each and top with 1 large or 2 small scoops of vanilla ice cream. Pour the remaining ½ cup of Cassis, equally, over the ice cream. Sprinkle generously with the toasted sliced almonds. Serves 6.*

*From Les Gourmets restaurant at Marsannay-la-Côte, Côte d'Or.

Or this:

Candied Fruit Soufflé

2 cups milk	2 tbsp. gelatin
2″ piece vanilla bean	½ cup cold water
16 egg yolks	2 cups whipped cream
1 lb. confectioners' sugar	1 cup minced candied fruits
	finely grated semi-sweet chocolate

Scald the milk, with the vanilla bean added, and discard the bean. Put the egg yolks and sugar in a large heavy saucepan and beat with a wooden spoon until the mixture begins to thicken and turn pale in colour. Add the scalded milk, a little at a time, beating constantly. Put the saucepan over very low heat, stirring, until it is thickened. *Do not let it boil.* Remove from heat, add the gelatin softened in the cold water, and stir until the gelatin is dissolved. Cool the mixture, stirring frequently to prevent a skin from forming on the surface. Fold in the 2 cups whipped cream and the minced candied fruits.

Fold a 16″-20″-long piece of wax paper in half lengthwise. Oil the band of wax paper and tie it, oiled side in, around a 1-quart *soufflé* dish to form a collar. Fill the dish with the *soufflé* mixture and chill it until it is set. Remove the paper collar carefully and sprinkle the top with the finely grated chocolate. Serves 6.

If not an AOC surely a VDQS?

$\mathcal{C}$ROSS TO THE other bank of the Garonne River at Langon and we are in the region called Entre-Deux-Mers, or Between-Two-Seas. The two "seas" that we are between are the Garonne, just behind, and the Dordogne to the north, ahead, the two of which join north of the city of Bordeaux, near a place called Bourg, and flow thereafter to the ocean as the Gironde. (The Garonne and the Dordogne aren't seas, you say? Go argue with the French, whose great national illusion it is to believe that they are logical, just as that of the British is to believe that they are unboastful, that of the Americans, that they are altruistic, and that of the Canadians, that everyone loves a Canadian.)

Every wine enthusiast *knows* that while both white and red wines are produced in Graves, and that while such places as Barsac and Sauternes are famous for their sweet white wines, the region of Bordeaux as a whole is mainly one of red wines. Claret is red, and claret is the very synonym for bordeaux. It is hard, in the circumstances, to adjust to the reality that if the annual production of the wines of Bordeaux comes to 100 million gallons, as it sometimes does, fifty-five per cent of it, and perhaps a little better, is white. (I know this, having been asked by a pillar of the industry for my estimate of the proportion of white to red, and having replied glibly, "Oh, twenty per cent," only to have yet another misconception stripped away.)

Here, Between-Two-Seas, is where a large part of that great volume of white wine comes from: sweet from such places as Loupiac and Sainte-Croix-du-Mont, which are directly across the river from the sweet wine country we have just left in Barsac and Sauternes; sweet-ish from the Premières Côtes de Bordeaux and Côtes de

Bordeaux-St. Macaire; dry under the general appellation Entre-Deux-Mers. Of these, the names most frequently to be found on wine-lists (where they ought not to be absolutely rottenly expensive) are the dry Entre-Deux-Mers and the sweet Sainte-Croix-du-Mont. It is also from this open-sided triangle between the Garonne and the Dordogne that a good deal of the wine labelled simply Bordeaux Blanc and Bordeaux Rouge comes from. Red wine from here of slightly superior quality, called Premières Côtes de Bordeaux, may also be looked for and occasionally found.

Turning farther inland to the north and east, we will pass near, or through, areas which give the world wines bearing the names of Bergerac and Monbazillac. These, strictly speaking, are outside the Bordeaux region, although they sometimes are listed under that heading. The grape types and the methods of making the wines are similar to those in Bordeaux. Bergerac wines, which are both red and white, are made with the same grapes and in very much the same manner as the red and non-sweet white wines of Bordeaux. The sweet white wines of Monbazillac are cousins of the dessert wines of Bordeaux. The Canadian liquor commissions have resisted the Monbazillac wines, which have more reputation, but Quebec, Ontario, Manitoba and Alberta have embraced those of Bergerac, which have less. Ontario, Manitoba and Alberta list a red wine of Bergerac; Quebec lists a rosé, and—not to say a word against them—one should not expect to pay a lot for any of these.

But all this is only in passing, for where we are headed is Cahors, where the vineyards rise in tiers along the river Lot and where the name will strike ten thousand ears as a clap of absolute silence. Cahors, which is due north of Toulouse, is noted for its striking bridge, a fact which will interest bridge-fanciers everywhere; for an agreeable climate, ditto, weather fans; and for its wines. About the latter, I seem somehow to be in possession of a note which says that they were greatly favoured by Peter the Great of Russia. Since Peter seems simply to have liked drink, and in stupefying quantities, the value of this as an endorsement of quality may be somewhat diluted. The wines of Cahors, sometimes referred to as the Black Wines of Cahors, admittedly are not going to be found on the wine card of your local steak-house. So far as I know, no bottle bearing the name of Cahors is to be found in this country at all. But there is in Cahors a story of a sort beloved of sports and theatre addicts—Success, Success Lost, Success Eventually

Regained—and it does give us entry into the question of the nomenclature of French wines.

The vineyards of Cahors are very old and at one time were much more extensive than they now are. Their wines enjoyed some widespread reputation of their own, at least well into the 1700's. They were known at that time in England. Subsequently, they came to be used mainly for improving other wines, notably those of Bordeaux, in years when the wines of that more celebrated region were deficient in colour and body. (The wines of Cahors, in addition to being dark, have remarkable keeping qualities.) As a consequence of this practice, the wines of Cahors were not themselves sufficiently renowned by the time the French government's laws of *Appellation d'Origine Contrôlée* (AOC) came into being, beginning in 1935, to warrant being included. It was only in 1949 when a second tier was created, this to comprise wines which would carry the designation, *Vins Délimité de Qualité Supérieure* (VDQS), that those of Cahors were brought within the quality-control framework. (Pause here to denote passage of years dedicated to relentless self-improvement on part of *vignerons* of Cahors.) Latterly, some experts had come to say that the wines of Cahors belonged in the first team, and in 1971 Cahors was elevated and given its own *Appellation Contrôlée*. The lip trembles at the telling of it.

What *Appellation Contrôlée* or the initials VDQS mean to the wine-buyer, basically, is that what is in the bottle is what the label *says* is in the bottle. It is his best assurance that there has been none of the bad old practice (which the wines of Cahors themselves were involved in) of beefing up a poor wine of a celebrated district to make it resemble a good wine of a celebrated district ... or at least to make it resemble a little less a poor, pale, thin one. Except that the words *Appellation Contrôlée* signify that the wine inside came from a place which generally produces some of the best wines of France (and VDQS that it came from one which generally produces good wines), they represent no promise about taste and bouquet; those will depend very much on the year. The designation constitutes simply a certificate of authenticity. While it would be vigorously denied in the Okanagan, even British Columbia (Eden West) on occasion will grow sour apples. But over the long term, it is generally expected that British Columbia will grow more good apples than will, say, Saskatchewan. So it is with wine regions.

Given all that, it is also the case that it does not follow automatically that a bottle which carries an *Appellation Contrôlée* designation will make more pleasant drinking than one which merely offers the VDQS seal —which, in case you are looking for it, resembles a postage stamp. There is no reason why anyone should agree with the French as to which are their best regions, and somewhere no doubt there is a man who prefers Minervois to the best bottle of Haut-Brion that was ever made.

By far the greatest volume of wine consumed in France in a year carries no certification at all. It is simply wine, red or white, and the closest thing to a statement of quality that can be made about it is to say that its strength is x number of degrees of alcohol. It is significant in this regard that France, as we have seen already, is the world's largest *importer* of wine. Some of this imported wine is drunk for itself alone—even a Frenchman, if pressed, can be made to admit the merits of the Rhine and the Moselle—but the great, great bulk of it goes into the making of the *vins ordinaires* which are sold across bars by the glass, or in screw-cap bottles from the lower shelves of the local grocery or supermarket.

Some, no doubt, finds its way into the non-appellation brand-name wines that dozens of producers put up. These wines are a long cut above the *vins ordinaires* that we have just been describing. Although they cannot lay claim to an *Appellation Contrôlée* or a VDQS designation because of their mixed backgrounds (and mixed is the word, as in stirred in), they do aspire to be regarded as burgundy *types* or bordeaux *types*. They are blends, in each case made to a formula existing in the mind of the shipper for a wine of a sort that will satisfy the greatest number of people at a predetermined price. Year in and year out, they will remain as true to that ideal in taste, colour, bouquet (if any), and price, as the shipper can manage. They are, in short, a standard product, like canned soup. There is nothing wrong with canned soup, and there is nothing wrong with a standard, blended wine, especially if the price is right. All wines, come to that, are in some degree blended wines. Even the wine of one vineyard and one vintage will be a blend of different pickings. (When we get to that point, however, what we are picking most of is nits.) Nevertheless, there is something inexpressibly dreary about the very idea of made-up wines, and the wine-lover's world would become a much duller place if suddenly those were all there were.

The name-branded wine—call it Export, call it Imperial Rouge,

Cuvée des Saints Pères, Red Flag, or whatever—will be made up of wines from any number of places, chosen mainly to offset one another's weaknesses. There is not a great deal to be said about these wines except that if you find one you like, you can stick with it in the reasonable assurance, as in the case of canned soup, that one bottle is going to be pretty much like another.

Perish the thought that I should seem to be suggesting so unadventuresome a course; that is a counsel of stick-in-the-muds. If you would scale the peaks—something which regrettably is becoming as expensive as ocean yachting—it will be necessary to enter into the true world of wines, where one goes looking for greatness in the places where greatness has been known over a very long time to happen. (Alsace, as we will see in due course, is the one notable exception in France to the rule that place names govern, and there is a particular reason for the Alsatian exception: the wines of Alsace are known first by the variety of grape used in the making of them.)

And so, to the *Appellation d'Origine Contrôlée* and the second tier, the *Vins Délimité de Qualité Supérieure*. What is it that is controlled? Principally, the types of grapes which may be used in the location named, the maximum number of gallons of wine that may be produced from an acre of ground (pruning is the control), the minimum number of degrees of alcoholic strength that the wine must attain, and practices in growing and vinifying. But first, what these laws do is to define the area to which each set of requirements applies. What happens then is that in any region, something like a set of concentric rings is created. This can perhaps best be illustrated by the following story, which has the great merit of being true.

It happened in an Ottawa restaurant where the sommelier, all posh, wore a tastevin slung from a chain around his neck. A tastevin is a shallow, dimpled silver cup which professional wine tasters use for viewing and tasting wine and which the sommelier in this case used for a slurp from each bottle served, to safeguard the clients against something—perhaps against drinking too much wine. On the wine card was a Château Margaux at a gratifyingly low price, one of the bargains of the age, in fact, if the wine had been what the list said it was. It wasn't, naturally. It was a bottle of the wine of the commune of Margaux, not *Château* Margaux. The difference is as between Belgravia and London, or Park Avenue and New York, which is to say that one is contained within the other, but to suggest that they are synonymous on that account would be absurd. Château Margaux is a single vineyard, one of the world's greatest. Margaux is the commune (township, in Canadian terms) in which it is located. In the same commune there are other vineyards, some of them nearly as illustrious as Margaux itself, which make, bottle and market their own wines under their own names—Château Rausan-Ségla, Château Lascombes, Château Durfort-Vivens, to name only three—but there are also lesser vineyards. These produce wines which go to market simply as Margaux. A bottle of Margaux may be very good, but it will not be *Château* Margaux.

Let us go back to our concentric circles. The outer ring in Bordeaux embraces the whole of the Bordeaux region, and stipulations as to wines that may be marketed as bordeaux, pure and simple, are the easiest to meet. (Precisely the same wine as will qualify for the *Appellation Contrôlée* Bordeaux, red or white, will qualify to be sold as Bordeaux Supérieur with one more degree of alcohol; in other words, to this point, we have not left the outer ring.) But within the Bordeaux region there are various districts of which the Médoc, Graves, St. Emilion and Pomerol, Sauternes and Barsac, are only the most important. While wine grown at an approved site in any of these can be sold as bordeaux, no wine but that grown in the Médoc can be sold as Médoc, nor any but a wine of Graves as Graves, and so on. And within the Médoc, to narrow matters now to that district, there are communes, or townships, such as Margaux, Pauillac, St. Estèphe, St. Julien (usually now referred to as St. Julien-Beychevelle). And again, while a wine of Margaux may be sold as Médoc or bordeaux, only a wine grown in the commune Margaux can be sold as Margaux. Finally, as we have seen, within the communes there are individual properties, the best of which are big enough, and rich enough, because they have world-wide reputations and their wines consistently command high prices, to function wholly on their own names, marking their labels "*Mis en bouteilles au Château*" (Bottled at the Chateau) so that the eventual buyer in Tokyo or Toronto knows that no one else has added anything to, or taken anything from, the contents of that bottle between the time the cork was put in and the moment he drew it out. This is the final ring.

Does all of this represent only so much mumbo-jumbo designed to create a sort of mystique for wine snobs to wrap themselves in? It is a question on which I am prepared to draw myself up to my full height and deliver an unequivocal, "Well, yes and no."

Although ways have been found from time to time of fiddling the French wine-control laws, as ways have been found of fiddling just about any other laws that have ever been enacted anywhere, in general the system seems to work fairly well. And it does add to the pleasure of trying to know something about wines to have a reasonable assurance that what is in the bottle in every instance is what the label says is in it. Here, of course, we are talking of the great generality of wine covered by the *Appellation Contrôlée*. Come to the rarified level of the great chateaux which hold responsibility in their own hands until the bottles are sealed in their cases, and there is the further assurance of their prestige. Convincing word that Château Lafite had doctored a bad vintage would be received by wine enthusiasts with something like the shock that would attend the report that the Archbishop of Canterbury had been caught filching shillings for the gas-meter from the poor box.

On the other hand—and it is something people in the Bordeaux wine-trade are concerned about—the whole matter of chateau-bottling, and the term chateau itself, may have been oversold. So much is the attention of the buying public riveted on the so-called Classified Growths, particularly those of the Médoc, and particularly the top few of those, that their prices are being driven to ridiculous heights. At the same time, while good, sound commune, district, and regional, wines do not quite go begging, they are neglected to a degree. As a member of *Le Grand Conseil de Bordeaux* complained privately during a visit to Canada in May 1972, "It is hard nowadays to sell anything that does not have the word *Château* in the name."

This kind of buying, of course, is snobbism, and like most snobbisms makes very little sense. It is also expensive. Both these statements are true even if we are talking only of chateaux which are outside the official classification. But they are even more true of the Classified Growths. For instance, if that venerable listing of 1855 were revised, some chateaux which were not included at the time would be included now; yet because they are *not* included, their wines sell for from a dollar to several dollars less than almost all those which made the lowest classified rungs in 1855 .

Some of the outstanding unclassified chateaux wines which are, or have been, available in Canada are Château d'Angludet in Ontario; Château Fourcas-Dupré in Newfoundland; Château Méyney, Pavèil-de-Luze and Gloria in Quebec. There are many others, which have never been seen here, which lurk just beyond the pale of the exalted classification. We could do with more of them.

But what the *Bordelais* already quoted was chiefly referring to was the relative lack of interest in commune and district wines, which is another aspect of the preoccupation with the big-name chateaux. And what he had in mind were wines bearing such names as Côtes de Bourg, Côtes de Blaye, Premières Côtes de Bordeaux, Côtes Canon-Fronsac, Graves de Vayres and the like—some of which, given a little time, if red, and served with due care and attention (that is, after having been opened for an hour or so, not stone cold), are more than just everyday wines.

But any name relating to the great Bordeaux region (the same is true of Burgundy and the Rhône, and even the Loire) is a household word as compared with those of the nearly seventy wines entitled to the VDQS seal. These are the sorts of *vins du pays* that cause visitors to return home from holidays in France muttering that there would be wine on their table at least twice a day (breakfast optional) if only.... (It is also the customary thing for them to say that the little wine which seemed so lovely when drunk on a hill overlooking the Mediterranean does not taste the same at home, and there is, perhaps, some truth in that, although it may have more to do with the traveller than with the wine.) The main problem is that it costs as much to ship a bottle of wine costing a few pennies as it does to ship one costing several dollars, and the duty on bringing it into the country is the same, since it is on volume rather than value. The provincial mark-up, of course, is related to value, and at something more than 100 per cent in places, that has its effect too. In the end, the price of our erstwhile little wine is nudging three dollars if not actually beyond that, and buying it has become a matter for mature deliberation.

In the summer of 1971, in an extended bout of research of an intensity and devotion which in more formal fields of study is rewarded with at least a Canada Medal, I made substantial inroads into the list of those *Vins Délimités de Qualité Supérieure.* Of the lot, I was particularly impressed with two bearing the VDQS place-name Rousillon dels Aspres—Rousillon is in the Midi—and named Château d'Aubiry and Château de Corneilla; and a third, Haut Comtat, from Provence. But then, at between thirty-eight-and-a-half and forty-two cents, I am easily impressed.

Some VDQS wines which are to be found in Canada are Corbières, Minervois and Caracous (Côtes de Provence).

The South, in a broad band behind the Atlantic almost all the way from the Spanish to the Italian border, is the great wine-producing area of France in terms of volume; there are some AOC wines in this extensive region, and rather more VDQS. But to reach the most southern of the really *great* names, it is necessary to travel a distance north in the Valley of the Rhône, to Châteauneuf-du-Pape and Tavel.

There are VDQS wines in all parts of France, but the greatest number of them are in the south, in Provence and the Midi. What to go with a Provençal wine but a Provençal dish? There are both red and white wines of Provence, but better than either of those are the rosés. A rosé bearing the VDQS sticker and the words Côtes de Provence would go well with this dish—or, failing that, any white wine which is not expensive. Provençal cooking, with its olive oil and garlic, needs a wine that can stand up for itself.

Brandade de Morue

2 lbs. salt cod	2-2½ cups oil
1 cup olive oil	1¼ cups cream
1 small clove garlic, crushed	salt and pepper

Wash and soak the salt cod to remove salt. Cut into square pieces and poach in water for 8 minutes. Drain and flake. Heat the olive oil in a heavy, flat-bottomed saucepan until it begins to smoke. Put in the cod and the crushed garlic and work the mixture until it is reduced to a smooth paste. Turn the heat very low and keep on working the *brandade* with a wooden spoon, adding, a little at a time, the 2 to 2½ cups oil and the hot cream. Stir constantly and add *very, very slowly*—over gentle heat. When the *brandade* is ready it should have the consistency of mashed potatoes and be very smooth.

Serve the *brandade* in a round bowl, moulding it into the shape of a dome. Garnish with triangles of bread fried in butter and slices of truffle.

*From the
new palace
of the Pope
to the ancient
roasted slope*

*G*LANCE AT THE map of France and the valley of the Rhône will be seen to look like something out of a wiring diagram: three arterial highways follow the river banks from Marseille to Lyon, the Autoroute and the N.7, which are on the east side, looping over and under one another as they run north.

The Rhône has always been a main means of access to the heart of the continent. The Romans travelled it, continued on beyond Lyon up the valley of the Saône into what we call Burgundy, and on beyond that to the Moselle and the Rhine. All of these, it will be noted, are wine areas, and it is true that where the Romans went, cultivation of the vine followed. (Clearly, the vine-stock travelled in the Roman soldier's packsack the way chewing gum and nylons did in those of some of his successors. Equally clearly, he was prepared to wait longer for the rewards of his enterprise.)

One theory to explain the discovery that the vine is best cultivated on hillsides runs this way: the valleys presented the path of least resistance in getting an army from Point A (Arelas, or Arles) to Point B (Burgundionum); where such highways of conquest were established, it became expedient to clear the lower slopes so as to lessen the danger of ambush; once the slopes had been cleared, what to do but grow things on them? Whether or not the discovery was made by some such happy accident as that, the fact is that over the intervening centuries it has been proved that slopes, and a climate which is brisk and bright rather than humid and oppressive, *do* provide the best conditions for the cultivation of wine grapes. For one thing, the vine is motivated by a spirit of *Per Ardua ad Astra*. It needs a struggle to reach the heights. Sedimentary basins may be all very well for the pallid likes of wheat, but the soil tends to be too fat and easy for the vine, with the result that fat and

Côtes-du-Rhône

Côte Rôtie
Château Grillet

St. Joseph
Tournon
Tain l'Hermitage
Crozes-Hermitage

Cornas
St. Péray
Valence

Rhône R.

Gigondas
Orange
Lirac
Châteauneuf du Pape
Tavel
Avignon

flaccid wines are made. Then there is the fact, which becomes more important the more northern the vineyards are, that a hillside which is canted towards the south and east so that it catches the sun from first thing in the morning until late evening, is necessary so that proper ripening can take place. Such a slope also will have its back to the first blasts of winter, and the fruit may go on ripening for several weeks after it would have perished on exposed flatlands.

This, admittedly, is not a serious consideration in the Rhône Valley, where growers and shippers are happy to boast that theirs are Wines of the Sun. That does not stretch the point, for during the long summer the Rhône Valley drily bakes—altogether pleasantly if you happen to have a picnic lunch and a cold bottle of, say, white Hermitage, hundreds of feet up on a steep hillside, with the broad-beamed barges, all fresh paint and flapping laundry, slipping by on the river below.

Sun or no sun, that adversity which the wine-grape thrives on, the Rhône provides, to meet the vine's most passionate masochistic tendency. In the middle portion of the Côtes du Rhône, for instance, where the already-mentioned Hermitage is grown (the red Hermitage is more famed than the white, by the way), the vines grow in a thin covering of not very encouraging-looking soil over basic granite. At the southern end of the Valley, where this tour of the Rhône begins, the wines called Châteauneuf-du-Pape are grown in circumstances that would cause a cactus to despair.

The story of Châteauneuf-du-Pape begins in a roundabout way, in Bordeaux, where in 1300 the Archbishop of Bordeaux, Bernard de Goth, planted a vineyard in the portion which is now referred to as Graves. (His vineyard is still there and doing well.) Nine years later the wine-loving Archbishop had not only become pope—Pope Clément v—but had moved the seat of the papacy from Rome to Avignon, in the South of France, where it remained until 1378. During all that period, the popes were French.

In Avignon there is still, and in a remarkably good state of repair, a massive, fortress-like building on high ground, looking down upon the Rhône. From its terraces there is an excellent view of the celebrated Pont d'Avignon, on which one might still dance, except in the middle, which is missing. North from Avignon a few miles, near Orange, there is a town, now called Châteauneuf-du-Pape, where, again on a hill, there is a ruin consisting of not much more than one end wall. This was the summer palace of the popes during the period of their stay in Avignon, the place in the country where they could get away from what may have been the heady vapours of the larger Avignon. And from that, we have the name of a wine which is grown today even at the base of the remaining walls—Châteauneuf-du-Pape, the wine of the Pope's New Palace.

Notwithstanding his credentials as a wine drinker and a wine-grower, Pope Clément seems not to have started the vineyards at Châteauneuf-du-Pape; that was left to a successor. Perhaps he was fully occupied with the building of his new castle. In any event, the vineyards at Châteauneuf-du-Pape flourished long after the papacy had been restored to Rome, but later—perhaps after 1502, when the summer palace was destroyed in the religious wars —they declined, until at one time they almost ceased to exist at all. It was only in the early 1800's that the wines of Châteauneuf-du-Pape began to be brought back again, and only in this century that Châteauneuf-du-Pape began to regain a reputation for honest wine of quality. (This was done by the application of strict codes, even before the *Appellation Contrôlée* laws were enacted.) There is some emphasis here to be put on the word "honest," for immediately before this reformation, Châteauneuf-du-Pape had been the subject of much stretching (as the practice is so delicately described) with inferior wines.

The vineyards of Châteauneuf-du-Pape cover about 6000 acres of as unpromising-looking land as can be in successful cultivation anywhere. The area might make an ideal rattlesnake farm. These acres are on a tableland above the Rhône. The Vaucluse, the department in which Châteauneuf-du-Pape is located, is generally fertile, market-basket country renowned for fruits and vegetables and especially for early asparagus. But on this high ground there is less of actual soil to be seen than of stones: there are great expanses of ground where the intersecting rows of vines form a sort of grid against an unbroken background of stones in all sizes from pebbles to rocks the size and shape of somewhat flattened small grapefruit. From a little distance, there are portions of ground which look as if they had been paved in cobbles. With a hot southern sun beating down and reflecting off this stony surface, the grapes bake. The vintage in Châteauneuf-du-Pape rarely suffers from insufficient sun, but quantity can be reduced by not enough rain.

The wine the vineyards produce is dark in colour, with a purple cast to it. It is a very full, winey wine, and one that is strong in alcohol. The minimum that Châteauneuf-du-Pape must reach in order to satisfy its *Appellation Contrôlée* law is twelve and a half degrees; it very frequently exceeds fourteen and is the most alcoholic of the French wines. Since it *is* robust, it is the sort of wine that goes well with strongly-flavoured dishes—game, if you are a game fancier (I am not); beef stews with lots of dark brown gravy (*boeuf-en-daube*, if you like); roast beef and steaks; or, if your ski-lodge supplies happen to include wine, with plebeian home-baked beans and brown bread. Whatever it is, if it is the sort of dish that is said to stick to your ribs, Châteauneuf-du-Pape is likely to be the very model of compatibility in sticking with it.

For reasons that the foregoing perhaps does something to explain, Châteauneuf-du-Pape has become a regular on wine lists everywhere. However meagre or however oddly chosen its offerings may seem to be, the card in that little-restaurant-that-hasn't-been-discovered-yet in Montreal, or in the Gem Cafe in Lilac, Saskatchewan, will have a Châteauneuf-du-Pape on it, if it has anything. Obviously, further reasons have to be found. It could be that there is something in its having a name that sticks in the mind; moreover, the name has rather an exotic flavour to it. Or perhaps it owes something to the wine's reputation for prolonging life, sustaining virility, and even being endowed with mildly aphrodisiac qualities. (I have been able to find no shred of support for the latter two of these, but still have hopes for the first.)

There is a story, told in *A Book of French Wines* by P. Morton Shand (as revised and edited by Cyril Ray), that the first revival of Châteauneuf-du-Pape in the early 1800's, was assisted by a certain Marquis de la Nerthe, who was a vineyard owner by occupation, and a rake of absolutely breathtaking capacities by inclination.

This marquis of the First Empire (as the story is told) was a famous and much-discussed viveur who continued his frivolities and debauches to an unprecedented and most unseemly age. When the curious asked him how he managed to maintain health and vigor in spite of the number of his years and the manner of his life, he invariably replied that the wine of his Château de la Nerthe was a veritable elixir for prolonging youth and even life itself.

It must be added that none of this elixir of the Domaine de la Nerthe, which remains one of the important vineyards of

Châteauneuf-du-Pape, reaches these shores. A pity. What there is in Canada to represent Châteauneuf-du-Pape as a whole is, in fact, very little. With the exception of Alberta, no provincial commission at all stocks the wine of any individually named vineyard; the rest offer simply Châteauneuf-du-Pape, which is to say a wine certified to have been grown in the delimited area, of the sanctioned types of grapes, which have been made to yield no more than the stipulated number of gallons of wine per acre and which have produced at least the minimum strength allowable in alcohol. The merit of a single-vineyard wine is that it is safely assumable that the grower keeps his best to put out under his own name. If he chose, he could sell off any year's wine or any part of it to the shippers, to be marketed under the *Appellation Contrôlée* of the commune (here, Châteauneuf-du-Pape), or, a step lower, of the region (Côtes du Rhône). But what carries his name expresses his individuality and makes his reputation.

In Châteauneuf-du-Pape, growers have even more than the usual room to assert their individuality because a dozen varieties of grapes are permitted to be used in the making of wines entitled to the *Appellation Contrôlée*. (The major wines of Burgundy are made of one, the Pinot Noir, for red, and the Pinot Chardonnay, for white; in Bordeaux, red wines are made mainly of the Cabernet Sauvignon and Merlot, although some others are permitted and used, in minor proportions.) The main grape in Châteauneuf-du-Pape, nevertheless, is the Grenache.

While most of Châteauneuf-du-Pape is red, and a full, *blude* red at that, there is also some white Châteauneuf-du-Pape made; after one brief meeting with the latter, I remain to be moved from indifference, but I should add that the wine then was not chilled nearly enough. It would be a surprise, too, if someone, somewhere, were not making a barrel of Châteauneuf-du-Pape rosé, which never enters trade. Perhaps the deterrent to such ambition is the fact that there is, a few miles away, the district that produces what many think is the ultimate rosé wine.

That district of course is Tavel. Here again, the vines grow in ground rocky enough, one would think, to discourage even the most persistent weed. Still, it is less awesomely rocky than at Châteauneuf-du-Pape. The same sun that Vincent van Gogh went south to find beats down, too, on the vineyards here. But while somehow it seems appropriate enough that out of this baking moonscape of the lower

Rhône should come the big, assertive red wines of Châteauneuf-du-Pape, it is hard to associate the delicate-looking pink wine of Tavel with it. It would be just as well to remember that Tavel is only delicate *looking*. Behind that pink complexion lurks a firm authority, and after a full lunch on some patio, with lashings of Tavel and the warm sun beating down on the head, there may be a distinct inclination to go bye-byes.

Nothing looks so good as a cool, bedewed bottle of rosé wine in the summertime, and hardly anything *is* so good, in the right place, as a good bottle of Tavel. The thing is to find the right place. Unfortunately—and I swear it is true—nine out of every ten bottles of any rosé that are sold in a year are sold in some such circumstances as these: it has been decided by both, or all parties—it is their considered judgement arrived at after full consultation—that they will have the *entrecôte marchand du vin*, and the host is running his finger down the list of red wines looking for a burgundy which he can order without actually going white at the price, or even a bottle of the much-more-moderately-priced Châteauneuf-du-Pape, or something else red. And just as his finger has come to rest, the others say, as if on cue, no, on second thought they will have (in order from the left) a broiled lobster, an *escalope* of veal in cream, and a mixed grill. Curses. Blast them for a pack of vacillating idiots. And he calls over the waiter and orders a bottle of rosé, thinking to bridge the old rule of red wine, red meat; white meat, white wine, by making a bow in both directions.

No harm done, but the better way out, assuming that it is not possible to tell them all to go to hell and ignore the revision, would be to order a bottle (a half-bottle?) of whichever red wine might strike his fancy to go with the steak and the mixed grill, and the same of something white to go with the lobster and veal. Rosé as a compromise has not a lot to be said for it; in any case, it is rather a waste.

Instead, as a pilot-study in how to get the most from a bottle of Tavel, try this: Present yourself at the door of Le Vieux Moulin de Tavel (Gabriel Roudil, Père et Fils, Proprietaire-Recoltant) and get from the hands of Gabriel himself, or from one of the three sons, a bottle of last year's wine which has not yet had its lead capsule put on to be ready for market, and which is straight from the cool bottling shed. Go straightaway to a place under a tree in any clear space among the surrounding vineyards, spread out the cloth, and on it the bread and cheese, and slices and bits of this and that from the *charcuterie*, and enjoy, enjoy. The same thing can be done in the backyard with almost equally gratifying results, although the bottle of Tavel will cost rather more than the dollar, give or take a few cents, that M. Roudil himself will charge.

Tavel looks good because it has a brilliant pale red colour that almost sparkles in the light, unlike so many other rosés, which are weak, washed-out pinks, or which contain large amounts of orange, like so much rusty water. The taste of Tavel is clean and fresh and, if you try, you might just find in the bouquet a hint of strawberry jam when first brought to the boil.

In 1958, Waverley Root, who even then had been a correspondent in Paris for thirty years, brought out *The Food of France*, cook-book, travel book, history text, and all-round guide for the enthusiastic eater in a country with a strong knife-and-fork tradition. *The Food of France* is great in itself, but its publication conferred an additonal benefit on the world in that it induced the late A. J. Liebling (whose other writings included the Wayward Press feature in the *New Yorker*) to write a series of reminiscent pieces which, as I recall it, he called "Memoirs of a Feeder in France". Mr. Liebling was a man who fed well, largely and often, and he liked his wine. He was writing of a time in his life—his young manhood—when he was absolutely in his prime at the table. And it emerged that he was a great fan of the wines of Tavel. It has been considered by many an eccentric tendency—it is generally accepted that there are good rosé wines, of which Tavel is the best, but that there are no *great* rosé wines—but the opinion of so practised a feeder has to be respected.

Unfortunately, there is very little Tavel imported into Canada. The liquor commissions of Ontario, Quebec, Manitoba, Nova Scotia and Alberta all list a Tavel. In the first four, the shipper is Père Anselme, a firm which is commercially very aggressive but which owns no vineyard properties of its own; in Alberta the shipper is Chauvenet, which is known primarily for a trade-name wine of burgundy-type which it calls Red Flag.

Next door to Tavel is the small community of Lirac, which produces red, white and rosé wines. Lirac is among the emerging nations in the world of wine. Until a few years ago, as a sort of colony of Tavel, the best of its rosé wines were marketed as Tavel. A note which I made on the spot says: "The wines used to be sold under the name of Tavel but apparently local pride prevailed, and some time past they decided that they were going to market them under their own name, and now there is a Lirac *Appellation Contrôlée*. . . . It is a very pleasant rosé wine; perhaps the rosé colour is not so clear and brilliant as it is with the Tavel, but a lovely summer lunch wine. . . . "

The centre around which this area revolves is Orange, an ancient city of not quite 26,000. It is one of those lusty sorts of southern places where in summer everyone and everything is in the streets, including in particular the scents of bakery, delicatessen, fruit store and café, escaping through the beaded curtains in the doorways. There is a cool small square with trees and a fountain where you can sit—it would be irrational not to—with a late afternoon drink and watch the people go by. For lovers of antiquities there is in Orange a great wheel of a Roman theatre in a remarkably good state of preservation in the centre of town, with buses snorting around it. (Run up to the highest row—the rake of the banks of seats is alarming—and see how the old coronary is coming.) And there are good places to eat.

One of them is Le Provençal, a restaurant I like. It is a good place to conduct your diligent research into the wines of the district. What the French reputation for good restaurants rests on is not the dozen with three stars in the *Guide Michelin*, but the large number like Le Provençal (which, incidentally, has one star). In places like this, the decoration perhaps begins and ends with a basket of fruit on a table inside the door, and the well-laid tables themselves, but the serving of food and wines is done with some respect for the fact that a meal should be something more than a response to a three-a-day reflex. The standard of Canadian restaurants has improved immeasurably in the past twenty years, for which praise be given, but it would go up more if proprietors would give a greater amount of time to their kitchens and cellars and less to the gimmickry of fake beams, carriage-lamp reproductions, and the burning of lumps of meat on the ends of swords.

The house wines of Le Provençal are, not surprisingly, Châteauneuf-du-Pape and the red wine of Gigondas. Châteauneuf-du-Pape is south of Orange; Gigondas, slightly northeast. The same grape varieties are grown in Gigondas as at Châteauneuf-du-Pape, and the two have a natural family resemblance. The *Appellation Contrôlée* here is Côtes-du-Rhône-Gigondas. Ontarians, but no other Canadians, can find an example of this good Côtes-du-Rhône wine in their stores. Although Gigondas, like Châteauneuf-du-Pape, does not need many years in bottle to be at its best, it needs some; then it can be a soft, billowy sort of wine with a taste and bouquet which may suggest raspberries. And then again, it may not; these things are highly subjective.

After our detour to Gigondas we return to the Rhône, a wise thing to do because the River, with its barges and other traffic, is pleasant to be beside. There is now a long stretch to the north where vineyards give way to such utilitarian things as cement plants. And then, about opposite the city of Valence (which is home to, among other things, the Restaurant Pic, of great renown), the vineyards recommence, those of St-Peray, Cornas and St-Joseph following one another in short order. (Cornas is a Celtic word meaning scorched ground. When you know that, and the fact that Cornas was the favourite wine of Charlemagne, there is not much else to know, given the fact that none of these wines enters Canada. Neither, for that matter, does a good, quite dry white wine called Chanté Alouette which is produced near here and which would do marvellously well in Canada, given the passion for unity in Toronto, Winnipeg, Calgary, Vancouver and such points, and the widespread English-Canadian notion that Alouette is the French-Canadian national anthem.)

As you come into the town of Tournon on the west bank, you can see the village of Tain across the River, looking for all the world like some of the places on the Rhine: a strip of town along the river front with a church and a steeple, and rising sharply behind it a very great sweep of vineyards in a sort of cup, facing south and perhaps slightly west. These are the vineyards of Hermitage and Crozes-Hermitage.

The red wines of Hermitage once enjoyed a much greater popularity than they now do. They were favourites of, among others, Edward VII, who had a number of favourites of various sorts, not all of them bottled. Wine books which contain glowing references to Hermitage usually are old wine books, and the term usually used is "Old Hermitage". What has happened is that the wine has gone out of fashion through no fault of its own. Hardly anyone anymore is laying down wine to be drunk by his son at age twenty-five or by himself at age sixty for that matter, and Hermitage needs time. In old age (the wine's, but perhaps also the wine-drinker's), Hermitage is supposed to scale the heights. By reputation, it develops great flavour, a soft, velvety texture, and with that a bouquet reminiscent of raspberries and gilliflowers. This latter reminiscence will necessarily be limited to those who know what gilliflowers smell like—of which I am not one. Nor have I much to say from experience about Hermitage wines of great age, due to my ancestors' regrettable neglect in the matter of laying any aside. Young Hermitage can be a little hard and even rough, but I can testify that at age twelve, the oldest bottle I have managed to put myself in the way of, it develops to a marked degree the characteristics of taste and bouquet (leaving aside the gilliflowers) already attributed to it. I have a few bottles of 1964 set aside and if they are willing to wait another thirty or forty years to be at their best, God knows I am willing to wait with them. (I have always looked upon a wine cellar as a form of life insurance, especially as one of those people of whom it might be said that he never left *anywhere* while there was anything left to drink.)

As well as its long-lived red wines, Hermitage produces white wines, of which the best-known is the already-mentioned Chanté-Alouette. The white wines of Hermitage often have a greenish cast to them and a little of the acidy tang of a not-quite-ripe apple in both taste and bouquet; it is a tang which goes beyond being dry. They, too, can stand a little time to get over an initial hardness. Red Hermitage is to be found in the commission stores of Newfoundland and Quebec; white Hermitage in Ontario. Crozes-Hermitage, which can only be regarded as a junior member of the family, is available in Nova Scotia and Ontario. Crozes is mainly red.

The wine area called the Côtes-du-Rhône—and of course the lesser wines drawn from the whole area are bottled and sold as just that—covers roughly 125 miles from Avignon in the south to Vienne in the north, the direction in which we are going. Approaching Vienne, which is noted for its Cathedral St. Maurice and its Roman theatre but more particularly for its Pyramide Restaurant —one of those dozen gastronomic shrines referred to earlier—we come to two of the Rhône's most renowned vineyards, those of Château Grillet and Côte Rôtie.

Château Grillet is a wine that is much talked and written about but not much drunk, for the very good and simple reason that there is not much of it *to* drink. It comes from what, on the lone prairie, would not even make a respectable kitchen garden—a patch of ground only a little more than three acres in extent. Some

Commissariat Général au Tourisme

Bottles stored for long periods in damp, cool cellars often become unappetizingly furred with mould, but the cool, dark aging makes the wine mellow.

When the grapes for these first bottles were on the vines, Napoleon was at Abukir. This is not the cellar of your provincial commission, but the library at Château Lafite.

Commissariat Général au Tourisme

Many owners have pieces of the coveted vineyard of Clos de Vougeot in Burgundy, but the chateau itself is the home of the Confrérie des Chevaliers du Tastevin.

Since the setting for this photograph is Burgundy, those grapes should be Pinot Noir, from which the fine red wines of the region are made. The kilt is not an indigenous costume of Burgundy.

Commissariat Général au Tourisme

Going south in Burgundy, the single, even slope that constitutes the Côte de Nuits gives way to country of small undulating hills. Here, we are in the Côte de Beaune.

The name on the stone marker, as will be recognized by every student of Champagne corks, identifies this magnificently barbered wine-region. Near Epernay.

Commissariat Général au Tourisme

Commissariat Général au Tourisme

Wine is not simply taste, or even taste and bouquet; it should also be of a rich, clear colour to delight the eye. Those barrels, wine-lovers, are at Château Lafite.

of its modest output goes to the Pyramide just across and up the River; most of what remains, I gather, is sold privately. It is a white wine which the ardent hunter might do best to track down at the Pyramide, where he may be able to bag a bottle armed only with his American Express card.

Côte Rôtie (along with Châteauneuf-du-Pape at the other end) makes one of the twin pillars of the Côtes du Rhône now that Hermitage is somewhat in the shadows. There is, however, very much less of Côte Rôtie than there is of Châteauneuf-du-Pape, and the likelihood is that there will continue to be still less, for the two dramatic slopes which comprise this so-called Roasted Slope, the Blonde and the Brune, have an escalator quality to them. They are quite as steep as any escalator and the terraces are hardly broader than steps. They are painfully difficult to work. Côte Rôtie is less well-known than Châteauneuf-du-Pape partly on account of its smaller volume, but partly no doubt because, like Hermitage, it is a slow-maturing wine in an age when houses are traded in like automobiles and a wine-cellar is any bottle not yet out of its brown-paper bag. Côte Rôtie is a wine of which it might be said that a sip makes a mouthful—it is very full, and it has a bouquet in which there is said to be a hint of violets. (I am not good about hints of violets.) It is a dark red wine which, for reasons not entirely clear, I find myself thinking of as glowing from great depths, like polished mahogany. It is, to my mind, a much overlooked wine and one worth rediscovering. It will be better if there is a ten-year gap between the date on the bottle and the date on the calendar.

Scholars have told us that the Romans (to end with them, as we began) thought highly of the wines of this part of their world and that Pliny the Younger, Martial and Plutarch praised the wines of Vienne, which very well may have been the wines of nearby Côte Rôtie's intimidating slopes. However, the Romans also liked their wines flavoured with odd additives, like pine resin and nuts, and were given to using spiced wine with snow in it as an agent to make them—not to put too fine a point on it—belch at table, so that they could eat more. In the circumstances, I am not sure that a wine's having borne the warrant, By Appointment to Imperial Rome, can be taken as the last word in recommendations.

The wines of Châteauneuf-du-Pape, Côte Rôtie, Hermitage and Gigondas each have their own characteristics. Côte Rôtie, I think, is the finest but they do have in common a warmth and heartiness that make them go well with hearty food. For instance, you might have a shot at something like this on a cold night:

Boeuf aux Olives
(Beef with Olives)

a *filet* of beef, trimmed and larded	1 tbsp. beef extract
¼ cup butter	3 sprigs parsley
½ lb. mushrooms, thinly sliced	1 bay leaf
2 medium onions or 1 large one, thinly sliced	pinch of thyme
1 carrot, thinly sliced	salt and pepper to taste
¼ lb. pitted green olives	2 tbsp. flour, mixed with a little water
2 cups water	1 cup Madeira
2 tomatoes, peeled, seeded and chopped	

Roast the *filet* of beef in a very hot oven (450°) for 10 minutes per pound for very rare, and 12 to 13 minutes for rare. Serve with the Madeira sauce.

SAUCE

Melt the butter in a heavy saucepan and add the mushrooms, onion and carrot. Cook until vegetables are golden in colour. Add the olives, tomatoes, water, beef extract and herbs and simmer for 20 minutes. Add the flour paste, stirring constantly, and cook until the mixture thickens. Strain, and then return to the heat. Add ½ cup Madeira and cook for 10 minutes over low heat. Add the second ½ cup, bring to the boil and quickly stir in 1 tbsp. butter.

Of course, if you weren't in your hearty peasant mood that night but were looking for something more elegant (though still hearty), you could accept the recommendation of Madame A. Vasse, the proprietress of le Provençal at Orange, who says that the very thing to accompany a robust (or *capiteaux*) wine such as Gigondas, or, even better, a fine Châteauneuf-du-Pape, would be these *tournedos* with a truffled (smack, smack) sauce:

Tournedos Sauce Truffée

Cut a *filet* of beef into good slices (about 1″ thick), allowing 1 slice per person. *Sauté* in hot butter to your individual taste (rare, medium, etc.). At the same time prepare an equal number of bread *canapés* (rounds of bread *sautéed* in butter). Place each *tournedos* on its *canapé* and keep warm.

Prepare an excellent brown sauce by adding beef stock to the skillet in which the beef cooked and stirring in Madeira wine, thinly sliced mushrooms, truffles and a large nut of butter. Spread the sauce over the *tournedos* and decorate with slices of truffle. Serve very hot with Dauphine potatoes or potatoes *sautéed* in savoury butter.

Drinka pinta every day light and fruity Beaujolais

*A*BOUT THE PART of France that goes by the name of Beaujolais, I am not at all a reliable witness. My bias is simply too strong to hide. I like the look, feel and smell of the place, and of course I like what it produces.

Remember Clochemerle? *Clochemerle* was the story of a French village that wanted to erect a monument which would be at once useful, and symbolic of the progressive mind of the local council—and chose a pissoir. The upheaval that ensued shook Clochemerle to its wine-filled cellars.

The village of Clochemerle (The Blackbirds' Bell) was in the Beaujolais*—*is* in Beaujolais, vibrantly alive and earthy as ever if you believe any of the various persons who from time to time have claimed to be able to put their finger on the very place. In fact, if you drive through the region, you can find it yourself—half-a-dozen times. In any case, the looking will be fun. In all of the wine towns —villages, really—there are cellars, *caves*, most of them run by the local co-operative, where you may stop for a glass of last year's wine. Some charge, some don't, but in all of them the woman behind the bar will expect a little something more than a smile of sublime satisfaction and gratitude.

Or you may buy a bottle—or a three-bottle carrying case, a case of 12, or a lot of 100 or 500 or more. In the summer of 1971, at the wine-growers' co-operative in Fleurie, 100 bottles of that very good wine of the Beaujolais would have cost $130. I did not price it in the 500-bottle lot; while pricing 100 bottles, which I would not be able to import anyway, might be put down as legitimate reportorial curiosity, to inquire about 500 would have been to stray into outright fantasy.

Leave one village and the road-signs point to two others with

*Beaujolais is shown on the map on p. 109.

familiar wine names. Decisions, decisions. But never mind. The road is easy and uncrowded and eventually it wanders its way around to them all. The trick, after a certain number of stops, is not to wander before the road does.

The real-life Clochemerle could be the village of Julienas, although I have never seen Julienas mentioned for the honour. But a place of so practical a turn of mind as to convert an old church into a temple of Bacchus, complete with murals of billowy-breasted maidens celebrating the vintage, somehow seems the sort to salute progress in the manner and with the weapons indicated in *Clochemerle*. It would be totally inadequate to say that the wine-tasting cellar in Julienas is a little out of the ordinary. At one end of the erstwhile nave, there is a centrifuge press. There are several fermenting vats in the old style, made of wood. Those are the customary artifacts of any cellar. But then there are the murals. There, on our left, we have a couple standing in the centre of a vat, where presumably they are treading the grapes . . .but perhaps to try to capture the scene more exactly it would be best simply to put down some notes as they were recorded in the heat of the moment.

> . . . *he is bare to the waist and has one hand around her waist. He is wearing what can only be described as a form of kilt; this seems to be the standard dress for the men in all these pictures. She has her skirt up and the front of her dress down, so that her bosom is hanging out. The other people in the scene include a girl naked to the waist with flowers in her hair, holding her ass—an animal in this instance.*
>
> *The picture on the end wall shows us Bacchus, I assume it is, with grape leaves in his hair and a large glass in his hand, sitting astride a barrel, and around him, all sorts of Bacchanalian revels going on. There's a goat rampant on a field of grapes and, over both, a girl with one foot up in the air and waving a scarf, which covers at least part of her.*
>
> *There's Pan playing his pipes. There are two children embracing one another. The female of the pair illogically has fully developed breasts, although she appears to be three years of age. On the other wall there is a man leaning into a vat of grapes pressing with his bare hands, and to his right, yet another topless grape-picker. The harvest here obviously is a time of great jollity, not to mention fun-and-games. . . .*

But on second thought, no; Clochemerle couldn't be Julienas. Gabriel Chevallier, the author, described Clochemerle's situation as follows:

To the west of the Route Nationale No. 6, which goes from Lyon to Paris, there lies, between Anse and the outskirts of Mâcon over a distance of about 45 kilometres, a region which shares with Burgundy, Anjou, Bordelais and the Côtes du Rhône the honor of producing the most celebrated wines in France. The names of Brouilly, Morgon, Julienas, Moulin-à-Vent have made Beaujolais famous. But side-by-side with these names there are others, with less splendor attaching to them, which are yet indicative of substantial merits. In the forefront of these names from which an unjust fate has withheld a widespread renown comes that of Clochemerle-en-Beaujolais. *

So the real Clochemerle can't be Julienas: Clochemerle is one of those unsung villages whose wines go to market simply as Beaujolais Villages. (The difference between a wine called Beaujolais and a wine called Beaujolais Villages we will come to in a moment.)

To me the whole of the Beaujolais is a delight, largely because, to a surprising degree, it remains true today even as when *Clochemerle* was written (it was published in English in 1936) that "Set apart in these hills, which act as a succession of screens, the towns and villages of Beaujolais, with their healthy, bracing air, enjoy an isolated position and retain a flavor of feudal times." For a start, the Beaujolais is on no main highway. Even so, it has an air of being more apart from the world than it is. It is all rolling hills, more and more now covered with vines, but with some wooded places left and with some room still for pastures. (For beef, no doubt; such milk as is considered necessary in the Beaujolais is taken, I suspect, without its being decanted.)

But let's begin at the beginning. Say that you are going from Lyon to Mâcon, travelling north from the vineyards of the Côtes-du-Rhône towards the glories of Burgundy's Côte d'Or. You *could* take the autoroute (it did not exist when *Clochemerle* was written). The autoroute is the French equivalent of the German autobahn, the Italian autostrada and the North American super-highway, a magnificent road on which any veteran of Indianapolis or the Grand Prix of Monaco would feel at home. Perhaps not happy, but at home. To say merely that the French produce an inordinate number of hairy drivers is like saying that there are trees along the Amazon.

I was on the Lyon-Paris section of the autoroute one day in the

*From *Clochemerle* by Gabriel Chevallier, translated by Jocelyn Godefroi (London, Penguin Books in association with Secker & Warburg, 1951), p. 18.

passing lane, doing a shifty ninety-five mph past half a dozen cars dawdling at eighty, when a Lamborghini behind let go a blast with his air-horns that almost stopped my heart dead in its tracks. He had not been anywhere in sight when I had got into the passing lane thirty seconds before. When I managed to get out of his way, he went by, horns blaring imprecations still, and shortly disappeared over the horizon. So *that's* what 150 mph looks like.

A much more sensible course would be to take the old highway, the previously mentioned Route Nationale No. 6, no distance at all to the west; most sensible of all would be to get off *that* at the first sign saying Route des Vins, or Beaujolais, or Route de Beaujolais or whatever. That way lies as lovely a wine area as there is, a place apart, with orange-roofed villages set amongst hills which rise gently at first, and then more steeply as you go west, until finally you climb to the village of Poyebead, from which you can see over all the Beaujolais, and even, on a clear day, as far as Switzerland—or so I'm told. (Seeing Switzerland on a clear day is a major activity in a considerable segment of western Europe.)

At the very peak of the tallest hill, well above the village of Poyebead, there is the *vignerons'* church, a chapel really. It's a tiny place with seven pews a side, room in all for perhaps fifty people. If the winegrowers make pilgrimages here to celebrate good harvests or to plead for divine intercession with the elements, as the visitor is told they do, obviously they don't come *en masse*. But it's a nice little church, a square belfry at the back, and at the front, a tower incorporating an arch in which stands a statue of the Mother and Child, looking out over miles and miles of vineyards which march in their orderly way up near to the crowns of the tonsured hills. Over the church door is the legend: "A Marie Protectrice du Beaujolais".

But that is the Beaujolais countryside; what about the wine? Among the great families of French wines which should be found represented on the list of any Canadian liquor control commission—Burgundy, Bordeaux, Rhône, Loire, Alsace, Champagne —the place to look for the wines of Beaujolais is under the heading, Burgundy. This is the proper listing, right enough, sanctioned by French practice, but there is no very evident good reason why it should be so. The Beaujolais country is remote from the region that usually comes to mind when the name Burgundy is mentioned. The topography is different—a gentle slope in the Côte d'Or, knobbly hills in Beaujolais. So also is the soil. Grapes, as we have seen before and will see again, flourish in inhospitable soils, and the particular form of this perversity practised by the vines of Beaujolais is to enjoy granite.

On top of that, the Gamay grape, from which Beaujolais wines are made, is considered very much a poor relation in Burgundy proper. In fact Philip the Bold of Burgundy (not to be confused with Philip the Bald) once decreed that the Gamay should never set root in the sacred Côte d'Or, the vinous heart of his dukedom. Of course, the heavy-bearing Gamay *is* grown in less-favoured locations in Burgundy proper (a wine identified as Burgundy Passe-Tout-Grains will have been made of a blend of Gamay and Pinot Noir grapes) but where it is, the objective is frankly quantity rather than quality. In the Beaujolais and in some places in California, and almost nowhere else, a peculiar affinity between this grape and a type of granitic soil causes the vine to surpass itself.

The hierarchy of the wines of Beaujolais is easy enough to master. The base name of course is Beaujolais. See the words, *"Appellation Contrôlée Beaujolais,"* on the label of a wine bottle and you know that what is inside was grown at approved locations somewhere within the whole of the Beaujolais region; that it was grown of the Gamay grape; that the grower did not produce more than 440 gallons of wine from each cultivated acre; and that the wine achieved a strength of at least nine degrees of alcohol.

Higher up the scale is wine entitled to be called *Beaujolais Supérieur*. Again, this will have come from any approved location within the region and it will have been made from the Gamay grape, but the number of gallons produced per acre must have been fewer— 396 to 440—and the alcoholic strength higher, ten degrees. Is alcoholic content important? Up to a point. To produce more alcohol, the grapes will have had to contain more sugar and hence to have been riper; the wine will have more body, which means that it will feel less thin in the mouth and will travel and keep better (although keeping qualities are not usually considered important with wines of the Beaujolais, which are made to be drunk young).

At the next plateau, we have the *Appellation Contrôlée, Beaujolais Villages*. We are coming up the scale; the requirements are becoming stiffer. The designation *Beaujolais Villages* is reserved for wines raised at some thirty stated localities in the district which are recognized to be especially favoured—but not quite so much so as to warrant their being allowed to identify themselves on the label. (The Villages are the wine-equivalent of the "and others" in a social note, mentioned after all the *really* gold-plated community leaders have been identified by name.)

The community leaders of the Beaujolais are named. Moulin-à-Vent is a wine of Beaujolais, although the word Beaujolais may appear nowhere on the label. Similarly Fleurie, Julienas, Côte de Brouilly, Morgon, Chiroubles, and Chenas. It is simply the case that the wines from around these particular villages are deemed to be of such merit that they may go to market under their own village names, without the addition of the family name, Beaujolais. In the circumstances, it won't do to say that while you don't care for Beaujolais (an unlikely occurrence) you are partial to Brouilly. Brouilly *is* Beaujolais. To be entitled to this mark of the first rank—an *Appellation Contrôlée* of the village itself—the wine, in addition to having been grown at the place named, must attain an alcoholic strength of at least ten degrees (ten and a half in some cases) and it must have been of a yield of not more than 325 gallons per acre. The rule observed in all wine-growing areas, or all that presume to a fine-wine rating, is that quantity is the enemy of quality.

The most respected of all the wines of Beaujolais is Moulin-à-Vent, ironically, because it is not the wine most people would pick as the archetypal Beaujolais. Moulin-à-Vent in particular, but also Morgon and Julienas, are recognized at their best to be bigger wines—fuller in taste and texture—than their named and unnamed brethren. Moreover, whereas the wines of Beaujolais in general are made to be drunk within two or three years—and vast quantities are drunk in France and elsewhere within a year—Moulin-à-Vent has a reputation for going on improving for four or five or perhaps more years, and to last at maturity for as many more.

The very great rise in the popularity of Beaujolais—there's a bottle of *something* called Beaujolais on almost every wine-list every-where—is attributable to the name, which has a pleasant sound to it, to the fact that the wine is relatively cheap (although that is changing) and also to the fact that it doesn't have to be laid down for years. You will never find Christies in London auctioning off a bottle of Beaujolais 1927 for a fabulous price, mainly because a Beaujolais 1927 wouldn't be worth any price. It is not a great wine of the sort to be cellared for years, brought out and carefully decanted, and poured appropriately (which is to say, reverently) only by a servitor in velvet knee-breeches. It's simply good to drink, and while age is good to the great wines of Burgundy, and even more so to the great wines of Bordeaux, Beaujolais supports the doleful proposition that the good die young.

Beaujolais has both benefited from and helped to foster the world-wide trend towards wines to be drunk young, a trend to which even the most exalted names in all France have had at least to *consider* making concessions. Methods of vinification in Burgundy and Bordeaux have not remained precisely the same over the years, and aged experts moan that claret will never be the same as when Grand-father put down his umpteen dozens of Château Margaux, the lucky dog—but then they have never been altogether happy since the phylloxera epidemic ravaged all the vineyards of Europe in the 1860's and 1870's.

Slow-aging wines require cellars, and private cellars, if not extinct, have become rarities. At Soames's new house at Robin Hill—for those who remember their Forsytes—there was to be a cellar with room for a modest six or seven hundred dozen—say 8400 bottles. Allowing himself a bottle a day (and none for guests, a selfish, but prudent exercise), a man could jog along on that for twenty-plus years without adding a one. Not bad. But in 1860, not so many years before Robin Hill was built, Madame Cliquot's sweet champagne *(à la Russe)* was being offered in London at 60 shillings a dozen ... say $1.25 a bottle—even at $5 to the pound.

Nowadays, prices come somewhat higher than $1.25 a bottle (certainly in Canada they do), and not just for champagne, or fine clarets and burgundies, but for even the most ordinary of *ordinaires*. The number of houses built'each year with wine storage for bottles numbering in the thousands does not seriously tax the statistical services of Central Mortgage and Housing Corporation. The next decade, not even mentioning the next generation, will have to look out for itself. (In any case, we are too mobile to be lugging around hundreds of clinking bottles. The son of the family that grew apples in the Annapolis Valley may make his living drilling for oil in the Arctic. And there are remarkably few wine-cellars dug in the permafrost under prefabs in the Arctic.) Hence the demand for such as Beaujolais, wines which will be as good as they are going to become in a year or two—no slight intended.

Already in any spring, the patrons of restaurants in Paris will have tasted the wines of grapes harvested in the Beaujolais only the previous September. Drinking the *vin de l'année*, in fact, has become chic. (In the Médoc, meanwhile, the finest wines will still have to rest in barrel for eighteen months, and may not be considered at their best for another ten years.) To this love affair with youthful wines I say, fine, but remember that ingratiating as a fresh bottle of Beaujolais may be today (and I *am* a devotee), real greatness takes a little more time.

Another characteristic of Beaujolais that has helped to ingratiate it with many beginning wine-drinkers is that it fits in very well in almost any company. The highest praise that can be given most of the Beaujolais that anyone is likely to encounter in a lifetime of devoted wine-drinking is that it's highly drinkable. It isn't to be pored over and analyzed, but, if not actually poured down, at least to be taken in generous mouthfuls and enjoyed. The words that are used most often to describe it are fruity and refreshing, and if they do not strike you as particularly apt as applied to the bottle in front of you, then barring the dread possibility that you are a victim of sluggish taste buds, what you have is untypical.

And Beaujolais is, as mentioned, accommodating. Red wine (there is a white Beaujolais which we can forget for a moment—or forever if you like) is not generally considered to do a great deal for fish, and vice versa, but that aside, a cool bottle of Beaujolais will do very well with cold chicken, a mixed grill, or with just about anything else that suits your fancy—including a *Coq au Beaujolais*, for which a recipe happily is at hand.

Coq au Vin (chicken in wine, not to make too much of it) is made with almost any kind of wine, not excluding the white Riesling of Alsace. Generally though, what is thought of when *Coq au Vin* is mentioned is chicken in a red-wine sauce. It should be made with the same wine that's going to be served with it at the table, but if you cheat a little and use a cheaper version of the same wine in the cooking, or even a merely similar wine, it is not an offence indictable under the Criminal Code.

With which, *Coq au Beaujolais*:

Coq au Beaujolais

A 3-4 oz. chunk of lean, slab bacon
butter
2½-3 lbs. cut-up frying chicken
½ tsp. salt
⅛ tsp. pepper
¼ cup cognac
3 cups Beaujolais wine
1-2 cups brown chicken stock
or canned beef bouillon

½ tbsp. tomato paste
2 cloves garlic, mashed
¼ tsp. thyme
1 bay leaf
18 brown-braised onions
(small white or yellow
cooking onions)
½ lb. *sautéed* mushrooms
flour

Remove the rind and cut the bacon into thin strips 1″ long. Simmer in water for 10 minutes; rinse in cold water and dry. Using a heavy 10″ fireproof casserole *sauté* the bacon in butter until it is lightly browned. Remove to side dish. Dry the chicken thoroughly and brown it in the hot fat. Season the chicken. Return the bacon to the casserole. Cover and cook slowly for 10 minutes, turning chicken once.

Uncover and pour in the cognac; light, and shake the casserole back and forth until the flame subsides. Pour the 3 cups of wine into the casserole and add just enough stock to cover the chicken. Stir in the garlic, herbs and tomato paste. Bring to a simmer. Cover and simmer slowly until chicken is tender. Remove chicken to a side dish and keep warm.

Skim off fat from the casserole liquid, then raise heat and boil down rapidly until about 2¼ cups remain. Remove from heat. Discard bay leaf and correct seasoning.

Blend 3 tbsp. flour and 2 tbsp. butter and beat into the hot liquid. Bring to a simmer and stir for a minute or two. The sauce should be thick enough to coat a spoon lightly.

Arrange chicken in the serving dish, place the mushrooms and onions around and baste with the sauce. Decorate with sprigs of parsley. Serves 4 to 6.

We can also make a bridge here between the Beaujolais and the district that follows, the Mâconnais, with a recipe, but alas, for Canadians it will be more illustrative than useful (unless they go where the dish is made, a thought worth entertaining). The recipe is *écrevisses à la crème*, and as prepared by M. Dalmaz, the chef/proprietor of Le Beaujolais at Belleville-sur-Saône, it's a dish to cause anyone to rush to the *escritoire*, still in his bib, to compose a poem, The question is, where to find the crayfish?

In any case, here it is, a dish that will be accompanied—to the mutual glory of *écrevisses* and wine—by a bottle of white Beaujolais, Pouilly-Fuissé, Mâcon-Viré, or, M. Dalmaz adds, Meursault, from the Côte de Beaune:

Ecrevisses à la Crème
(Crayfish à la Crème)

3 lbs. crayfish
2 tbsp. butter
4 oz. cognac
2¾ oz. Cherry Rocher
1½ oz. whiskey
½ cup chopped shallots
fresh cream
salt and cayenne pepper

To clean live crayfish drop them into a pan of very hot water and leave for 2-3 minutes. Drain them and pull out the central flap at the base of the tail to draw out, along with it, the intestinal tube.

In a copper fry pan, slowly cook the chopped shallots in 2 tbsp. butter until golden but not browned. Throw in the cleaned crayfish and stir quickly until they are a deep red colour. At this moment pour in the liquor and allow the liquid to reduce by about half. Add enough fresh cream to cover, salt and cayenne pepper to taste, and cook for about 10 minutes. Serve immediately.

Going north (as we have been doing), there is another considerable wine area after the Beaujolais before we bump into the bottom end of what must be called classical Burgundy—an area less well-known than it used to be and perhaps even less well-known than it deserves. This is the area roughly between Mâcon and Châlon-sur-Saône. From it comes a lot of quite good red wine and one very good and widely admired white wine, Pouilly-Fuissé.

At its southern end, the Mâconnais fades into the Beaujolais. As a matter of fact there is no knowing where the one leaves off and the other begins, and no compelling reason, so far as can be seen, for trying to know. Some villages, practising a quiet sort of viticultural separatism, have managed to slide themselves out of the less famous (the Mâconnais) and into the more famous (the Beaujolais). Wine drinkers may wax sentimental and even poetic about what they drink, but *vignerons* and wine shippers are hard-headed men, at least during business hours, with a fine eye for a buck, a pound, a mark, or a krone—and Beaujolais, as we have just seen, has been a rising star these twenty years and more. Consequently, vineyards around places like Romaneche-Thorins (Moulin-à-Vent) and Saint Amour (Saint Amour) which enjoy a species of dual citizenship have opted for Beaujolais. In the same way, much of the white Beaujolais that is to be found on the market now would have been sold, at another time, as white Mâcon. (Even now, the name Beaujolais almost automatically brings to mind a glass of highly drinkable red wine. How long any Beaujolais other than red has been recognized I do not know, but the first bottles of white Beaujolais I saw, in Washington in the early sixties, I did not believe.)

There is no fraud or fakery in this sort of sideways slide of some communities' into Beaujolais; it is a matter of pure—if that is the word I am looking for—commerce. The two areas do more than just meet, and the wine authorities have been persuaded that wines from localities that actually overlap should be entitled to the appellation they think will do them the most good.

In the Mâconnais proper, a wine sold simply as Mâcon cannot be expected to be great, but it should be cheap, and given the fact that the area is somewhat out of popularity, it may even be a good buy. Most of the red Mâcon is made of the same Gamay grape as is used in the Beaujolais, but here it produces a stronger-tasting wine. The best idea would be to try it alongside a bottle of Beaujolais and see what you think. Perhaps you will be the making of a Mâcon fad. The only other red wine of the whole Châlonnais-Mâconnais that will be encountered in Canada will be the wine from the small town of Mercurey, which is well to the north within the area. This, though, is a different article (and at a different price) from the wine bearing the broad name, Mâcon. It bears a closer relationship to the fine wines grown farther north, in the Côte d'Or.

Red and white wines are produced about equally in the Mâconnais and on the whole, the whites probably are better value than the reds. The unchallenged star of the whole area is the white Pouilly-

Fuissé. Another wine, with some similarity to Pouilly-Fuissé but a good deal cheaper, is the wine of a place called Viré. It is used as a carafe wine in the excellent Restaurant Greuze in Tournus in the heart of the Mâcon district. This constitutes a sort of recommendation in itself.

All of this brings us at last to Pouilly-Fuissé—about which it is obligatory to say that it is not to be confused with Pouilly-Fumé, which is grown around the town of Pouilly on the Loire. (Having said that, I can't think what harm it would do anyone *to* confuse them; they are not the same, true enough, and Pouilly-Fuissé generally is awarded the palm as the better, but they are both white, both good, and both will go appropriately with most of the same things. Pouilly-Fuissé is pale gold in colour, with a greeny tint, and very dry, with a taste more to be described as clean and fresh than flowery and fruity. It is a good wine to accompany oysters and all seafood, as we'll see in a moment.

The Châlonnais-Mâconnais, unlike the Beaujolais, is not a country of winsome personality, although it is by no means unhandsome. It strikes me, however, that in this regard my judgement may be suspect; I cannot think of *any* wine area which is unhandsome. This is, in any event, pleasant country to poke around in. For the fisherman there are, here and there, streams with visible fish in them. For the historian, there are the partly restored ruins of the great medieval (early tenth-century) monastery at Cluny, an early bastion of civilization, for which may also be read, wine-culture. For followers of Nicephore Niepce, there is his birthplace to be visited. (Nicephore Niepce, who invented *la photographie* in 1822, has no place in this narrative—but how often does the opportunity arise to get so glorious a name into print?) And for all, there is the fact that it is splendid eating country, as is elegantly demonstrated by the Restaurant Greuze, already referred to, where Sunday lunch is a thing to be lingered over but not (z-z-z) to be driven on, after.

Here is a little something—or rather a number of tasty little somethings—that would go admirably, for starters, with a bottle of

Pouilly-Fuissé, or Mâcon-Viré, or just plain white Mâcon or white Beaujolais, or just about anything else white and dry that happened to be both cool and at hand. The recipe comes from Jean Ducloux, the *chef de cuisine* and boss at the aforementioned Restaurant Greuze.

Feuilleté de Brochet à la Greuze
(Pike in Flaky Pastry)

Use a thin slice of pike fillet, approx. ½ lb. Cook in a frying pan with a small amount of white wine, a nut of butter, a pinch of chopped shallots, and 3 raw mushrooms, thinly sliced.

Cook 10 minutes on low heat and add, without boiling, a cup of cream thickened with 3 egg yolks.

Cut fish in small pieces and fill patty shells that you have either prepared beforehand or bought ready-made at the pastry shop. Reheat in oven and serve very hot.

Not from Chef Ducloux, but good nevertheless with any of the same white wines, would be this:

Soufflé de Saumon

FOR 4 PEOPLE	FOR 6 PEOPLE
A 6-cup *soufflé* mold buttered and sprinkled with 1 tbsp. grated Parmesan cheese.	An 8-cup *soufflé* mold buttered and sprinkled with 1½ tbsp. grated Parmesan cheese.
2 tbsp. minced green onion	3 tbsp. minced green onion
3 tbsp. butter	4½ tbsp. butter
3 tbsp. flour	4½ tbsp. flour
1 cup boiling liquid—milk and the juice from canned salmon	1½ cups boiling liquid—milk and juice from canned salmon
½ tsp. salt	¾ tsp. salt
pepper	pepper
1 tbsp. tomato ketchup	1½ tbsp. tomato ketchup
½ tsp. oregano	¾ tsp. oregano
4 egg yolks	6 egg yolks
¾ cup canned salmon	1¼ cups canned salmon
½ cup grated Swiss cheese	¾ cups grated Swiss cheese
5 egg whites	7 egg whites
pinch of salt	pinch of salt

Cook the onions in the butter for a moment; add the flour and cook 2 minutes. Remove from heat and beat in the boiling liquid, then the seasonings, ketchup and herbs. Bring to boil, stirring for 1 minute. Remove from heat.

Beat in the egg yolks one at a time. Then beat in the salmon and all but 1 tbsp. of cheese. Beat the egg whites and salt until stiff and fold into the *soufflé* mixture. Turn into prepared mold and sprinkle with remaining cheese. Set in middle level of oven pre-heated to 400°; turn heat down to 375° and bake for 30-35 minutes. Serve immediately.

Josephine, you are my queen but Burgundy is king

*F*OR REASONS WHICH I have not analyzed (fear not, I'm not about to embark on it here) the very name of Burgundy has for me the ring of heroic deeds. I see pictures of rosy-cheeked, ample men with upcurled moustaches raising large bumpers in gauntleted hands—goodness knows why the gauntlets—to salute their rosy-breasted womenfolk before riding out to start skewering the foe on whacking great swords.

> *On-ward, on-ward, swords against the foe,*
> *For-ward, for-ward, the lily banners go,*
> *Sons of France around us,*
> *Break the chain that bound us,*
> *And to hell with Burgun...*

Sorry, wrong troops; those are the other chaps. In any case, you get the idea. Burgundy just plain sounds hearty and vaguely martial. Something about it inspires the sort of drinking song that Hillaire Belloc, a hearty gent himself, wrote to its excellence. The song finished up with this flourish:

> *Outside you may hear the great gusts as they go,*
> *By Foy, by Duerne, by the hills of Lerraulx,*
> *But the Devil's above, there's good liquor below,*
> *So it abound,*
> *Pass it around,*
> *Burgundy's Burgundy all the year round.* *

*"Drinking Song on the Excellence of Burgundy Wine" from *Collected Verse* by Hillaire Belloc (Harmondsworth, Middlesex, Penguin Books, 1958), p. 117.

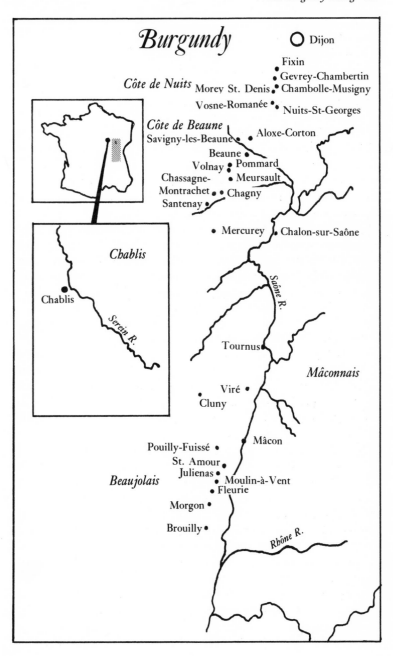

Burgundy

◯ Dijon

Fixin
Gevrey-Chambertin
Côte de Nuits Morey St. Denis Chambolle-Musigny
Vosne-Romanée Nuits-St-Georges

Côte de Beaune
Savigny-les-Beaune Aloxe-Corton
Beaune
Volnay Pommard
Chassagne- Meursault
Montrachet Chagny
Santenay

Mercurey Chalon-sur-Saône

Chablis

Chablis

Serein R.

Saône R.

Tournus

Mâconnais

Viré
Cluny

Mâcon

Pouilly-Fuissé
St. Amour
Julienas
Beaujolais Moulin-à-Vent
Fleurie
Morgon
Brouilly

Rhône R.

Yes. And it is also ghastly expensive. If Belloc had been cast upon the tender mercies of the liquor commissions and had had to find his drink here in the True North Strong and Free, he would have been forced to conclude that the undeniable merits in letting it abound and passing it around are somewhat offset by the poignant ache that kind of generosity leaves in the wallet. But for the moment, let us concentrate on the wine.

The Dukes of Burgundy were fond of referring to themselves as, among other things, the lords of the finest wines in Christendom. The claim was not modest of them, but it was not impossibly wide of the mark. And it is to be said for them that at least they confined themselves to Christendom when they *might* have claimed all of the known world, given the fact that the benighted heathen outside Christendom either got no wine or refrained. In any case, there is no name more evocative of wine than Burgundy. For most people, wine will be the first and perhaps the only thing that will come to mind when the word is mentioned—a wine of a particular deep, clear red colour, taken in big generous-bowled glasses from which comes a bouquet that would cause a corpse to rise up and tip its hat.

Bordeaux, for contrast, *may* mean wine, or it may mean only a commercial city with a handsome Grand Threatre in the southwest of France. In fact, a large part of the world has adopted another word, claret, for the wine of that region so as to leave no doubt when it is speaking in oenological terms and when in geopolitical.

But Burgundy's Burgundy all the year round, as Belloc said, and all the world over. Hear another enthusiast on the matter, the late Charles Edward Montague, English novelist and critic: "Burgundy was the winiest wine, the central, essential, and typical wine, the soul and greatest common measure of all the kindly wines of the earth." The winiest wine, burgundy. Beef and burgundy. Pheasant and burgundy. Roast wild boar and . . .no, not roast wild boar, not for me, not a second time anyway. Fine, rich, robust stuff for fine, rich (especially rich), robust men.

The martial associations of burgundy suggested at the beginning of this section are not entirely fictitious. There is the story of a General Bisson, presumably one of Napoleon's (it is always a safe guess; he had so many), who was marching his regiment hot-foot to the Rhine when he ordered a halt and had full military honours paid to the ranks of vines at the famed Clos de Vougeot. The story has always suggested to me that the General may have been a little taken in wine himself at the time, but there it is, a military man's gesture of homage to greatness. I am told that the French army has gone on doing the same thing every time it has passed the Clos since, but it has never done so in front of me so I cannot swear to the truth of the story.

And then, of course, it is well known that Chambertin, the very king of burgundies, was as mother's milk to Napoleon. If the Marshal had laid down, intending to drink later, one one-thousandth part of the brandy that subsequently came to be called "authentic Napoleon brandy," he would have had to be one of the monumental boozers of all time. But the fact seems to be that he was a moderate (half-a-bottle of wine with dinner) and a discriminating (as witness the Chambertin) drinker. And where Napoleon went, his Chambertin was sure to go. A marriage counsellor, or his best friend even, might have told him that he would do better to take along Josephine (and events proved them right), but no wine-lover would have faulted him for a moment.

But we digress.

All of this air of heartiness and muscularity which has come to surround the name of burgundy has had an unfortunate effect, or rather, two. It has led a lot of people to look for something extraordinarily powerful—powerful in taste, bouquet *and* alcohol—in any wine called burgundy, and there are whispers that this expectation has sometimes led wine firms to try to give nature a hand. But while good burgundy means a wine with a rich bouquet and rich taste, it does not at all mean that it is heavy, or that it is what your dear old grandmother would mean if she said it was a *strong* wine (just before she said it was making her all giddy).

Experts have helped along the misconception by referring to burgundy as the masculine of the pair when talking of burgundy versus claret. It is true in general that the taste and scent of a great burgundy will be less subtle (that's how you put it if you are a claret-fancier) or more positively glorious (what you say if you are a burgundy-fancier) than an equivalent claret. But whichever side of the argument you lean to—as for me, I am inclined to lean towards both as opportunity may provide—it is not to say that anyone should try to find in good burgundy an approximation of that fortified taste that port has. Port has it because port has a dollop of brandy in it. Burgundy is not port. To avoid suggesting that burgundy is sweet, it might be left as a handy generalization simply to say that it is less dry than claret.

Red burgundies, mythology aside, usually are not strong in alcohol. In fact, in very many years, sugar must be added to the fermenting juice—never to the wine itself—so as to ensure the wine's reaching the required minimum alcoholic content, which in the greatest of them all is eleven and a half degrees. (Others may be as little as eleven, and even ten and a half degrees.) This practice of sugaring is common in other northern vineyards, not just those in France. It is called *chaptalisation* after Napoleon's Minister of Agriculture, who was named Chaptal, and whose game, incidentally, was not primarily to improve wines but to get rid of a surplus of beet sugar. In any case, it enables good wines to be made in years when the weather has not given the grapes enough sugar of their own, and it does no harm so long as it is not overdone. If it is, it makes a much heavier wine than nature at its best ever intended. The practice is carried out under the eyes of government inspectors for the very good reason that some producers, as mentioned earlier, may be tempted to give the public the heavy wine the public thinks it wants—especially since sugar, being cheaper than wine, also can be used to extend the quantity.

(What happens in the making of wine is that natural yeasts, which form on the skins of ripe grapes, act upon the sugar which is in the grapes to convert it, firstly, into alcohol, but not alcohol alone. Where there is not enough sugar, there will not be enough alcohol and the wine will not keep. Moreover, because of the deficiency of alcohol and other elements, the wine will be thin and tart, lacking in any of that velvety quality which characterizes great wine. When sugar is added to the fermenting juice, or must, it is converted in the same way as natural sugar—sugaring the wine itself would merely add to its sugar content. The process is not needed in all years, but it is needed in very many; Burgundy is about as far north as Quebec City, which as anyone knows who has been there in winter, is far enough north to be a hazard not only to grapes, but to other similarly configured objects on brass monkeys.)

As we will see when we get to it, the part of Burgundy which suffers most from its northern location is Chablis—and here it is necessary to make the point that Burgundy is not a cohesive whole: Beaujolais is a world apart to the south; Chablis is even more tenuously related to the rest of Burgundy, off by itself nearly halfway to Paris, to the northwest.

The heart of it, the Burgundy of Burgundies, the part that produces the great red wines and the equally great white wines which the world's wine enthusiasts think of when Burgundy is mentioned, is the Côte d'Or, a narrow band of low hills running between a point just below Dijon in the north and the vineyard village of Santenay in the south, for which Chagny, not very large itself, makes perhaps the best map reference. It was fully 1500 years ago that it was discovered that this slope—the Slope of Gold as it is called, with as much truth as poetry—was uniquely suited to the growing of grapes. Maps in the wine museum at Beaune show that vineyards were located in the portion called the Côte de Nuits, the nortern portion, in the fourth century. By the sixth century, others had been planted below and above Dijon. These, although they hardly proved fly-by-night, have since gone. They petered out in the past century, done in mainly by the phylloxera epidemic which swept across the vineyards of all Europe in the second half of the 1800's, but also by the encroachment of the city.

The Côte d'Or begins with the town of Fixin (pronounced Fee-san, by the way), virtually a suburb of Dijon, on the city's southern doorstep. But Dijon itself is worth more than just a look in passing. This is the ancient capital of Burgundy. Here in the splendid and recently refurbished Palace of the Dukes of Burgundy, anyone who snatches a moment from the art treasures (which make it a museum second only to the Louvre in France) can glean some idea from the massive installations in the ducal kitchens of what sort of feeders the dukes (all of whom seem to have been named Philip or Charles) were. Tucked in around the Palace, there are the remaining streets of ancient shops, many of them now appropriately the places of business for dealers in antiquities.

Dijon as recently as the 1950's was described by so notable an authority as Waverley Root as one of the great gastronomic centres of France, and a place that seemed to have no bad restaurants. It is still good, but perhaps he would not praise it so highly today. Dijon's most famed restaurants are the Pré Aux Clercs et Trois Faisans, facing the Palace, and the Chapeau Rouge, located in what is also a good hotel. Both are expensive, although not by North American standards. I have favourable recollections of the restaurant in the Nord Hotel (where, however, it is necessary to ask for the *proper* wine-list and not the one automatically handed to boob tourists), and the Rallye.

If history and restaurants are not enough to lure the visitor to Dijon, it does not seem likely that he will be drawn by the three Dijonnaise specialties—mustard, gingerbread and cassis, as mixed a bag of culinary delights as one could wish for. Cassis is a blackcurrant cordial, available incidentally in Ontario and Alberta liquor commission stores. Mixed to taste with a chilled Burgundy Aligoté, or any other dry, and not very expensive, white wine, it makes a wonderful light summer drink, called Kir, after a one-time Mayor of Dijon. (The Mayor's name is also attached to a man-made lake in Dijon, the city's only body of water, excepting a piece of the Burgundian canal. The lake is good to look at, but like the man-made lake at Tashkent in the Uzbekistan Republic, is yucky to swim in.)

Without a doubt, the great vineyards of Burgundy are familiar by sight to more people than any other vineyards in the world. Almost every traveller making for the Riviera and Italy passes at least a corner of them—and that, nowadays, means almost every holidaying Briton, Belgian, Netherlander, Luxembourger, German and Scandinavian, plus such Frenchmen as can manage to find a piece of their own road.

Top to bottom, Fixin to Santenay, the length of the Côte d'Or is not more than thirty-five miles, and that would take in every bend in the road. When it is added that the best .portions of the slope, or slopes, are nowhere very deep, and when it is further added that not *all* the ground is used for vineyards (just below Nuits-St. Georges the vineyards yield to, of all unlikely things, quarries for building-stone), it becomes evident why fine burgundies are not cheap. The acreage is small, the yield is, by design, low, and the demand is world-wide.

There is something about a great sweep of the ordered greenness of vineyards that is always satisfying, at least to me, and the visitor setting out south from Dijon may find himself suitably impressed as he gazes to his right up the great scallop of the slope to the treed rim. He may, on the other hand, simply wind up in hospital. The N. 74, which is the Dijon-Beaune-Lyon highway, is surely—in its Dijon-Beaune section at least—as miserable a piece of over-crowded, fume-enveloped road as there is in France. (French trucks seem to run on the distillate of a fluid made by dissolving old truck tires in the effluent of paper mills.) Efforts go on being made to improve the N. 74, but because of an inelastic engineering principle—that a wider highway requires more ground, which no one presumably wants either to take or to give up—these efforts have come to little, a situation which seems likely to continue.

Fortunately, for most of the distance there is, roughly parallel, the Route des Grands Crus just to the west, and as we will discover eventually, there are more reasons for taking it than just to escape the N. 74—not, goodness knows, that any other reason is needed. But first we should try to sort out some names, for although fine burgundy is remarkably easy to drink—there is a local saying that has it going down "like little Jesus in velvet pants"—it is not easy to know, partly because of the Burgundian hyphen, which we will come to in a moment.

The so-called Golden Slope is divided into two parts—the Côte de Nuits in the north, and the Côte de Beaune in the south. In a world in which order ruled, *i.e.* in *my* world, the Côte de Nuits, which takes its name from Nuits-St. Georges, would run from a beginning at Fixin to the city of Beaune, where the Côte de Beaune would begin and would run to Santenay. Unfortunately, order is not the Burgundian long suit, with the result that the Côte de Nuits peters out indecisively just beyond a place called Corgoloin, and the Côte de Beaune straggles into being at or near a place called Ladoix-Serrigny. Neither of these is a household word, even, one suspects, in the households of Corgoloin or Ladoix-Serrigny. There are, in any case, the two slopes, the Slope of Nuits and the Slope of Beaune.

Within those, the next unit of interest to us is the commune. A commune is an administrative unit which might be compared with a township if that, in Canadian terms, does not imply something larger than is intended. A commune—the commune of Gevrey-Chambertin, for example, the first such of *great* importance in the Côte de Nuits—will embrace a number of vineyards, some great, some less great, some, in poorer locations, merely members of the family. In Burgundy it has been the custom of the natives, wily *commerçants* that they are, to appropriate to the name of the commune the name of the commune's best vineyard. Without the addition of Chambertin, what fame would be attached to Gevrey? Without Romanée, what would be the standing of Vosne? Without Musigny, how many would remember Chambolle? The matter becomes more than merely an interesting curiosity when the exercise is one of making a selection from a wine list. A wine called Gevrey-Chambertin is not *the* Chambertin. A wine called Nuits-St. Georges is not a wine of *the* St. Georges vineyard. A wine called Vosne-Romanée is not *la* Romanée. That is not to say they will not be very fine; in the whole great ranking of the world's wines, they will be found well up towards the top, but they are not the wines of the particular vineyards whose names add lustre to their own. Consider:

On the special order list of the Alberta Liquor Control Board there were—and may still be—two items: first, a 1966 Chambertin Clos de Bèze, bottled by Bouchard Aîné & Fils, at $10.90, and next under it, a 1966 Vosne-Romanée, bottled by Sichel & Fils, at $5.25. Both Chambertin Clos de Bèze and Vosne-Romanée are from the Côte de Nuits. The wines are made solely from the same noble grape, the Pinot Noir. The year is the same. The commune of Gevrey-Chambertin is no more than a morning's stroll from Vosne-Romanée—not far enough, the layman would have thought, to produce any marked difference in sun or moisture, or perhaps even in soil. And yet, the price of the one is better than twice that of the other.

The main part of the answer, as indicated, is that Clos de Bèze is a single great vineyard, the one alone among the vineyards in the commune of Gevrey-Chambertin which is considered the equal of the great Chambertin itself. In the case of the other, matters are turned around. What the simple *Appellation Contrôlée*, Vosne-Romanée, tells us is that the wine in the bottle was raised at one or more locations within the confines of the commune of Vosne-Romanée and therefore has kept company with greatness. The difference, therefore, is between proven greatness and mere physical proximity to a place where it occurs. There may be ten apple orchards or ten potato patches in a township and, collectively, they may give that township the reputation for producing the best apples or potatoes in the province. But their produce is not averaged in that way, and while the lesser of them prefer to market under the township name because it enhances their prestige, the best of them prefer to market under their own name because it is their prestige which enhances the rest. But can what comes off one piece of ground differ that much from what comes off another, a stone's throw away? I am less sure about apples and potatoes, but with wines, the record over not just decades but hundreds of years has shown that, yes, it can. But can the difference be so much as to warrant the great difference in price there may be between a bottle from a single great vineyard and a bottle of the wine that is marketed under the commune name? There, of course, we are into a judgement which everyone must make for himself. A good production-line car will get you around with great reliability and in some considerable degree of comfort, but a Ferrari is still a Ferrari.

Unfortunately for the beginner trying to make a modicum of sense of what he may find in a list of burgundies, there is another use of the hyphen than the one just referred to. Consider the case of Chapelle-Chambertin. Chapelle is a vineyard of high repute which might be thought not to need the name of its great neighbour to recommend it. But so great is the fame of Chambertin that *all* the great growths of the commune of Gevrey-Chambertin at some time in their history have sought and been given the right to tack on the name of Chambertin after their own. There does not seem to be any way out but to remember that Gevrey-Chambertin is the name of the commune within which they all dwell, and then to learn to recognize the rest.

(The urge to embrace the name, Chambertin, evidently is irresistible. In his monumental *Encyclopaedia of Wines and Spirits*, Alexis Lichine records that at one time a man named Jobert had the great good fortune to own both Chambertin and Clos de Bèze, which in viticultural circles would be roughly the equivalent of having in your private possession the combined treasures of the Metropolitan Museum of Art in New York and the Winter Garden in Leningrad. Ownership of the two vineyards nowadays is shared by about two dozen persons. In any case, so affected by it all was M. Jobert that he hyphenated the vineyard name to his own and became M. Jobert-Chambertin. Other proud vineyard owners, including M. Lichine himself, who is the proprietor of Château Prieuré-Lichine, in the Médoc, have attached their names to those of their properties, but Mr. Jobert-Chambertin must be the only one to have done it the other way around.)

A further cause of confusion about burgundies arises from the fact that the wine of any one vineyard may appear under a dozen labels at as many prices. (This is a confusion that exists where the wine buyer has the luxury of a choice of merchants. It is one from which the provincial governments thoughtfully have spared

Canadians. The number of single vineyard burgundies that are available in all of Canada can be counted on one set of hands, with enough fingers left over to make an obscene gesture at the liquor commissioner of your choice.) The reason for the multiplicity of labels is that almost all Burgundy vineyards, or *climats*, as they are called, are split up among a number of proprietors. These may make and bottle their own wine, or they may make the wine and sell it for bottling to as many *négociants* in Beaune, Nuits-St. Georges or elsewhere as may bid for it. (Many of the *négociants*, of course, also own pieces of vineyards themselves, some of them at various locations along the length of the so-called Golden Slope.)

The result is that Burgundy presents a face to the world beside which that of Bordeaux is simplicity itself. Order a bottle of, say, Château Palmer, 1962, in Sydney, Australia, and it will be indistinguishable from another bottle of Château Palmer, 1962, bought in London or San Francisco the next week. The explanation is that Château Palmer is a single enterprise. The grapes from all the vines of its sixty-four acres are tended under one direction; the decisions about when they are to be picked and how they are to be vinified are the same; so are those about how long the wine should remain in barrel and when it should be bottled for market. And when the cases eventually are shipped away, the bottles in them all carry the same gold-on-navy label.

In Burgundy, where any given, named property may be divided up among a dozen owners, the proprietor of a corner of, say, Les Vaucrains—whose corner may be the *inferior* corner to begin with —picks early because his bones tell him that frost is coming, and produces a wine which is thin and acid. The man at the better corner takes a chance and is rewarded with two weeks of long days of glorious sunshine and cool, dewy nights, and makes a wine that connoisseurs will rave over from Aberdeen to Walla-Walla, Washington. Both of these wines will be on the market somewhere as equally authentic examples of Les Vaucrains, 1972—which of course they will be. But they will be far from the same, and because professional buyers know something of what they are about, they will be at far from the same price. The poor retail customer may very well shake his head. In a competitive market he will take his wine-merchant's advice, and if it turns out to be bad, will find another merchant next time.

Certainly no such frivolous inconstancy is encouraged by the Canadian system. But the essential trouble with the commissions as wine merchants, as particularly revealed in the case of burgundies, is that they are too large and too inflexible to be able really to deal with anything which comes in necessarily short runs. Gin is one thing; there will be a zillion bottles of Auntie's Ruin London Dry Gin (The Gin With a Heart) on call at any one time, every last one of them identical down to the last eye-dropperful of juniper juice. Burgundy is another matter.

The output of Burgundy in *total* is small—perhaps 140 million bottles a year of all wines, from the least to the greatest—well under half the output of Bordeaux. At the base there will be wine bearing simply the *Appellation Contrôlée*, Burgundy, good, as ranked among all the world's wines, but with nothing more required of it than that it have been grown at approved locations within the whole of the area and made of the Pinot grape, and that it have achieved a modest ten degrees of alcohol (ten and a half if white). Next up the scale come the wines of one or the other of the slopes; look, for instance, for Côte de Nuits, or Côte de Nuits Villages. Then come the wines of individual communes (Gevrey-Chambertin, Nuits-St. Georges), and finally the wines of single, named vineyards. We are now at the pinnacle. We are now at the point, too, where we are explaining to the bank manager about the overdrafts.

These name-vineyard wines are made in ridiculously small quantities. Study the descriptions of the *climats* of Burgundy and what you see are such figures as five acres, twenty acres, seven and a half acres, fifteen acres, two and a half acres. The great vineyard of Romanée-Conti covers four and a half acres. Scarcely more than a dozen vineyards are more than thirty-five in extent. And most of them, as we already know, are divided up among a number of proprietors. This is a great nuisance to so large a bureaucratic mechanism as the liquor control board of a big province—perhaps one hundred cases of this will be available, seventy-five cases of that, two hundred of the other thing. The board's solution to these nuisance quantities is not to bother with them. The best the wine buyer can hope for in most places is a commune wine, which of course can be very, very fine and will be by no means cheap, but should he have a wild urge to blow the bundle and see what the Aristotle Onassis's are drinking, he has few opportunities for such folly.

The output of Burgundy is low, as well, because of the type

of grape planted—the Pinot Noir for red wines, the Pinot Chardonnay for white. In Bordeaux, several varieties are grown. Châteauneuf-du-Pape in the Rhône is a veritable convention of grape types. In most places, more than one is used. But in Burgundy, the Pinot, a small bearer, is the one vine and the only vine for all the better wines. Lesser wines, such as Bourgogne Passe-tout-grains (red) and Bourgogne Aligoté (white), are made only in part of the Pinot grape and they are, as a result, less expensive.

It is accepted literally as law in France, and therefore must be considered tested by time, that the more the wine in quantity, the less the wine in quality. For instance, it is laid down that the yield from an acre of vineyard can be half again as much for a wine that is to be sold as a plain and simple burgundy as for one of the named *Grands Crus* of the Côte d'Or. In other words, the proprietor, or proprietors, of one of the certified noble pieces of ground must be content with getting fewer gallons of wine from it. The vines must be pruned accordingly; some buds, which would become shoots and which eventually would support bunches of grapes, are simply rubbed off. The theory is exceedingly simple—the less the fruit, the better the juice that will be derived from it.

Obviously, in some years, when everything comes right, the yield will exceed the stipulated maximum per acre, conscientious pruning or no. What then? There was such a year in 1970. Where the higher yield is obviously just the result of Nature's bounty and has not been contrived at by the proprietor, the authorities may make some relaxation of the rules; they may allow more wine to be marketed under the appellation than otherwise would be permitted. Nevertheless, in such years, some wine which otherwise would be entitled to a higher title will be sold with a lower one—wine of a *Grand Cru* vineyard, for instance, will be sold under a commune name. As a result, it is no bad business to look for commune wines of what were known to be prolific years. A year which is very big in quantity—assuming it was not dismally bad in quality, and that is not often the case—will raise the quality all down the line.

Somewhat the same result flows from precisely the opposite causes in bad years. Suppose the permissible amount of *chaptalisation* does not succeed in bringing the alcoholic strength of the wine of, say, Les Haut Baux (which does not exist, by the way) up to the eleven and a half degrees which is the stipulated minimum for it as a *Grand Cru*. What then? What then is that it is denied the right to be sold under its own designation and is, in effect, banished, to find its place on someone's list as a *Bourgogne Grand Ordinaire*, or perhaps to be beefed up with a certain amount of a heavy, high-in-alcohol southern wine and sold as someone's trade-name (non-Appellation) burgundy-type, or even to be made into sparkling burgundy. A modest nine degrees will do for any of these uses.

What with it all, a burgundy list may be a hard thing to become comfortable with. The wines themselves are in relatively small supply, and painfully expensive. Still, I have found that wonders can be done with a Presbyterian conscience by explaining patiently to it that an occasional good bottle is not altogether a wicked extravagance, but simply a prudent measure towards the preservation of one's health. Burgundies *do* come so frightfully well-endorsed—by Louis XIV, for instance, whose recovery from an operation for a fistula was assisted by draughts of Romanée-St. Vivant. I had come across the story of the King's operation in a dozen places before encountering the graphic account of it—graphic enough for me—in *The Sun King*, by Nancy Mitford, after which any lay reader might find himself reaching for the Romanée-St. Vivant, too, if not for something a good deal stronger. In any case, Louis survived. Whether or not the wine did it may be debatable. His doctor, Guy-Crescent Fagon, who prescribed it, had what must be described as a somewhat equivocal record. But as for me, I'm prepared to give the burgundy the benefit of the doubt. In almost any circumstances.

If you are thinking of bringing two or three bottles of 1953 Chambertin up from the *cave*, there are two things you should do: (1) Have the chef prepare something beefily magnificent, such as a *Boeuf Wellington*, the recipe for which will be at his fingertips if he is worth his salt; and, (2) Phone. However, if your taste runs to something simpler, here is a recipe—from Burgundy—which would be magnificently accompanied by a wine from either Côte, Nuits or Beaune.

Le Rôti de Porc Farci aux Pruneaux
(Roast Pork with Prune Stuffing)

1 3-lb. boned roast of loin pork	1⅔ oz. fresh cream
12 large prunes	a small glass of brandy
1⅔ oz. butter	salt and pepper
2 tbsp. oil	

Stone the prunes and put them to soften for some minutes in very hot water. Make a cavity in the middle of the roast with a pointed knife. With the help of an instrument such as a skewer, make a sort of canal in the cavity by moving it to and fro to widen the opening.

Dry the prunes on absorbent paper and one by one, insert them into the inside of the roast. Pack the cavity tightly, pressing the prunes with the handle of a wooden spoon until it is completely filled. Close the opening with the fingers; shake some salt and pepper on a plate and roll the roast in it.

Put the butter and oil into a pan and when very hot, place the roast in it and allow it to brown on all sides. Averting your face, pour the brandy over the roast and light it immediately. Next add the cream. Cover, and allow to cook for one and a half hours in a moderate oven. Remove the roast from the oven and strain the gravy. When serving, cut in slices so as to show the prunes in the centre. Serve the gravy separately. Serves 4 to 6 people.

Served cold, this roast is equally excellent.

Through the Côte de Nuits in a glass-bottomed bottle

A KILOMETRE OR SO outside the southern limits of Dijon, a sign comes up on the right pointing to Marsannay-la-Côte, which, viticulturally, is a sort of rump of the old Côte de Dijon. The wines of Marsannay-la-Côte are red, white and rosé, of which the rosé is the most acclaimed. They are not found very far from home nowadays, but the town itself is pleasant; the beginning of the wine road that runs through the Côte de Nuits can be picked up here (although Marsannay is not properly part of the Côte itself), and getting off the N.74 is reason enough in itself for coming this way.

But there is another and better reason. Find your way to the centre of Marsannay (the trick would be not to; it is that small) and just behind the church, there is a square where you can park. Walk back fifty yards and you will come to a restaurant called les Gourmets. Here, if you arrive early, you may find a couple of waitresses, a waiter, and perhaps an apprentice from the kitchen, a napkin knotted at his neck, standing in the courtyard beside a massive copper pot which looks as if it were the sort of thing cannibals used for making their missionary-au-vin.

The fact that the names of the towns, or villages, along the Côte d'Or are world famous leads to enlarged expectations, and the fact that they are famous for *wine* leads naturally enough to visions of every one of them harbouring a jewel of an eating place on which will have been bestowed galaxies of stars, and other symbols of merit. Not so. These are small, very quiet, ordinary-looking little towns, very much closed in, where people live whose apparent relationship to what they produce is about the same as a gold miner's is to what *he* produces. In other words, they are not conspicuously consumers of their own produce; nor is much of it consumed by others in the neighbourhood. Most of it is destined for more distant tables. The tourists and the wine buyers, for their part, make do in Dijon and Beaune, both of which provide a level of making-do well above that of camping out, and the little places with the famous names doze brownly in the sun by day and roll up the sidewalks by night.

Still, let us keep a sense of proportion. This *is* Burgundy, and Burgundy as a whole has a reputation for good and substantial food not far behind its reputation for glorious wines. The traveller need not perish while covering the roughly eighteen miles that will take him from one end of the Côte de Nuits to the other. The first, and to my mind most satisfying, of the oases (of which others are Chez Jeannette at Fixin, which is a great bargain as a restaurant *and* as an hotel, and la Rotisserie du Chambertin at Gevrey-Chambertin) is the already-mentioned les Gourmets, at Marsannay-la-Côte. Most often when French cooking is talked about, what the speaker has in mind is *haute cuisine* as practised by a handful, and a *small* handful, of restaurants with soaring reputations and prices to match. But its real glory is in the hundreds of places that are to be found in the unlikeliest-looking towns, where with no frills, excellent basic ingredients are translated with skill, but even more, with respect for the art, into fine food. Les Gourmets fits this description exactly.

The house wines of les Gourmets are, of course, Marsannay wines: the red, Pinot Noir; the white, Pinot Chardonnay, and the rosé, also Pinot Noir, but differently vinified. They come to the table without labels because when they reach the restaurant they have come as far as they are going anyway, and need no more identification than appears on the menu. They are by no means great wines and at least the *young* red has a sharp edge to it (which time might soften); but a bedewed bottle of the dry, light rosé goes down very well with just about anything on a summer evening, especially at just a little over two dollars a bottle at the table. Les Gourmets and la Rotisserie du Chambertin, incidentally, both rate one star in the *Guide Michelin*.

The Côte de Nuits proper begins at Fixin, home of the previously mentioned Chez Jeannette, which, while it has not been awarded a star, does enjoy the *Guide*'s recommendation for providing a good meal at an astonishingly low price. To this I readily testify. It also has an excellent wine-list. And if you arrive too early for dinner, there is, higher up behind the town, above the vineyards, a piney park in which is to be found an heroic statue of Napoleon by François Rude, the man who also did the monumental relief on the Arc de Triomphe. (Napoleon, except for his endorsement of Chambertin, had no particular connection with Fixin or Burgundy, but Rude, a fervent Bonapartist, did; he came from Fixin.) Napoleon is said in this work to be awakening from a dream of greatness, but the attitude that Rude has conveyed has an unfortunate similarity to the tentative look of a man getting up after a bad night. For a start, the Marshal appears to be fully dressed; also, he is on one elbow, as if considering whether or not it would really be a good idea to go further. So much for art, or in any case, the sculptural art; we are here for the contemplation of an art of a different sort.

Among the luminaries of the Côte de Nuits, Fixin dwells in comparative anonymity. Whether or not any of its wines have come to Canada at any time, none do now, unless they are privately imported. Nor is it a name that leaps out at the diner from the wine-lists of restaurants even in Europe. Still, Fixin is not totally unknown, as witness the listing of Fixin les Hervelets (one of the better properties of those which cluster round the village) in the wine catalogue of the Peter Dominick stores in Britain. It was £1.60 when I checked—say $4.00. "Do not waste it on guests who don't notice what they are drinking," was Peter Dominick's advice, having previously said that the wine "will show you the real perfume and taste of true Pinot Burgundy". Alas, Canadian wine-enthusiasts are unlikely to get the opportunity to see if that is true, short of going to the place to find out (no bad idea in itself—and Rude's dyspeptic Napoleon will be pure lagniappe).

Next beyond Fixin is Brochon, which again is a small island amidst vines, as in fact all these communities are. But the wines of Brochon enjoy no identity of their own. They disappear into the anonymity of bottles that go out to the world labelled simply Côte de Nuits or Côte de Nuits Villages, and some no doubt are sold as generic burgundy. In fact, Brochon is merely a sort of roll of the drums before the great Chambertin comes on stage.

Through most of its length, the wine-growing area of the Côte de Nuits is divided into three parts—four, really, although the fourth part is less clearly defined than the others. The part to the east of the Beaune-Dijon highway, left as you go south, is on flat ground;

that is the least of them. Between the N. 74 Highway and the wine road, the ground rises gently; the space between produces secondary wines. To the right (the west) of the wine road, the rise of the ground is quicker, curling upward as the side of a saucer, to a rim which for the most part is covered with scrubby growth, but which here and there shows bare rocks where faults have been exposed. Towards the top of this rise—this is the fourth section—quality tails off again. It is from the wine road to half way up the slope, or more, that the prime wine-growing portions are to be found.

The soil is light brown, and salted with pieces of stone; these are faintly burnt orange in colour and certainly as large as the one with which David slew Goliath. (Given the fact that they are sharp-edged, they would do the trick, too.) And here, tended by twenty-some owners with the sort of every-blade-is-sacred care that greens-keepers lavish on championship golf-courses, are le Chambertin and its neighbour and sole peer, Chambertin-Clos de Bèze. Between them in years of average quantity, the two produce 90,000 bottles; they may not, even in the most bountiful, produce more than roughly 120,000 without exceeding the limit imposed by law. Did someone say something about the doleful effects of too much money chasing too few goods? With every wine-merchant in the world wanting to offer his customers a few bottles of genuine Chambertin, those relatively few thousand bottles naturally fetch breath-taking prices. (However, the prices take the breath more completely in some places than in others. Reference has been made already to that Chambertin-Clos de Bèze in Alberta at $10.90 a bottle, certainly a price to reflect on. At the same time in Ontario, a bottle of the equivalent Chambertin, of the same year, 1966, cost the buyer $16.75.)

The maximum number of gallons of wine which may be produced from each acre of ground in the vineyards of le Chambertin and Chambertin-Clos de Bèze is 267. In the other vineyards which are entitled to attach the name of Chambertin after their own—of which Chapelle-Chambertin, Latricières-Chambertin, Charmes-Chambertin are a few—the maximum gallonage permitted per acre is 285. Contrast that with 312 gallons per acre, which is the yield allowed for wines entitled only to the commune name, Gevrey-Chambertin, and with the 400-gallons-per-acre yield that is permitted in the case of those which may carry the generic name, burgundy; and the importance of the relationship which French law finds between quantity and quality will be seen. The lesser the name, the more wine there can be of it—half as much again of the wine which is entitled only to the regional name, burgundy, as of the grand seigneurs of Burgundy, exemplified by such as Chambertin, Richebourg, Romanée-Conti, Clos de Vougeot, and Musigny, among others.

(As an incidental note, of which anyone may make what he will, it is worth observing that notwithstanding the great vineyard tracts of the Midi, which deliver rivers of *vins ordinaires* to the corner bistros and grocery stores of France, France produces relatively less wine than does Canada. In average circumstances, from every acre under vines in Canada, something over 410 gallons of wine are produced; for every acre in France, something under 385.)

The commune of Gevrey-Chambertin gives way to that of Morey-St. Denis at about the garbage dump—a *small* garbage dump, it is true, but as incongruous to find on this sacred soil as a service station on Parliament Hill. The communes of the Côte de Nuits, in fact, run together with nothing really to distinguish where the one leaves off and the next begins until a vineyard sign—Clos de la Roche, for example, in Morey-St. Denis—proclaims the fact that you have moved on from Gevrey-Chambertin.

Clos de la Roche is one of those relatively few single-vineyard burgundies with which at least some Canadians have been enabled to develop a familiarity on their own home grounds. As bottled by the firm of Joseph Drouhin, it has been available for some time in Quebec. Clos de la Roche, by Burgundian measurement, is a large property—not quite forty acres—and produces perhaps 60,000 bottles in a good year. It is worth a note in passing that while the common practice in the Côte de Nuits has been to attach the most famous vineyard name after that of the commune, in Morey-St. Denis this is not quite the case. Bonnes-Mares and Clos de Tart, in particular, but also Clos de la Roche, enjoy rather more fame than does the vineyard St. Denis. Presumably this was not always so—unless, perhaps, the chief proprietor of St. Denis was mayor at the time the decision was taken to hyphenate Morey with St. Denis.

A propos what was said earlier about the communes here running indistinguishably into one another, Bonnes-Mares has its smaller part in Morey-St. Denis and its much larger part in the adjoining commune of Chambolle-Musigny. Bonnes-Mares therefore may be found listed with either affiliation, but it will be at the top of the class in both, sharing the honour in Chambolle-Musigny only with le Musigny itself.

More so than its neighbours down this route of the great wines, the village of Chambolle-Musigny sits back into the hill, on which, in this part, sheer rock faces show towards the crest. Here and there, soil is being brought in to make new patches of vineyards in front of these faults; in fact, in places, new vines already are growing. This land can only be reclaimed with some difficulty; there never will be much of it, and it is on the uppermost portions of the slope, which do not make the most favoured locations, but the prospective returns evidently make the effort worth-while.

The village itself is more attractive than most in the Côte de Nuits. Notwithstanding the fact that the great wines of Burgundy are grown by a myriad of small growers, obviously not all of them are constantly in difficulties to find two francs to rub together. Still, if they yield at all to ostentation, they limit it to within the family group, for most of what they offer to the outside world are blank walls. The purpose may be to divert the tax-collector's gaze. In any event, it makes for a certain drabness. Chambolle-Musigny has a modicum of charm, partly the result of its setting, with a wall of rock rising abruptly behind and seeming to lean over the village. There is, too, a church, very old and with a little court in front of it, which has a curious sort of cupola roof on the steeple. And as if to bear out the suspicion that there is more in this neighbourhood than meets the eye, there is the Château de Chambolle-Musigny en Bourgogne, which, behind the customary inscrutable stone wall, turns out to be an elegant white building, very much in the French style, with shutters beside the doors and windows, wrought iron lamps in the park, and grounds laced with gravelled drives.

Wine professionals say that the wines of all these communes, their vineyards standing cheek by jowl (even, in the case of Bonnes-Mares, overlapping), have their own distinguishable characteristics, that those of Gevrey-Chambertin have an austere majesty whereas those of Chambolle-Musigny are infinitely softer, more elegant and feminine. But these are nuances—nuances the identification of which the lay-enthusiast can have great fun pursuing while his nearest and dearest go barefoot in the cold. The difficulty, particularly in Canada, is to assemble for comparison purposes even a decent representation of commune wines, far less those of individual great vineyards. There is, in fact, no province which affords the individual, or the wine club (the best way of arranging affordable tastings), the opportunity to buy bottles of all the principle communes in the Côte de Nuits—Gevrey-Chambertin, Morey-St. Denis, Chambolle-Musigny, Vougeot (which we come to next), Vosne-Romanée and Nuits-St. Georges. It would be done as well as it could be done in Newfoundland, Quebec and Ontario.

The actual chateau of the Clos de Vougeot, which arises out of its vineyard like an ocean liner sailing through a placid green sea, is one of the great institutions of Burgundy. To know something about its background is to catch a glimpse of the association of the Church with the greatest vineyards of France, which occurred more particularly in this part than in any other. The Clos de Bèze at Chambertin, already referred to, owes it origins to an Abbey de Bèze created at Dijon in the seventh century. The property now known as the Clos de Vougeot passed into the hands of the Abbey of Citeaux early in the twelfth century and Clos de Tart was acquired by the Bernardine nuns in the same century. And there are many others throughout the whole of the region Côte de Nuits and Côte de Beaune which became sophisticated vineyards and remained church properties until the French Revolution and the dispossession of the monasteries at the end of the 1700's.

During the period when the popes were sequestered in Avignon in the fourteenth century, wines from Burgundy were delivered to them there, a practice which says two things: first, that while they had their own vineyards, as we have seen, at Châteauneuf-du-Pape and other places nearby, they also recognized a superior source of supply; and second, that there may have been some warrant for the apparent canard of a contemporary observer that their reluctance to return to Rome was not unconnected with the wine that was available to them where they were. Certainly they were not unappreciative. In the mid-1300's, the Abbot of Citeaux, who was the head of the Cistercian Order, sent thirty casks of wine of Clos de Vougeot to Pope Gregory XI, at Avignon, and four years later he was made a cardinal. It has been suggested in some places that the interval was just long enough for the wine to have reached an honest maturity—which of course implies a dreadful suspicion, but then, as H. W. Yoxall observed in *The Wines of Burgundy*, cardinals have been made for worse reasons.

What the visitor now sees at Clos de Vougeot is the result of several buildings, rebuildings and renovations. While it is in the chateau style, Vougeot was never a chateau in the sense of a country home. It began, as it is now, as a building associated with the making of wine. It was created by the Abbey for the purpose. As best can be determined, the property was walled in the 1300's, and the chateau was built in the 1600's—various dates are given for both—but the important fact for all present purposes is that the restoration responsible for the building's present well-kept state results from the formation of the *Confrérie des Chevaliers du Tastevin* in the middle 1930's. The order was established in the beginning for the purpose of boosting the flagging fortunes of the Burgundy wine-trade—there was a world depression on, as may be recalled —but it has since assumed more fraternal connotations. In the third week of November, when the annual sale of the Hospices de Beaune wines takes place (we will come to it later), one of the three grand dinners known collectively as les Trois Glorieuses is held in the chateau of the Clos de Vougeot.

The property enclosed within its celebrated wall—125 acres in all—is the largest single vineyard in all of Burgundy. Owning a portion of those 125 acres, as some 100 or more individuals and firms do, has become a mark of prestige. It is not something for which any base readily is to be found in logic, but again, logic is not all-compelling. The quality of the wines that are produced from grapes grown within the walls is recognized to be decidedly mixed, and it is rarely suggested that the best of them in the best of years surpasses all others. Still, to own a piece of the famous Clos is not only to have a piece of superb wine property; it is to have prestige even greater, and that is enough. The result has been to create a most odd wall.

It is made of stone and is six feet high, give or take a few inches. The owner of the portion of the vineyard touching the wall is responsible for the upkeep of that part of it. Thus, there are portions which are in as good condition as when the monks first built the wall; there are others which look as if they had not been given more than a lick and a promise since. There are bits with cement copings, tile copings and slate copings, and everywhere there are gates, most of them with the name of the property owner proudly displayed. There are, of course, almost as many wines of Clos de Vougeot as there are property owners, and in passing judgement on a bottle of 1966 Clos de Vougeot it would be essential to say whose it was, for an entirely different verdict might be warranted on a bottle made by someone else in a different corner of the 125 acres.

At the Clos, the wine tourist is pitched willy-nilly back on to the Dijon-Beaune Highway, the N. 74. The first wine commune he then touches is the only one in the Côte de Nuits on the wrong, or left, side of the road. This is Flagey-Echezeaux. If a commune wine of Flagey-Echezeaux is marketed as such anywhere, I have neither seen nor heard of it, and the wines of its principal vineyards—Echezeaux, Grands Echezeaux and Beaux Monts—evidently for convenience's sake, are chucked in with those of its nearest neighbour, Vosne-Romanée. It is under that heading that they will be found listed. It has been suggested that Flagey-Echezeaux hangs back because its own name is difficult to pronounce (Fla-jhee Ay-shay-soh); this may or may not be the case. Certainly the commune has no cause to be reticent on account of the quality of its principal properties, which is very high indeed. As it is, they enrich the already rich list of names which travel under the imprimatur of Vosne-Romanée: Richebourg, La Romanée, Romanée-Conti, Romanée-St. Vivant, La Tâche, Echezeaux, Grands Echezeaux, and in the next tier, a shade below, Beaux Monts, Malconsorts, Gaudichots and Suchots, among others.

Romanée-Conti very often will be the most expensive wine on earth, partly because it is one of the greatest of all vineyard properties, but also because it is small (four and a half acres) and therefore produces less wine in a year than would quarter-fill a fifteen by thirty foot swimming pool. Even if its output were reserved for the owners of hundred-foot yachts (which is not ridiculously far from the case), they would not have a great deal of wine. Whether or not one of Romanée-Conti's numbered bottles from a superlative vintage is worth the price that will be asked for it, is a matter which anyone must settle with his conscience at the time and his accountant thereafter. It is *très snob*. Romanée-Conti, incidentally, is one of those properties to which an owner's name has been attached. It once belonged to the Prince of Conti, who served Louis xv as a diplomat. He outmanoeuvred Madame de Pompadour for possession of the property, an accomplishment which suggests that he had some considerable talent in his profession, given Pompadour's presumed talent in hers. In any case, Romanée-Conti, and the others of the principal growths of Vosne-Romanée, are among the greatest in Burgundy. None is available in Canada. In three provinces,

Alberta, Quebec and Ontario, a commune wine of Vosne-Romanée is listed; in Quebec, it comes from two shippers, one of them the firm of Leroy, which is a partner in the syndicate that owns Romanée-Conti.

Next below Vosne-Romanée, and completing the roll of the Côte de Nuits, is the commune from which the slope takes its name, Nuits-St. Georges. No doubt because its 950 acres of vines are more than there are in any other commune, Nuits-St. Georges is an omnipresent name in wine lists. Every railway-station hotel in Britain has been said to have its bottle of Nuits-St. Georges, whether it has anything else or not, and the name enjoys very nearly equal ubiquity in Canada. It may be that the name has become too familiar, for the wines of Nuits-St. Georges are not now so highly thought of as they once were.

Only in Newfoundland is the wine of a single-named vineyard of Nuits-St. George to be had—les Roncières. In Ontario and in Nova Scotia, Close des Forêts is listed—correctly—as a Nuits-St. Georges, although les Forêts actually is in the commune of Premeaux, a step down the road from Nuits. (The premier wines of Premeaux are permitted to lump themselves in with those of Nuits.) The firm which ships Clos des Forêts, Jules Belin, also makes and markets a marc de Bourgogne under its own name. Marc, which is made in most of the wine-growing areas, but best, to my mind, in Burgundy, is made in the same spirit which resulted in its being said that the hog butchers of Chicago marketed everything but the squeal. When wine is made, the grapes are only lightly pressed, so as to avoid crushing the seeds and macerating the skins, either of which would release more tannin into the must than would be desirable. Thus, there is a considerable pulpy mass left, and some time after the vintage it is stewed up into a broth and distilled. The result is marc, an *eau-de-vie*, or light spirit, with the leathery taste of a well-worn saddle—a description which will identify it precisely for all those who have ever chewed a well-worn saddle. Marc is an acquired taste, and one I have acquired. On this note, and with nothing left but the marble quarries of Corgoloin, which are outside our terms of reference, we take leave of the Côte de Nuits.

The marc can wait until after dinner; right now, to knife and fork. Say burgundy and it is almost necessary to say beef, and if the rule has not been enunciated before, perhaps, Mr. Chairman, I might be permitted to do so now: claret and lamb, burgundy and beef. (Of course, that is hopelessly narrow, but what generalization isn't?) And if the beef isn't always going to be simple, thick cuts of rare roast beef, a way out might be the following:

Tournedos Sautés aux Champignons
(Filet Steaks with Mushroom and Madeira Sauce)

6 *filet* steaks 1-1½ inches thick
2 tbsp. butter
1 tbsp. oil
salt and pepper
½ lb. mushrooms, sliced
2 tbsp. butter
1 tbsp. oil
2 tbsp. minced shallots or
green pepper
½ cup canned beef bouillon
1 tbsp. tomato paste

6 crustless rounds of white
bread
3-4 tbsp. clarified butter
¼ cup Madeira mixed with
½ tbsp. cornstarch
2 tbsp. minced parsley

Sauté the bread rounds in hot butter till lightly browned on both sides. Reheat in oven just before serving.

Sauté the mushrooms in hot butter and oil to brown lightly. Stir in the shallots or green pepper and cook slowly for 1 to 2 minutes. Season and set aside.

Dry the steaks well. Place butter and oil in a heavy skillet, and when the butter foam begins to subside add the steaks and *sauté* them for 3 to 4 minutes on each side. Immediately remove from heat and place each steak on a bread round. Keep warm while preparing the sauce.

Pour the fat out of the skillet; stir in ½ cup of canned beef bouillon and 1 tbsp. tomato paste. Boil rapidly until liquid is reduced to 4 tbsp. Pour in the starch and Madeira mixture; boil rapidly for a minute. Add the *sautéed* mushrooms and simmer a minute more to blend flavours. Correct seasoning, and spread the sauce and mushrooms over the steaks. Sprinkle with parsley and serve. Serves 6.

*The closer
the Beaune,
the sweeter
the meat*

*I*T IS CUSTOMARY, when the question comes up, to say that, well, yes, the red wines of the Côte de Beaune are fine, very, very fine indeed, but they do not, of course, achieve the supernal heights of the luminaries of the Côte de Nuits, the likes of Romanée-Conti, Chambertin and Musigny. The colour (the robe, in the parlance of the trade) is not quite so splendid, nor the bouquet (or nose) so intense, or the taste (which, unaccountably, comes out, baldly, as taste) either so velvety or rich. They are rather more subtle wines, less opulent. (Some people take dope. Some lock themselves in their rooms and drink up the cooking sherry. My escape, at least when the cooking sherry is gone, is to read about wine. This has equipped me not simply with one of the world's great stores of utterly useless information, but with some glimmerings of comprehension of a language which frequently strikes the layman as baffling, and almost always as precious. For instance, there was a comparison of the wines of Burgundy and Bordeaux in which such characteristics were attributed to the former as being more downright and substantial, of having generosity, fire, warmth, velvety softness and rich fragrance, not to mention the splendor of liquid sunshine, although it was admitted, on the negative side, that sometimes if *chaptalisation* were resorted to, too liberally, this could produce a dumb wine, and that some other heinous practices in the vinifying could give the wine a cooked taste. Bordeaux, on the other hand, was described as showing a classical self-restraint, serenity, austerity, dryness, a nice balance of light and shadow, and infinitesimal gradations of taste and scent. It is neither here nor there whether I agreed; what is important is that some meaning was conveyed. Praise the Lord, I exclaimed; I have arrived.)

But this is an aside—and a longish one at that. Let us not flout custom in considering the characteristics of the wines of the Côte de Beaune and the Côte de Nuits: the more regal *are* those of the Côte de Nuits. But this is so much a matter of degree that any dedicated amateur might spend the better part of a lifetime, not to mention a fortune, compiling cases to prove or disprove the point, according to whim. Where, of course, there is no argument, is in the matter of white wines: the Côte de Nuits has none, or none of consequence, and the Côte de Beaune, in Corton, Meursault and Montrachet, grows what are widely acclaimed (the Germans vigorously dissenting) as the greatest white wines on earth. (Since the German and Beaune white wines have each their own attributes and since there is room for both, and many more besides, this is another of those pointless arguments which there need be no rush to settle.)

But another area in which the Côte de Beaune has it over the Côte de Nuits like a blanket, is in the handsomeness of its countryside. The fact is that once you have taken in that great swoop of hillside with its ordered ranks of precious vines, the Côte de Nuits is, scenically, nothing much. On the other hand, the traveller is no sooner into the Côte de Beaune, going south towards the town itself, than off to the right, set into folds in the base of the hills, are two villages whose bosky charm from afar is borne out close up, as is not always the case. These are the villages of Aloxe-Corton (pronounced Aloss, as in Aloss, poor Yorick. I knew him, Horatio; a fellow of infinite jest... etc.) and Pernand-Vergelesses (pronounced vairje-eh-less). Although Pernand-Vergelesses is relatively little known, I am prepared to testify that at least the best of what it produces deserves to be better known. As for Aloxe-Corton, of course, the name rings like a Chinese gong, and moreover, it rings in both basic colours.

Here, on the small back road that leads into the village from the Dijon-Beaune highway, the first outpost of the village that the wine traveller comes upon is Château Grancey, the property of Louis Latour, one of the most respected names in Burgundy. The chateau itself is a three-story building, cream-to-buff in colour, with a roof of reddish tile and white shutters at the windows. It is set in a treed park to the left of the road and facing it on the other side is the substantial *cuverie*, where the wines are made and bottled. Vineyards surround both. The firm of Louis Latour owns several of the best portions of the vineyards of both Corton and Corton-

Charlemagne. Latour wines from these properties are to be found in Canada only in Ontario, under the proprietary name Corton Château Grancey for the red Corton, and Corton-Charlemagne for the white, with the additional identification, "Ancien Domaine des Comtes de Grancey". If the purpose is to find examples of the best that Corton has to offer, these will do admirably (as the prices posted beside the names will suggest they very well might). But in general in Canada, the pickings are slim. They are summed up in this short list: Quebec, Corton, red, and Corton-Charlemagne; Newfoundland, Corton; Alberta, Aloxe-Corton, the commune wine. The Corton available in Quebec, incidentally, is from the Caves de la Reine Pedauque, in Beaune, which owns property at Corton adjacent to that of Château Grancey. The red wines of Corton are usually considered peers of the best in the Côte de Nuits, and Corton-Charlemagne rates with Meursault and even Montrachet among the unequalled white wines of the Côte de Beaune.

Aloxe-Corton itself is a comfortable little place with a look of being quietly well off. Its most impressive monument is the chateau of (what else?) a wine-firm (J. M. de Saissey), a great pile behind high wrought-iron gates. Burgundian architecture has a florid side to it, reflected mainly in intricately-patterned and multi-coloured roof tiles. At the premises of M. de Saissey, the roof is tiled in diamond-shaped tiles which are so arranged as to outline yellow diamonds in brown tiles; each diamond in turn has at its centre a cross of brown tiles. Nor is that all, for what this covers is a roof further adorned by one square tower and a pair of smaller, conical towers.

The principal ornament of the village of Pernand-Vergelesses, of which, in truth, there are not many, is its most unusual church. Pernand-Vergelesses is a small place, all up and down hill, inhabited almost entirely by small wine-growers who go out to the fields in the morning and come home at night. There are no chateaux here. Rather, the village is dominated by the church with its squat, square tower, from one side of which grows a sharp-pointed steeple with a weathercock at its top. The tower is tiled in a psychedelic display of blue, red and yellow tiles. It is really quite a handsome little church. Inside, it has a vaulted ceiling, and a heating system consisting of a stove from which radiate pipes that look as if they have been rescued from an auto-wrecker's. The few pews have dates carved in them going back, at a cursory look, at least to 1754. The church may be two or three centuries older than that, but even that is not old here, where the vineyard now known as Corton-Charlemagne, in which many of the people of the village work, had already been given to the Abbey of Saulieu by the Emperor Charlemagne before the end of the eighth century. It is true not only of Burgundy, but of Bordeaux, and of the Moselle and Rhine in Germany, that when a piece of slope is said to have a long history of producing superior wines, it is a l-o-o-o-ng history.

Although Pernand-Vergelesses finds no place in the lists of the Canadian provincial liquor commissions, the next wine village on the way to the city of Beaune does; that is Savigny-les-Beaune. In the company of Corton, Beaune itself, Pommard, and Volnay, the wines of Savigny-les-Beaune occupy a place a step or more below, being lighter in all respects. (The same may be said of those of Santenay, the southern terminal of the Côte de Beaune.) If the price makes some gesture towards that fact, they are worth remembering, for they will give a fair demonstration of what burgundy is about. What Savigny there is to be had in Canada—the commune wine, needless to say, not a named vineyard—is to be had in Newfoundland and in Ontario (the very good firms of Calvet and Drouhin, respectively, are the shippers).

The village of Savigny-les-Beaune has neither the setting nor the out-of-the-way charm of the two we have just left; however, it does have a large, and very much a spit-and-polish, wine establishment —that of Henri de Villamont, who took it over only in 1964 and plainly is bent on making a name for it. Savigny-les-Beaune makes a small quantity of white wine, as well as red, and a sign leading into town says it also makes a mousseux wine, presumably a sparkling red burgundy, of which it is only appropriate to say—as of all sparkling burgundies—uh-huh.

Here, by my scheme of things, for which the French so far have given no sign of awareness or concern, is where the Côte de Beaune should be about to begin—with Beaune. But as we have just seen, perhaps four miles and a bit of the Côte de Beaune (and an important four miles and a bit, particularly when one thinks of Corton and Corton-Charlemagne) already lie behind when one reaches the gates of Beaune—or where the gates would be if Beaune had remained a walled city.

I am an unabashed enthusiast of the town of Beaune, not altogether because of its greatest architectural treasure, the celebrated Hospices de Beaune, but because it has a mellowed air of having been around forever (which it has, if you will accept the fifth century as a reasonable date from which to begin counting); because of its good restaurants and at least two good hotels, its outcroppings of medieval walls under shady trees, its warren of cool cellars to visit, and its sense of vibrant busy-ness, which is attractive, especially if you have nothing to do with it except observe it. To all that you might add the farmers' market, where a good deal of the busy-ness is generated, especially on Saturdays, and where the tomatoes, *aubergines*, *haricots verts*, and peppers come in riotous mounds, and the adjacent market building is odorous with cheeses displayed on straw mats, and sausages in all sizes and most colours. And you might add as well the wine museum, where, among other discoveries to be made, is the discovery that the patron saint of the wine-grower is St. Vincent. (St. Vincent, it seems, was in Heaven when he was visited by a poignant memory of the wines he had left behind. He returned to earth, had rather more of the wine than he needed, overstayed his leave, and was turned to stone on the spot. The appalling aspect of the story is that it suggests that there is no wine in Heaven, which is enough to cause a man to give up and to inquire about alternative bookings. But it also raises the question of what St. Vincent can do for the struggling *vigneron* if he remains among the mortals, imprisoned in stone.) The calcified St. Vince, it needs to be added—and quickly—is not to be found propping up an archway, or otherwise employed in a utilitarian way, in the wine museum. What is to be found there, along with numerous charts and maps, are all manner of ancient artifacts of the *vigneron's* and the wine merchant's trade. While most wine enthusiasts know in a general way that such things as bottles and labels were not always as they are now, it comes as a small surprise to discover that they have been as they are now for comparatively so short a time. Bottles at one time were broad in the base, and dumpy. It is only in the past 150 years that something like the present-day bottle—in Burgundy, with sloping shoulders; in Bordeaux, with square—has evolved. Labels not so long ago said simply, in plain black and white, that what was in the bottle was Chambertin, or Volnay, or whatever; perhaps because bottles passed directly between grower and consumer, this was all that was necessary. When the shipper came into the picture, the labels became larger and more colourful.

By no means all the antiquities of Beaune are in the museum, nor are they at ground level. Beneath the city are some kilometres of cellars—Joseph Drouhin and Company have a kilometre of them of their own—and some of these are of ancient date. Portions of the Drouhin cellars were built in the 1200's and originally were church property.

But there is no need to pursue history in the museum or underground; a great piece of it rises impressively in the centre of town to smack the visitor in the eye—the renowned Hospices de Beaune. This hospital for the poor, built in 1443, is not simply a splendid sight under its steep-pitched roof of multi-coloured tiles; for the wine student, it has the further interest of an intimate connection with the wines of Burgundy, and more specifically, with those of the Côte de Beaune. The hospital was founded as a charity by Nicolas Rolin and his wife, Guigone de Salins. While there is no reason to believe that the lady was moved by anything but piety and an instinct for good works, it may be that her husband felt the prickings of conscience, for as Chancellor to the Duke of Burgundy, he was also the tax collector. It has been suggested, uncharitably, of poor Nicolas that it was appropriate that he should aid the poor because he had created so many of them. (Present-day finance ministers, please note.)

Of the bequests that have been made to the hospital over the centuries, many—enough to support it—have been made in the form of choice parcels of vineyard properties. There are 120 acres of these in all, producing red wines in the vineyards attached to Beaune itself, and in Corton, Savigny-les-Beaune, Pernard-Vergelesses, Pommard, and Volnay, among other communes; and producing white wines mainly in Meursault. The wines of the Hospices de Beaune are sold at an auction which takes place in the third week in November, while the wines are still so new that only an expert could foretell their future, and perhaps even he depends on a certain amount of rapping on wood and crossing of fingers. An ancient method is used for regulating the period within which each sale must be completed: a lighted candle burns down while the bidding goes on, and when the candle flickers out, the last bid is in. For the same sort of partly mystical reasons that every wine shipper seems to want a corner of Clos de Vougeot, so do buyers in the trade and restaurant proprietors want to have a little bit of the annual output of the Hospices de Beaune vineyards to offer their clients. Perhaps they are motivated somewhat by a spirit of generosity towards a charitable institution, or, perhaps, the buyers are somewhat under the influence (in not too literal a sense) of the three big dinners which take place that week, one each in Beaune, Clos de Vougeot, and Meursault, and which are known collectively as les Trois Glorieuses. In any case, the prices tend to run high. Consequently, in buying a bottle of Hospices de Beaune wine, the sense of self-indulgence may be abated somewhat by the knowledge that what you paid, and even overpaid, went in part to a good cause. (To reflect on the fact that an even larger part of it went to your provincial treasurer could only serve to turn the wine sour.)

The prices realized at the Hospices de Beaune sale, coming when the wines are new in barrel, help to set the pattern for the whole of that vintage in the Côte de Beaune, and in Burgundy as a whole. They are a barometer.

Conducted tours through hospitals, even hospitals rooted in the wine business as well as in the healing arts, do not come high on my list of things to do. This makes it harder to account for—not the first visit—but the second and the third. Perhaps it is because the place *is* impressive, inside and out. The architecture, barring a seventeenth-century bit, which is something else, is described as Gothic. So be it; it is not to my untutored eye notably Gothic, but then perhaps I am misled by that Flemish-looking woodwork, the open gallery surrounding the courtyard, which suggests something faintly Venetian, and the Hospices' justly-famous roof, the patterns on which look like the interior lights experienced after a punch in the nose. The hospital is not simply a museum; there are still patients, although after the third visit to the place, I had begun to have stirrings of an unworthy suspicion that the one or two wandering about were really dress-extras, hired to give an air of verisimilitude to the place.

Beaune is the capital of the whole Burgundy wine-trade. There are *négociants* with substantial establishments in Nuits-St. Georges, in Meursault and in Dijon, but Beaune is the place around which the whole trade of the region revolves. It therefore is awash with the offices and cellars of the men who buy, bottle and ship wine, many of whom (such as the firm of Joseph Drouhin) also own extensive vineyard properties in their own right. Most of these firms invite the visitor to come in to see and taste. (I have the impression that the insistence with which the invitation is extended is in inverse proportion to the firm's standing in the wine world, another unworthy suspicion, I am sure.) Go; feast your eyes upon thousands and thousands of bottles growing old gracefully in the cool half-light, but do not expect them to trot out rare old bottles for your delectation at the end; promotion-minded these firms may be, but philanthropic institutions they are not. But the taste you do get is fun, nevertheless.

For a fine bottle of Beaune wine of your choice, at your own table, there are places enough, the best of them the Poste and the Marché. The Poste is the better known to tourists, but also the more expensive. The Marché is not only excellent, but also remarkably reasonable, and I will be content if I never do worse than a dinner I had there in the summer of 1971, melon, *escargots* (Burgundy, of course, is their native heath), *salade Niçoise*, and *carré d'agneau*, with a bottle of Beaune Bressandes (Chanson Père et Fils) 1964, all of this beautifully served in pleasant surroundings for the equivalent of seventeen dollars and change for two. Both the Poste and the Marché enjoy one star in the *Michelin*.

Draw a line southwest-northeast through Beaune; the prime vineyards press in along the whole of the 180 degrees above the line. Take the road out of town in the direction of Bouze-les-Beaune (a wonderful name, but not one which appears on any label so far as I know) and you are in the midst of the Beaune vineyards. There are a lot of them—thirty-four rate as *Premiers Crus*, a good half of which are unusually large properties by Burgundy standards —but only two of these *Premiers Crus* are represented in Canada, Clos des Mouches (which produces both red and white wine) and Beaune-Teurons. Both of these are ranked among the best. If they cannot be marketed by vineyard name, the wines of Beaune may be marketed as Beaune, or as Côte de Beaune Villages, or Côte de Beaune, in descending order.

Leave Beaune by its southwest axis—Bouze-les-Beaune lies more directly west—and Pommard is to be found immediately on the doorstep. It seems to me that when I first encountered wine in fiction, perhaps in the *Strand* magazine, sophisticated men of the world, when they were not ordering champagne, were summoning the waiter to bring a nice bottle of Pommard. Such men always drove Alfa-Romeos, which barked and scattered gravel from the driveway as they roared off into the night, along the Grand Corniche, as I recall it. (Twenty years later I bought an Alfa-Romeo. Not only would the damn thing not bark; on cold mornings it frequently would not even grunt.) From those heady days, Pommard's reputation went somewhat into decline, for reasons which perhaps may be discerned in the following few lines from Alexis Lichine's *Encyclopaedia of Wines and Spirits*: "Before the laws of *Appellation d'Origine* brought a measure of control into the wine business, a Burgundian writer estimated that the amount of Pommard sold throughout the world each week was more than the commune could make in ten years." Obviously, not all of what those Johnnies with the waxed moustaches were buying—and paying for as Pommard—*was* Pommard (and if the truth were known, their Alfa-Romeos probably did not bark any more readily than mine did).

Some suspicion has continued to linger about Pommard which is sold simply as Pommard, which is to say, not by the name of a particular vineyard. Still, if prices may be taken as indication, demand flourishes as well as ever. In Canada, not only are there six provinces retailing various bottlings of Pommard (Ontario and Manitoba, two each; Newfoundland, Nova Scotia, British Columbia and Quebec, one), but at prices which run the gamut between the merely indefensible and the absurd—and $10.10 for a commune wine of Pommard (as in Manitoba) is absurd. Volnay, next door, which produces similar wines, although perhaps a shade lighter, offers infinitely better value. Still, an Hospices de Beaune Volnay that finds a ready market at over $10 the bottle in Ontario may be regarded by the rest of the country as reassuring evidence that the Certified Boob is not yet extinct, even in the supposedly worldly canyons of Bay Street. Apart from the Hospices de Beaune, there is not a Volnay or Pommard available in Canada which is dignified by more than the commune name, and although the shippers of those that are shipped here are reputable, the prices of the Pommard wines are not warranted. The ordinary wine buyer, curious for a taste of a genuine burgundy but with a pocketbook not up to the great names—as whose is?—probably will find the most reasonable compromise between price and quality in a Côte de Beaune Villages.

After Volnay, we enter the realm of white. It is true that some white wine is produced where we have just been—the Clos des Mouches, at Beaune, for instance, may be either red or white—and equally true that there is still some red wine in the communes of Meursault and Chassagne-Montrachet, which are ahead. But what red wine is produced in Meursault is sold as Volnay, and the red wine of Chassagne-Montrachet (and very good, too) is rather a rarity in foreign markets.

Meursault, the town, is a sort of commercial consort to Beaune, the white queen to the red king, perhaps; it is a power in the Côte de Beaune, too. Not all the *négociants* are in Beaune; nor, as can be gathered from occasional glimpses of gracious living through not-quite-closed gates, is all the money. This is a prosperous looking town. The vines which are the source of its prosperity, here trimmed and trained like parallel hedges, come marching right in within the town limits.

Meursault is one of the great white wines of the world. Nevertheless, another which is universally held to be greater—greater, very many professionals have declared, than any other dry white wine anywhere—is le Montrachet. (The Alberta commission on its special order list not long ago offered a 1969 Montrachet, Marquis de Laguiche—the Marquis being the proprietor—at $14 a bottle. Ah, the happy oilman, extracting one liquid gold from the ground in order to put another back down his throat. I go on, enviously, drilling my hole in the backyard in hopes of being able to emulate him in both, but especially in the latter.)

It is some small mark of the standing of le Montrachet that not one, but two, communes have attached its name to theirs, Chassagne-Montrachet and Puligny-Montrachet. The two are hardly a mile and a half apart; le Montrachet straddles them and they share its glory, although not quite equally, for Puligny-Montrachet is associated exclusively with white wines (and therefore with *the* Montrachet), whereas Chassagne-Montrachet as a commune is more closely associated with red. There is not much to be had of the Montrachet, for the vineyard covers just under nineteen acres of ground. Its neighbours, great in their own right, include Bâtard-Montrachet, Chevalier-Montrachet, and Bienvenue-Bâtard-Montrachet. It is true of all the great vineyards that they are beautifully kept, but these are barbered to the centimetre, each row trimmed to the same height (about three feet), and as precise as any hedge in an ornamental garden.

Below Puligny-Montrachet and Chassagne-Montrachet, the Côte de Beaune changes; the hills become more broken and steeper, and there remains only the village of Santenay, a health spa as well as a wine centre. An example of its wines—the waters must be tested on the spot—is to be found in Ontario, shipped by the firm of Louis Latour.

As a footnote to the Côte de Beaune, it might be added that at Pommard, set smack in the middle of vineyards, there is, of all unlikely things, a motel, quite as North American, in every detail but one, as any Holiday Inn or Quality Court. And that one aberrant detail is that in each room there is a refrigerator, and in every refrigerator—on an honour system—there are two large bottles of mineral water, two small bottles of Perrier, two bottles of tonic, two each of soda and Pepsi-Cola, two Pschitt, two bière Encro lager, one whisky Haig, one gin Beefeater, one liqueur Izara, one cognac Rémy Martin, one Porto Croft, one aperitif Americano Cora, one Pernod 45 and one Pastis 51. Or according to the list, there should be. I have never been sure how the French pronounce their soft drink, Pschitt, anyway. But how does an Anglophone go to the front desk and say that there is none of it in his icebox?

Not to snoot the red wines of the Côte de Beaune, which are excellent, but to raise a further cheer for its whites, which are matchless, here are a couple of go-withs to go with, say, a nice, softy, fruity Meursault, or whatever you may have going. The Restaurant Couronne in Rouen makes *filets de sole Normande*, the mere recollection of which is enough to bring a look of wistful longing to the eye. This is a simpler version:

Sole à la Normande

2½ lbs. sole fillets
1 quart fresh mussels
dry white wine
½ lb. shelled cooked shrimp
½ lb. mushrooms, sliced and
 sautéed in butter

3 tbsp. chopped shallots or
 green onions
3 sprigs parsley
salt, pepper

TO STEAM MUSSELS:

Scrub mussels with a strong brush; wash thoroughly. Trim off the tuft of hairs around the edges. Set the mussels in a basin of fresh cold water for an hour or so, drain, and they are ready to cook. Put them in a large saucepan with ½ cup dry white wine, chopped shallots or green onions, parsley and a pinch of pepper. Cover and boil quickly for 5 to 6 minutes, shaking the pan occasionally so that the mussels will cook evenly. When the shells open, the mussels are done. Drain, reserving the liquid. Remove from the shells.

TO POACH FISH:

Arrange the fillets in a large skillet which has been buttered, and sprinkled with chopped onion. Season with salt and pepper, then barely cover with 1½ cups liquid—dry white wine and water mixed. Cover with a buttered piece of wax paper. Bring just to the boil; cover and reduce to a simmer. Simmer 8 to 12 minutes depending on the thickness of the fillets. Do not overcook. Drain carefully, reserving the liquid, and remove fish to a warm serving platter. Surround with the mussels, shrimp and mushrooms. Cover with buttered paper and set aside. Just before serving, reheat by placing the platter, covered, over simmering water for a few minutes. Drain off any liquid before covering with sauce.

SAUCE

3 tbsp. butter	2 egg yolks
4 tbsp. flour	½ cup whipping cream
reserved fish-liquid	salt and pepper
¾ cup milk	6 tbsp. softened butter

Combine the reserved fish and mussel liquid and boil down to 1 cup. Melt 3 tbsp. butter in saucepan; add flour and cook slowly for 2 minutes. Remove from heat and beat in the hot fish liquid and then the milk. Cook for 1 minute. Combine the egg yolks and the whipping cream in a bowl; then slowly add the hot sauce. Return to saucepan and boil for 1 minute, stirring constantly. Remove from heat and beat in softened butter, 1 tbsp. at a time. Spoon the sauce over the hot fish. Decorate with whole shrimps, truffle slices and small *croutons*. Serve immediately. Serves 6.

And the other go-with:

Crabmeat Quiche

1 cup canned crab
2 tbsp. chopped green onion
3 tbsp. butter
¼ tsp. salt
pepper
1 8″ partially cooked pastry-shell
¼ cup Swiss cheese, grated

3 eggs
1 cup whipping cream
1 tbsp. tomato ketchup
¼ tsp. salt
2 tbsp. sherry or Madeira

Cook the green onion in melted butter over moderate heat until tender; add crabmeat and cook for 1 minute. Salt and pepper, then add the sherry or Madeira and boil for 1 minute. Cool slightly.

Beat the eggs; add the cream and seasonings, then the crabmeat. Pour into prepared pastry shell. Sprinkle with grated cheese and bake in preheated 375° oven for 30 minutes or until the *quiche* is browned. Serves 6.

*The oyster
is
Chablis' world*

*C*HABLIS BY THE glass in London is very
nearly as common as Guinness; almost any wine bar has it. Once,
in one of these, in the late afternoon of a hot day, a glass of the
steely, greeny-yellow Chablis seemed just the thing to rest the feet
over, at however many pence the glass it was listed at on the slate
standing amidst the clutter of barrels and bottles on the back bar.

What I got was pleasant enough. In fact, it was doing my feet
and intermediate portions no end of good when the notion began
to take hold that it didn't taste like any other Chablis I had ever
tasted. So, after a few more sips, and plucking up my courage,
I said to the gent in the director's suit who had served me, "Look,
this is quite good, and I'm not asking you to do anything about
it (tug of the forelock), but I would bet all the money I have on
me that it's not Chablis." And, suddenly come all over matey, he
leaned towards me, had a quick look both ways down the bar,
and said, confidentially, "Well, no, actually. But that's what we
call it. Actually, it's rather a good Meursault." I think if it had
not been contrary to management policy, he might even have called
me, Sir.

Whether or not the wine was Meursault, I would hesitate to say;
it could have been, in which case the substitution did not spring
entirely from crass concern for profit—not *entirely*—but sprang in
part, as well, from the desire to give the customers what they thought
they wanted and what the place did not have any of the real thing
of, there not being all that much of the real thing to be had.

In any event, there is a very great deal of what purports to be
Chablis sold in London. Not only do the little wine bars have it

by the glass, but every fish restaurant that aspires to rise above the -and-chips category lists a Chablis, which the customer is invited to believe was bottled for the proprietor by the grower's own loving hands. It is impossible not to wonder a *little* about this ocean of wine in one city alone, on seeing where the wine is supposed to come from. The loaves and the fishes were a parlour trick by comparison. Chablis, the town, is a little grey-brown place, an easy hour and a half southeast from Paris by autoroute, between Auxerre, where the Cathedral of St. Etienne may be visited in passing, and Tonnerre. It would be hard to say whether Chablis is sleepier than the stream it is on, the Serein, which is overhung with willows, supports a flotilla of lilypads, and is so slow-moving as to give scarcely a sign of the direction in which it is going.

Chablis, the town, is notable mainly for its gate, which is about all that remains of the old town wall; for the substantial homes and business establishments (the two are combined) of some of its leading vineyard proprietors and wine shippers (also combined); for l'Ecole Communale, a three-story building with a mansard roof, from which rises a wrought-iron clock-tower whose bells ring with the flat sound of an iron frying pan being struck with a hammer; and for the Hotel de l'Etoile-Bergerand, just off the town square, where the former King Alfonso of Spain once stayed, or at least ate. There is a picture commemorating his visit in the lobby. Notwithstanding its manifest innocuousness, Chablis was bombed and severely damaged during the Second World War, happily not by our side. As a result, there is quite a bit of new building. This, however, has blended in well, which is to say that it is dun-coloured like the rest.

The town lies in a sort of basin. There are hills all around it, close in, to the north and east, farther away, to the south and west. The best of the vineyards begin just across the Serein from the town, within a short walk of the main square, and most of them face between southeast and southwest so that they get as much sun as may be going, which this far north is rarely more than enough.

The first characteristic of Chablis, the wine, is its clean taste. Sometimes it is called flinty; this, if it strikes a note at all, does so more in the imagination than in whatever mechanism it is that records taste recollections. But it does—doesn't it?—suggest a clean taste. Chablis is an altogether dry wine, rarely with anything about it that would be described as flowery or fruity—certainly not flowery—and when it is young, it can be hard. The 1970 vintage was both a large one, and by local account, an extremely good one in all respects, but a sample of the wine of a first-class vineyard of that year, taken within a year of its being made, was astringent enough to leave the mouth with a feeling—remember eating chokecherries as a kid?—of being faintly puckered.

So there it is—clean, dry, flinty (if you like). The bouquet is delicate. The two, fresh scent, clean taste, make it, at a better age than the young wine just described, an excellent companion for anything fresh from the sea, especially oysters, with which it forms a combination like ham and eggs. There is something of the same sea-freshness of the oysters in the wine itself. In fact, Chablis has a tenuous connection with at least *ancient* seas if I interpret correctly (a point I do not absolutely insist upon) the following description of the geology on which it rests from *The Wines and Vineyards of France:* "The strata is composed of alternate beds of clay and marl with intercalations of greyish marly limestone and grey and pink shell beds. The soil is extremely calcareous (50 per cent on average). One finds by the thousands the characteristic Kimmeridgian fossil, ostrea virgula." Whether or not they are of the characteristic Kimmeridgian fossil, ostrea virgula, I cannot say, but I can testify to the presence of numerous fossilized shells. From shell-bearing soil to shell-bearing tables in one not-so-easy hop—that is the Chablis story.

There is surprisingly little to the whole Chablis wine area. Climb to the top of the nearest vineyard just down the road from the town—a long climb, but not a back-breakingly steep one—and all the rest of the fields which comprise Chablis are to be seen spread out around the town. There are fewer than 5000 acres in all, and if 4,000,000 bottles of Chablis, in all grades from best to least, are taken from them in one year, it is not a bad year, for Chablis is prone to failures.

The hazards are several. For instance, the first thing the visitor is likely to notice is that over the top of every sixth line of vines as it runs up the hill there is a pipe, and that here and there higher up the slopes are white-painted storage tanks with the names of makers of bottled gas on them. This is the Chablis *vigneron's* answer, and not always a successful one, to the killing frosts of winter and spring. This heating system is his equivalent to the smudge pots of the California and Florida orange-groves. In mid-summer, very often there is hail, a plague to winegrowers everywhere but a more regular occurrence in Chablis than in some other places. Hail does not seriously affect the quality of the wine that subsequently may be made from a hail-struck vineyard, but it virtually ensures that there will be a good deal less of it. Grapes are knocked from their bunches, or are broken open and thereafter are scarred and less filled with juice. If his vines have survived winter-kill, if late spring frosts have not nipped the blossoms, or if cold, wet weather has not interfered with the necessary idyll with the bees, if hail has not battered the formed bunches, then the Chablis winegrower may find that what is sent to try him is a torrential summer rainstorm, which will sluice the precious vineyard soil down the slope to the bottom.

This may seem an exaggerated catalogue of woes; it is not. In the growing season of 1971 there were frosts; there was unusual heat in April; there was wet weather during the blooming of the vines; there were hail storms in mid-summer, and following close on those, days of heavy rains. (The vintage, while small, in the end was quite good.) The heavy rains had left furrows cut between the vines, which in Chablis run on wires up and down the slopes rather than across them, and vineyard proprietors patiently shovelled up the soil and chips of stone that had washed down, and carted them back up to where they belonged.

Chablis is one of the most northern wine districts of France. Champagne and Alsace are both farther north, but Chablis seems particularly exposed to the elements, and most dangerously, to frosts, which in some years have permitted almost no crop at all. It is no wonder, then, that another of the difficulties with which the winegrowers of Chablis have had to contend is the steady departure of the local young men for less chancy occupations. Paris, after all, is not far away, and in Paris it is not necessary to carry mud and stones.

None of this, of course, affects those fish restaurants with the special, private bottlings of Chablis; they go on getting it in uninterrupted plenty... from barrels which in many cases, inescapably, must be marked something else. So, the question: If there is a good deal of fakery of Chablis, how do you know, how does anyone know, when he goes into his liquor store and lays down his not insignificant sum, that he is getting the real McCoy?

It probably would be unwise to say that fakery takes place *only* where bottling is done outside the jurisdiction of the inspectors who enforce the French laws on controlled place-names. No law anywhere always goes unbusted. But the *Appellation d'Origine Contrôlée* laws are as good as any of the food, drug and other product, safeguards that we rely on daily, and if the words *Appellation Contrôlée* appear on the label, what is in the bottle can be accepted with some assurance as being what is *said* to be in it. On the other hand, where the wine, Chablis or any other, is bottled outside the country of origin, the buyer must rely on the seller's word. In the case of numerous long-established wine merchants in Britain, where a large amount of domestic bottling continues to be done, nothing could be better. The proprietor of the little fish restaurant around the corner with his very own Chablis from the cask may be another kettle of, um, fish.

The question does not arise in Canada because no really fine wines are imported in cask and bottled in this country. (The Régie des Alcools du Québec imports and bottles some French *district* wines which are good for everyday drinking, although the quality tends to be up and down. But these, essentially, are carafe-quality wines—a comment which is by no means intended as a disparagement; wine-drinkers in other provinces probably would welcome similar enterprise.) The best bottle of Chablis that is available to Canadians is to be had in Ontario, at a price—a price $1.50 (or more) dearer than the same bottle could be had for in Boston, New York or San Francisco. The wine in question is Chablis Les Clos, grown and bottled by the excellent firm of Moreau. The vineyard called Les Clos, which is within a long stone's-throw of the centre of the town of Chablis, is one of only eight in the Chablis district which are accorded the rank of *Grand Cru*. Since the district is a small and compact one, the hierarchical structure of the wines of Chablis is simply set out. From the bottom up, it is as follows:

First there are the wines—and these represent the great bulk of the whole production of Chablis—which are entitled to be called simply Petit Chablis or Chablis. Wines so designated come from the lesser slopes of the district. They are not to be disdained on that account; nor are they cheap. To be entitled to be called Chablis, the wine must come up to a minimum alcoholic strength of ten degrees; Petit Chablis may be one degree less. Chablis, it will be observed from this, is basically a wine that is very light in alcohol, as tends to be the case with all northern wines.

Next come the *Premiers Crus*, First Growths so-called, single vine-yards which because of their long-term excellence are considered worthy of being sold under their own names—Chablis-Fourchaume, for instance, to identify probably the best known of them. They must attain ten and a half degrees of alcohol. If they do not, they have to be sold off simply as Chablis. (It is the general rule: a wine may always be sold *down* to the next, broader category the requirements for which it can fit, but it cannot be sold *up*; Fourchaume may be sold as Chablis, but no Chablis but Fourchaume can be sold as Fourchaume.) None of the twenty-two wines which compose the list of First Growths of Chablis is sold as such in Canada. However, again in Ontario, the liquor commission lists a Chablis *Premier Cru* put up by the firm of Poulet. A wine so designated is not necessarily, and in fact not likely to be, from any single *Premier Cru* vineyard—otherwise the name would be given—but is a blend of wines of several *Premier Cru* vineyards, and only of those. The year being stated, it is also necessarily of one year's production, and not a blend of years. This, then, can be regarded as a wine of high quality.

After, and above, these come the *Grands Crus* already mentioned. In addition to Les Clos, they are, in a highly arbitrary order of fame, Vaudésir, Grenouilles, Blanchots, Valmur, Preuses, Moutonne and Bougros.

As I've already mentioned, Chablis is pre-eminently a wine for sea-food, although with any dish that might strike anyone's fancy as calling for a clean, fresh-tasting altogether dry white wine, why not? So go butter yourself some thin, thin slices of brown bread, cut a wedge of lemon, open a dozen oysters, and you are in business. Or, if that was lunch yesterday, you might try the following, created by André Roy, chef at the Hotel de l'Etoile-Bergerand in Chablis itself:

Soles Glacées au Chablis

4 sole	salt
mussels	pepper
Chablis white wine	butter
onion rings	

Remove both skins from the sole; clean the fish and break the backbones towards the middle with a knife, to flatten them. Steam a handful of mussels in Chablis or other white wine and reserve the juice. Butter the bottom of a baking dish; add 4 or 5 onion rings. Arrange the sole on top so that they touch as little as possible; sprinkle with salt and pepper. Add a cup of Chablis white wine, the reserved juice from the mussels, and enough water barely to cover the fish. Cover the dish with buttered paper. Cook in the oven for 10 to 15 minutes.

SAUCE

cooking liquid from the sole	2 egg yolks
butter	juice of half a lemon

Drain the cooking liquid from the sole into a saucepan (keep the sole warm) and boil until it is reduced to half the original amount. Combine with a little softened butter and let cook for 5 minutes. Remove from heat and, using a whisk, beat in 2 egg yolks which have been thinned with a drop of water. Return to high heat and bring to the boil again, stirring constantly in order to prevent the sauce from curdling. Add the juice of half a lemon and stir in 4 ounces of fresh butter. Do not let the sauce boil.

TO SERVE:

Place the sole in a baking dish and pour the sauce over it. Put the baking dish in a pan of warm water and brown in a very hot oven. Serve immediately. Serves 4.

Diane
of Poitiers
had a bust glass

*T*HE LOIRE, THE Loire, the beautiful Loire. The Loire has been described as the most French of French rivers, in part, no doubt, because there is more of it than there is of any other. If you are on the Rhône, well to the east in France, and well to the south of Lyon, you are only a short drive from the beginnings of the Loire, which at that point will be found running contentedly north. And yet, on the Atlantic coast, clear across the country, there it is emptying into the ocean, having come the last part of the way flowing east-to-west.

Mention the Loire and by a reflex action out comes the word, "chateaux". And sure enough, it has them, great fairy-tale places, all placid moats, pointy towers, and sculptured, formal gardens— Chenonceaux, Amboise, Chambord, Beaugency, Azay-le-Rideau, Chaumont, Château-la-Vallière. (Poor Louise La Vallière; Louis XIV, the Sun King, gave her her chateau on the Loire, but as was his way, he lost interest. Before she left, however, he also gave her a baby. Louise became a Carmelite nun.)

The chateau country, of course, reeks of romance, rather a lot of it, unfortunately, *ad hoc*. Chenonceaux, the most improbable castle of them all, spanning as it does the tranquil Cher (a tributary of the Loire), was the love nest of Henry II and the hearty Diane of Poitiers. Henry, however, had a wife, Catherine de'Medici, who, when Henry had the bad luck to die of wounds received in a tournament, turfed Diane out and occupied Chenonceaux herself. But while their relationship existed (*relationship* having been the term in use at the time), we are told, Henry and Diane greatly favoured the wines of Chinon—which brings us again within what may be laughingly referred to as our terms of reference. (I seem to have

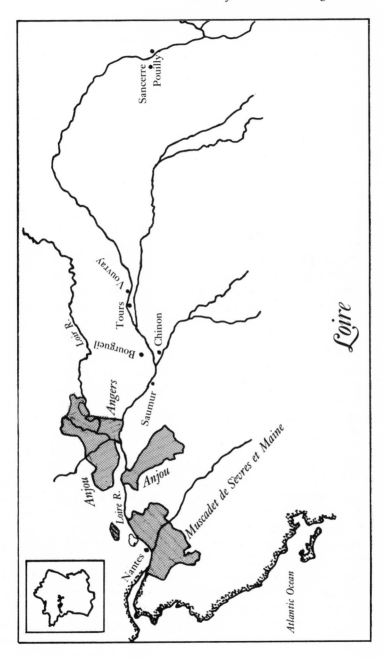

here a vagrant note to the effect that Henry, while at Chenonceaux, had a drinking glass made for himself, modelled after Diane's breast, left or right not specified. This gives rise to wild visions of the glass-blower pulling up at the drawbridge—Chenonceaux has a splendid drawbridge—presenting his compliments, and saying that he has come to rehearse. But that is clearly *outside* our terms of reference.)

Touristically, the Loire is awkward for the wine-enthusiast. First, there is the problem of where to fit it in. Following a sort of great circle route, clockwise or anti-clockwise, it is possible to touch upon all the other major wine-growing regions of France in a more or less orderly progression. The Loire, in its meandering way, is laid on the country crosswise, and approached from either end, can only succeed in taking the traveller miles away from somewhere else that he was planning to go. In addition, there is the fact that there is no real family to the wines of the Loire. It is impossible to say that the wines of the Loire are . . . because the wines of the Loire aren't. They are a bit of everything. They are red, white and rosé; they are dry and sweet; they are still, *pétillant* and sparkling.

But that is part of the reason for going. On top of that, this is country in which a man can punish his cholesterol count until it screams for mercy; Tours, for instance, is a gastronomic centre of standing. And then, for those addicted to architecture, history and similar pedestrian studies, there *are* those chateaux, poking their Disneyland profiles out of the trees. Finally, though the Loire is hardly a day's drive from almost anywhere, an important wine part of it is nowhere nearer for the traveller than at Chablis; so, this is the time to go.

From Chablis, it is an easy morning's drive, southwest by Auxerre, to Pouilly-sur-Loire, about which the most remarkable fact is that it has three one-star restaurants within the town limits and a fourth just outside them. True enough, there are just over 550 of these in France, but for a town of 1850-odd people to have grabbed off four of them makes rather more than its fair share. It is instructive in the matter of the dishes that go with Pouilly—if you approach the choice of food according to the wine that will go with it, a method of proceeding that has a lot to be said for it—that all four of these restaurants have fish dishes among their specialities. These include turbot cooked in Pouilly, *écrivisses à la nage* (crayfish swimming in a bouillon that is basically made of wine, which of course will be Pouilly), and sole *soufflé*, with which the only conceivable wine, at least here in Pouilly-sur-Loire, would be Pouilly-sur-Loire or Pouilly-Fumé.

There is not a great deal to be said for the town of Pouilly except for the eating places in it and the vineyards on its doorstep, most of those in the direction of Cosne, to the north and a bit west of the town. Set in concave surfaces of the slopes, the vines are situated to get the most of the sun from first light to last. Still, it would be ungracious not to mention that there are also numerous little places in the neighbourhood where the traveller can drop in and, perhaps calling the *vigneron's* wife away from the cellar where she is putting the capsules (mostly plastic now) on the heads of bottles, taste the wine and buy a bottle—or fifty cases for that matter, there being a lot of direct-from-producer-to-consumer selling done here.

Two distinct wines are made at Pouilly, both of them dry and both of them white, but of different grapes, and different in style. The better of the two is called Pouilly-Fumé (not to be confused—the obligatory mention—with Pouilly-Fuissé from the Mâconnais). The grape used in making Pouilly-Fumé is the Sauvignon Blanc, the basic grape of the white Graves. The other wine is called Pouilly-sur-Loire, for which the grape is the Chasselas. There is a difference in quality, and there should be a difference in price. The Pouilly-Fumé, though dry, is more rounded and has more of the taste of the fruit to it; beside it, the other may seem sharp. As a final note, it might be added that Pouilly-Fumé is sometimes called Pouilly-*Blanc*-Fumé, for no very good or apparent reason since the only Pouilly-Fumé there *is* is blanc and the Pouilly-sur-Loire is white as well—but these things are sent to try us.

Cross the Loire by a long, skinny iron bridge—the Loire has no depth, but it is wide—and in addition to being, like the chicken, on the other side, you are pointed in the right direction for the next of the wine towns of the Loire, Sancerre. About the wine of Sancerre, my opinions are hard to define. It might be as well to admit that white wines so dry that they do not admit of even a little of the taste of the natural, ripe fruit are not quite my dish, although at the right time, and in the right place, that sort of razor's-edge crispness is just the thing. Sancerre is that way. If you like it—Ernest Hemingway did; it was a favourite of his—you are likely to like it very much. And it has to be admitted that the sort of bone-dryness that I associate with Sancerre is very much the *in* thing.

But about the town of Sancerre itself, there is simply no question. It is one of those wine towns that restore your faith in wine towns, which, it is my particular idiosyncracy to believe, ought not to look like the sorts of places that specialize in growing mangel-wurzels; just a little glamour is surely in order. And there you have Sancerre, a genuine delight. To get to it, you climb away from the flat country of the river-bottom, up and around and about, by way of a road that leads through vineyards to what turns out to be a sort of butte, on which stands (or rather, clings) Sancerre. All the streets in the place are narrow; they all run up and down hill; there is nowhere to park, but those problems aside, it all turns out to be very much worth-while.

There are ramparts to lean over—the *remparts des Augustins*, for example, and the *remparts des abreuvoirs* (you could water your horse) —an esplanade, the *Esplanade de Port Cesar*, a couple of fifteenth-century towers, and far below, the Loire itself, leisurely and shallow, making its way placidly around corners where the silt has accumulated to make white banks.

The name of Mellot is an important one in Sancerre: the wine of Sancerre listed by the Ontario liquor commission is shipped by a Mellot, and Alphonse Mellot has an *auberge* in the centre of town that puts up a light, fixed-price lunch designed especially for winetasters. It begins with a *terrine d'auberge* to go with the red wine, follows with an omelette to go with the rosé and ends with a goat cheese to go with the white. There are at least two surprises here: Sancerre is so much associated with white wine that not everyone will have heard of the red and the rosé, although it is a rare thing in any wine district that there will not be at least a small quantity produced of whatever happens not to be dominant. Still, I confess a rosé Sancerre remains new to me. Then, it is a surprise to find wines being offered in this order, from red, through rosé, to white—and a surprise to find the white paired with cheese at all. However, it is also a general rule with wine that the best is served last, and no doubt the people of Sancerre know what they are about. It is the white wine that has the reputation.

My notes on the red Sancerre from a single tasting are that it was quite dark in colour, with a tinge of purple, that it did not have a great deal of bouquet, and that in the taste there was a hint of something that reminded me of the tonic given kids to build up their blood. That last, I realize on rereading, does not make it sound terribly appetizing; perhaps it should be added that the same notes said that the wine was a bit young, being then under one year, and might benefit from being left. I have seen the rosé of Sancerre extravagantly praised, but confess that I do not share the enthusiasm. In any case, I doubt that much, if any, is exported. As to the white, I have already admitted my indecision. The main vineyards at Sancerre are not those that the road leads through on the way up from Pouilly (nor are they, strictly speaking, *at* Sancerre); but from the proper rampart they are visible—as is everything else for miles around—mainly to the west of the town.

Following the Loire north from here a bit, and then west, where it eventually settles into its long run to the Atlantic, the next vineyard area of major note that we come to is Vouvray. For reasons which would be hard to explain (a euphemism I sometimes use for, "I haven't a clue...") there is a widespread tendency to think of Vouvray solely as a lightly effervescent wine, as of course some of it is. But by no means all. Aside from that variety as between *pétillant* and still, Vouvray also will be found to be both dry or semi-dry—and sometimes so labelled, a practice which is unusual except in Champagne. However, this is done more often with the sparkling Vouvray than with the still, and the buyer of a bottle of unadorned Vouvray may be left to guess whether what he has purchased is going to be bone dry or verging on the absolutely sweet. It can be very good either way, but sometimes it is disconcerting not to know in advance what to expect. In years when the growing season has been especially bright and long, the entire vintage may be semi-sweet, but in other circumstances the same grower may make both dry and semi-dry by keeping separate the ripest latest-picked grapes for the less dry wine. I find the driest Vouvrays a little acid for my taste; by the same token, others call them stimulating, refreshing and goodness knows what else. (The first rule of wine, to be cited as required, is that you satisfy your own taste and let everyone else tag along as best he may—selfish, perhaps, but effective.) The pale, sometimes almost colourless, wine of Vouvray is left in barrel for six to eight months after the vintage, and is bottled the following spring or early summer. It is then ready for drinking. A lot of it is sold as a carafe wine in France.

Vouvray, the town, is a quiet, grey, comfortable-looking place, with some substantial homes, cherry, pear, apple and peach trees in many of the backyards. The Hotel Grand Vatel is not grand, but adequate and inexpensive. Climb the hill that rises steeply behind the town; the vineyards start towards the top. On the way, you pass the establishments of the Vouvray wine growers; they live, and make their wine, down the hill from the plots they tend. Signs outside the courtyard gates invite you to stop for a tasting.

At Vouvray, what lies below the soil, and not far below it, is solid chalk. Very many wine cellars and some homes have been burrowed into it. For instance the cellars of Gérard Nouzillet, a well-known grower, go back deep into the hillside; at the farthest point, a long chimney, perhaps fifty feet high, has been drilled upward to the surface so as to permit a current of fresh air to circulate. Even so, the walls and ceilings are black and velvety and damp to the touch, with a sort of mould. Some of these *caves* are known to have existed from the fifth and sixth centuries.

Vouvray lies to the east of Tours, the capital of the Touraine. The principal, and very nearly the only, red-wine areas of the Loire are to be found not far to the west of Tours. These are Bourgueil, north of the river, and Chinon, south of it. The wines in these areas are made from the Cabernet Franc grape, the same one used in St.Emilion. Consequently, they serve as an illustration of the fact that the same vine in different circumstances will produce dissimilar wines. These are wines which visitors to the chateau country may look for. They will not often find them elsewhere, although I have seen Chinon and Bourgueil on the lists of some London wine-merchants at about one pound a bottle. The two are, to my mind, very much the same, being dark in colour, and soft, and with a bouquet and taste in which are reputed to lurk hints of raspberries. In moments of diligent application, I have been able to persuade myself that these hints actually exist. However, I also find something faintly herbal about the taste, stirring a dormant memory of catnip tea or something equally exotic. These are red wines which, contrary to the usual rule, are served cool.

Seen from a distance, there is a family resemblance to all the towns on the south bank of the Loire: there is the road along the River, and behind it, a line of houses and shops two or three storeys high, in a sort of dove-grey; the town rises behind that again, and somewhere, lording it over all else, is the chateau. Saumur, though

larger than most of these towns, is like that. It was a fortress once.
Saumur comes at the end of a string of small wine-towns which
together constitute the Côteaux de Saumur. The district makes
mostly white wine and rosé, some of the white, sparkling, some
of the rosé, *pétillant*. The first bottle of wine I remember buying
was a bottle labelled Anjou Saumur rosé, which turned out to be
very lightly bubbly and delicious.

Saumur is a part of the general wine-district of Anjou, for which
Angers is perhaps the best reference point, although the town itself
is north of the River, while the vineyards lie to the south. Angers phys-
ically presides over the several areas which collectively make up
the Anjou wine-region: the Côteaux de la Loire, Côteaux de
L'Aubance, Côteaux du Layon, and a little farther away, towards
Tours, the Côteaux de Saumur. With the exception of Saumur,
and perhaps the Côteaux du Layon, these are not names that will
be encountered every day, even in the most sophisticated wine lists.
Mostly, what they describe are dry white wines. Nevertheless, the
most distinctive of all—and of those, one, particularly, Quarts de
Chaume—are the sweet wines of the Côteaux du Layon, which
are similar in style and use to those of Sauternes.

Otherwise about Anjou, except to say that it is green, gardenish,
gentle sort of land, and beautiful, I would add only two items for
collectors of esoteric information. One, is that Anjou once was ruled
by my very favourite among the world's rulers, Fulk the Good
(if he had been Fulk the Bad, it might have been equally a name
and a declaration of principle); two, is the following, from *The Wines
and Vineyards of France*, an encyclopaedic work by Louis Jacquelin
and René Poulain:

> *The soil is hard rock, siliceous or schistose, of silurian or precambrian
> formation. The arable top soil is very shallow. . . . In the eastern section
> the soil is of a later secondary and tertiary formation. The zincs are
> grown on limestone rocks of the cenomanian and turonian cretaceous order.
> A little senonian strata is to be seen and a few fissures of jurassic limestone.
> It is in the limestone masses that famous underground caves of the region
> are to be found. . . .*

Caves, I know. Nor is that all: in some of those *caves* there is
wine, cultivating serenity. The jurassic limestone I am prepared
to leave to others.

Finally, around Nantes, almost at the mouth of the Loire, there are the wines called Muscadet. Probably because the name starts out the same way, there is a tendency to associate these wines with the Muscat grape, which in the south of France, either alone or in company with others, goes into the making of sticky-sweet wines, some fortified, others not. If there is one thing that Muscadet is not, it is sweet. The wine, Muscadet, is made from a grape of the same name, and thus is one of the rare wines in France (the principal exception being in Alsace) which are named by other than place of origin. However, in the case of Muscadet it is only a partial exception. What is now generally considered to be the prime area in which Muscadet is grown, lies southeast of the city of Nantes, and bottles from there will be labelled Muscadet Sèvre-et-Maine or Muscadet Region Sèvre-et-Maine, instead of simply Muscadet.

In this part of the Loire, the grapes are picked early so as to avoid overripeness, and the wine, which rests no longer in barrel than the early spring following the vintage, has a good deal of that acid-freshness which you either like or do not like, and no trace at all of sweetness. Its natural affinity, as is the case with all such wines, is with fresh seafood, especially with such things as oysters and clams. Since the Second World War, and accelerating rapidly in just the past few years, it has enjoyed a considered fad, first in Paris, now in the United States, with consequent effects on the price. Muscadet is made to be drunk young, so any thought of stocking up against further price-rises is to be dismissed.

We have now exhausted the River and are on the Atlantic. In this we have not covered *all* the wines of the Loire, which along a length of about 600 miles of river, number quite a few. Montlouis, a white wine similar to Vouvray, is made across the River from Vouvray and, in fact, at one time was sold as Vouvray. There are wines of the Touraine sold as that, or with that name in association with the name of a locality, but these are likely to be met only on the spot. And then of course there is the fact that some Muscadet wines come not from the region Sèvre-et-Maine, but from a region described as Muscadet des Côteaux de La Loire, the Côteaux de La Loire, in this instance, being different from the Côteaux de La Loire, near Angers, which in turn, are something else again from the Côteaux du Loir a little distance to the northeast, le Loir (m) being a different river from la Loire (f). But that way lies madness.

Notwithstanding its Chinon and Bourgueil, which are red, the Loire is mainly a white-wine river, or perhaps white and rosé. And the white wines—the *dry* white wines, for not all of them are, remember—go very well with seafood. A Muscadet, for instance, would do these *moules* proud, but so would a wine of Pouilly, or of Vouvray (still) or Sancerre. And having said that, the same can be said for the *Coquilles St. Jacques*, here in southern, or Provençale, dress.

Moules à la Marinière

6 to 8 dozen fresh mussels	1 small bay leaf
scrubbed well and de-bearded	¼ tsp. thyme
2 cups dry white wine	salt and pepper to taste
½ cup chopped green onion	6 tbsp. butter
parsley sprigs	1 clove garlic, chopped

In a large, deep kettle, heat the butter; add the garlic and cook over low heat for 1 minute. Add the rest of the ingredients and bring to a boil. Add the mussels; cover and boil over high heat until the mussel shells open—about 5 minutes. Remove the mussels and arrange in soup plates, then ladle the hot liquid over them and sprinkle with chopped parsley. Serve immediately. Serves 6 to 8.

Coquilles St. Jacques à la Provençale

1½ lbs. scallops	pinch of thyme
salt and pepper	⅓ cup finely chopped onion
sifted flour in a dish	1 clove garlic, crushed
butter	2 tbsp. chopped green onion
1 tbsp. oil	¼ cup grated Swiss cheese
⅔ cup dry white wine	
small bay leaf	

Cook the chopped onions and garlic in 1 tbsp. butter until tender and set aside.

Wash and dry the scallops and cut into slices. Sprinkle with salt and pepper and roll in flour. Shake off excess. *Sauté* quickly in hot butter and oil for 2 minutes; brown them lightly. Pour in the wine; add the herbs and the garlic/onion mixture. Cover and simmer for 5 minutes, then discard the bay leaf and correct the seasoning. Spoon the scallops and sauce into 6 buttered scallop shells and sprinkle with ¼ cup grated Swiss cheese. Dot with butter and place under broiler for 3 to 4 minutes to brown the cheese. Serve immediately. Serves 6.

The
breakfast wine
of champions

*T*HE GERMANS HAVE a saying (which I suspect is one of those sayings that are quoted endlessly without anyone's ever actually having said them a first time) that the vine will grow where no plough can go. Their own Moselle (or Mosel) Valley illustrates the point. Beautiful, it undeniably is, with its great loops and bends between steep walls, but it would discourage a mountain goat. And not only are the sides steep; what passes for soil in the Moselle is mostly slate—and slate, moreover, with a wayward tendency to wash down the slopes, only to have to be painfully humped back up again.

The Swiss vineyards of the Valais are no better, capable of being worked only by stubborn men, science having not yet produced a horse with two short legs on one side adapted to working precipitous hillsides. The same can be said for some of the best vineyards of the Côtes-du-Rhône, which are terraced in terraces only a few yards deep. The Douro Valley in Portugal, where port comes from, is no more accommodating. Chablis, as we have seen, although it does not thwart the plough, is enough to make strong men weep.

All of which brings us, by a devious route, to Champagne. Come by car to the region of this best-known name in wines from almost any direction and you do so over plains which disclose nothing of the adversity of topography and soil which wines are supposed to thrive on, and do. Let us say you come from the south, through some such place as Troyes, Brienne-le-Château or St. Dizier. You pass through bountiful agricultural land, covered to the horizons in late summer with golden grain; rich prairie. The Canadian could be excused at this point for thinking himself back again clasped to the equivocal bosom of Mother Saskatchewan. These hundreds

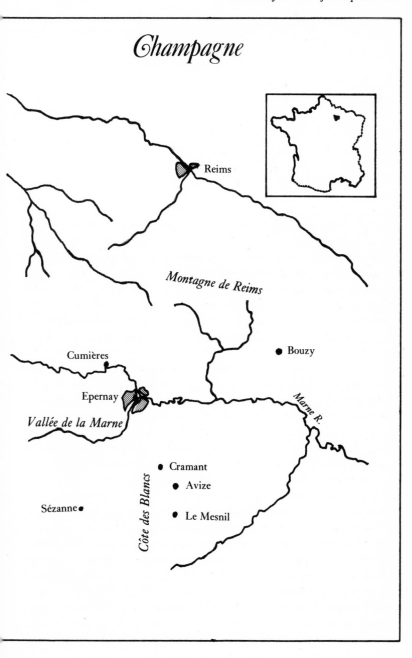

of *hectares* of prospective *baguettes* are all very well, but man does not live by bread alone, not even French bread, so continue; above and below the city of Epernay, but also extending in a great hook up to the city of Reims to the north (Reims and Epernay are the twin capitals of the Champagne wine district), there are vineyards, situated, as is only appropriate to all vineyards, on slopes. But these, though often sweeping, are still gentle slopes; impeccably tended, cultured-looking slopes as befits champagne, the wine for impeccably tended, cultured-looking people. The wines grow on them in soil which is to all appearances the amenable, everyday stuff of back-gardens and window-boxes, except that it visibly contains large quantities of chalk.

This is as chalky a chalk as ever teacher screeched on blackboard, the real thing in its native state, and it is the dominant factor in Champagne. It is largely responsible for giving the wine its character, which by nature tends to be dry and rather acid. It is also the stuff in which are cut the great underground tunnels—galleries, they call them—of the champagne firms, in which literally millions of bottles of champagne are stored. Under the city of Reims there are reputed to be 120 miles of tunnels. The firm of Mumm & Co. has 11 miles of them of its own. The small city of Epernay similarly sits on top of a series of what amount to wine mines.

The scheme of growing, making and marketing wine as it exists in Champagne may foretell the future for all the great wine regions; it will be a pity if it does, but there are influences in that direction. In Burgundy, as we have seen, already-small vineyards almost invariably are divided among numbers of vigorously independent *vignerons* who make and market the wine from their own few acres, or even in some cases from their own few rows, or sell it in barrel to the big *négociants* in Beaune or Nuits-St. Georges or Dijon, to bottle and sell abroad.

Whatever the small grower may do with the wine he produces, the one thing that is certain is that it will be sold with as specific a geographical designation as it has a right to under the *Appellation Contrôlée* laws. For example, wine grown in the vineyard of Bressandes at Beaune, if it does not exceed the stipulated number of gallons that may be produced per acre, and if it does not fall short of the minimum number of degrees of alcohol, will be sold as Beaune Bressandes, never by the vaguer name, Beaune Villages, nor by the still less specific name, Côte de Beaune, far less by the generic name, burgundy. And if the proprietor who raised it also bottled it, that will be proudly stated on the label too.

There is something very agreeable in this for the wine enthusiast who is seeking, among other things, a refuge from standardization, but as any specialist in mass marketing might say, it is, commercially, grossly inefficient. Let us take the case of Bressandes, at Beaune, as an example of a typical top-flight Burgundian vineyard, and make the comparison with the situation in Champagne. Bressandes encompasses forty-four acres, on which may be produced about 80,000 bottles of wine in a good year. These do not go to one market but enter into world trade, and do so under the different labels of various proprietors and shippers. The enthusiast who has concluded that of all the wines of the world, this is the one he loves best, will have to seek out his small share where he can, even in a large market such as London or New York. But the essential thing is that he *can* do it.

In Champagne, the situation is very nearly the opposite. There, for all purposes of identification in the market, vineyards do not exist; individuality gives way to standardization. Some makers, of course, standardize at a very high level of quality, buying their grapes mostly if not entirely from the top-rated vineyards, but even in those cases this will be from vineyards located over the whole district designated for wine purposes as Champagne. Thus, there is a process of averaging. The highs are lopped off and the lows are filled in—filled in, in great years, when a vintage is declared, from entirely within that one year's production; and in the non-vintage years, from the production of several years, so that by skilful blending, one wine's strengths are used to counteract another wine's weaknesses.

In most cases, the grower in Champagne is simply a grape farmer; what he sells are grapes. The winemaker, far from being the little man with a patch of vines which he cultivates, picks and makes into wine himself, as in Burgundy, is a large, and in some cases a very large, firm, with a beautifully kept, splendidly equipped plant and miles of galleries in the chalk below, in Reims or Epernay. The wine that is made (with minor exceptions that we will come to) is called by one name: champagne. What distinguishes one champagne from another, then, is the name on the label—Mumm's, Moet & Chandon, Krug, Veuve Cliquot-Ponsardin, Bollinger, Lanson, Pol Roger, Perriet Jouet, are a few of the best known—and each of these firms has its own very secret blend of so many gallons of wine from grapes grown in this location, so many from that, so many from a third, fourth and fifth. And of course each has millions of bottles to market a year, under a label advertised world-wide.

The first thing a champagne label tells the buyer is the maker's name. In the circumstances, it is the one thing that determines the buyer's preference. The label may or may not state the year of the wine. There cannot be any rule about the frequency with which good years, worth being identified by vintage, will occur, but the champagne makers seem to find their arcane standards are met three or four times a decade. Very probably it will say something about the degree of sweetness which the wine has been given, running from very dry to quite sweet as indicated by the terms brut, extra sec, demi-sec, rich. (Sec means dry, but here it nevertheless denotes a wine which is sweet, or sweetish: even in highly efficient Champagne, wine has its little idiosyncracies.) If the wine was made only of white grapes, the label may identify it as a *blanc de blancs*. *Blanc de blancs* champagne has been enjoying a fad, which like most fads has no very apparent explanation. And that about exhausts the information to be found on a champagne label.

But let us go back to those elegant slopes, say to those at Epernay; they make a great semi-circle in front of the town, to the north, so that the town sits as if it were the stage and the vineyards the tiers of some vast amphitheatre. The vineyards in Champagne—these and all others—are divided into classes according to quality, as proved over a long time, and each year before the picking begins, representatives of the growers and representatives of the champagne houses meet to bargain over a price for the grapes of vineyards of the top class. The prices for all the rest are stated in percentages of the first.

All the champagne-makers start, theoretically, on an equal footing; it is when it comes to buying grapes that they first part company. Obviously, the firm that buys the larger proportion of top-quality grapes will make better wine than the one which obtains most of its needs more cheaply from vineyards in less favoured locations. When the grapes are picked, they are trucked at once to press-houses located near the vineyards, and within hours the juice, or must, is transported in tank trucks (even as Esso or Shell) to the plants of the wine firms, mostly in Reims and Epernay. There it is made into wine, blended, induced to foam and fizz as a good champagne should, dosed to the desired degree of sweetness, corked, labelled, wrapped in tissue, and sent off to the world to launch marriages, ships and various other unstable enterprises.

Wines with bubbles in them are a drug on the market—and anyone who is inclined to take the term literally should not let any feelings of mine stand in his way. There is no trick in making a fizzy wine. However, that is not to say that everything that fizzes is champagne, including any of the numerous imitations which are made around the world. Apart from the fact that they do not taste like champagne, which is important, they rarely come remotely close to the frothing excitement of champagne. They bubble briefly and in a desultory way, perhaps, but they do not foam; nor are they, in most cases, very good. The reason for that is dead simple: they are inferior wines to begin with. Sparkling burgundy is made exclusively for the boob trade—it is notable that the meagre British Columbia list of burgundies manages to include not only a *red* sparkling burgundy but, ye gods, a white—and *sekt*, the German champagne, is generally made from the secondary wines of the Rhine and Moselle.

For ages before there was any sparkling champagne, there was still wine called champagne, good enough to have attracted the agents of Henry VIII, among others. There is still today still champagne—we had better settle for saying non-sparkling champagne—although it is not often encountered outside the district itself, and there is at least one very good non-sparkling *red* wine of Champagne; it goes by the delightful name of Bouzy Rouge. Bouzy is the name of a small community. Its wines would enjoy a wider reputation but for the fact that they do not stand shipment well and are made from grapes that otherwise would be used to make champagne, which fetches a higher price. It is a victim, then, of economics.

While no doubt it partly represents more profit, the higher price of champagne is not *all* profit, for champagne is a slow, and, consequently, costly wine to make. The grapes picked in October 1972, miraculously transformed, will not be ready to be sipped from actresses' slippers for at least four years, and very likely longer. (A slipper makes an extraordinarily poor thing from which to drink champagne. For a start, the large opening for the foot permits too rapid release of the bubbles. If the slipper, in addition, has open toes, the result may be disastrous to the shirt-front.)

Champagne, not alone among white wines, is made from black

grapes as well as white. Since the colouring matter in a grape is in the skin and not in the juice, what is required is simply a light pressing (folk tales to the contrary notwithstanding, grapes for wine are broken open to let the juice run out rather than wrung dry), and the juice is separated from the skins without delay so that it does not become tinted. And if it does? Right. Pink champagne. And lovely, if you go in for that sort of thing, although in most places it went out with black cami-knickers and garters with rosettes on them.

Once out of the tank trucks and into the vats, very probably having been sugared along the way, the juice begins a vigorous fermentation, during which all sorts of miscellaneous muck are thrown up to form a head at the top, or, if heavier than the juice, are cast down to form a sludge at the bottom. All in all, fermentation lasts from about three weeks to a month, subsiding rapidly after the first ten days, and before Christmas the new wine is ready to be given the first of the three rackings which it will undergo before bottling. Racking simply means separating the clear liquid from what's left.

Up until now, the process has been as for any wine, and the wine itself, for that matter, is indistinguishable from any other white wine of like age. It is now ready to be treated according to the secret that Dom Perignon unlocked (or is supposed to have unlocked; some say he was simply a skilful cellarman who benefited by the arrival of reliable corks), namely, the secret of how to get the bubbles in and the sediment out. (It's not the bubbles that are the trick, it's the sediment.)

But first the bubbles. What we have in front of us now is a young, still, white wine. It is a common thing with wines that a secondary fermentation begins spontaneously the following spring. If the wine is bottled, this secondary fermentation will take place in the bottle. If sugar syrup made with ordinary cane sugar and wine is added before the wine is put into the bottle, the fermentation will be vigorous but contained. What is needed, then, is a strong cap and a strong bottle. Nowadays, crown caps similar to those on soft-drink bottles are used at this stage; champagne bottles are always new so as to be better able to withstand the strong pressure built up, but even so there is always a lot of breakage.

The bubbles are now in the bottle, right enough, but so, after a while, is a fine, gritty-looking sediment which is precipitated in the new fermentation. This, for the sake of the appearance of the wine, has to be got out. There is no hurry about this because the bottles at this stage lie stacked like cordwood in the galleries, as for some time they will remain, to their profit, quietly maturing. But the problem is not to be avoided: the gunk has to be got out, while the precious bubbles have to be kept in. This difficult feat—and it was an *impossible* feat until the trick was discovered—is performed as follows:

Bottles of the wine are stuck, neck-first, into a simple device called (God knows why) a *pupitre*, or desk, which is something like an old-fashioned street-advertiser's sandwich-board in that it has two sides inclining so that they are spread at the bottom and joined at the top; but this sandwich-board has rows of pigeon-holes all over it. The bottles, heads down, bottoms up, are stuck into this sandwich-board, and every day or so a highly skilled cellarman comes along, gives each bottle a bit of a shake and a turn, and leaves it fractionally turned around from the position in which he found it.

That pop-bottle cap which is on top of the bottle has inside it a sort of plastic cup, facing inwards to the bottle, and what the mover/shaker will do over a period of weeks is: (a) gradually alter the attitude of the bottle in the *pupitre* until it is absolutely standing on its head, and (b) by leaving it turned around a little more each time than the way he found it, ensure that no sediment is allowed to collect on any side. Thus, in the end, the bottle is perpendicular, upside down, and all the sediment is in the little plastic cup. Now the neck of the bottle, and just the neck, is popped into a freezing solution; the cap is yanked off (the cup containing the now-frozen sediment is attached to it); the bottle is dosed with a sugar-and-wine mixture in order to make good the loss and give the wine the desired sweetness; the cork is bunged in and wired; and that, except for a further period for rest and maturation, is about that. Dead easy.

Scarcely any champagne in that last, deft series of events goes without its dose of sugar, notwithstanding the fact that the knowing thing with champagne, as with every other drink, is to demand it dry. (It must be that I am an irretrievable square, but the very, very, very dry champagnes do nothing much for me except to leave me feeling like an ad for Tum's.) But there are markets and there are markets. The best market of all for champagne at one time was Russia; the Russians developed their taste for it when they followed Napoleon into France after the Battle of Leipzig in 1813, and they liked it sweet. The cattle millionaires of the Argentine liked it sweet. In fact, the French market takes it rather sweeter than does the British or North American. In any case, the final dosing with a syrup of sugar, wine, and just a trace of brandy—it is called *liqueur d'expédition*—takes place as the last thing before the cork goes in. Champagne labelled brut, which is intended to suggest that it is absolutely dry, should contain none of the *liqueur d'expédition*, but it does, a little. So far as I know, no champagne labelled rich or sweet (the same thing) is sold in Canada, and although I have never tried it, I cannot imagine that our loss is very great. In fact, demi-sec (semi-dry, semi-sweet) is about the sweetest that is likely to be found in English-speaking countries.

It was no great feat of salesmanship which caused champagne to have so large a market in Russia. The Russians simply took what they wanted that first time, which was quite a bit, including some 600,000 bottles of a more-than-usually-sweet wine from one firm's cellars. It was this which set the taste. But the fact is that the great champagne houses of France are not only excellent winemakers; they are, and always have been, merchants of great skill.

It perhaps does not tell us very much about champagne, but it does tell us something about people that the fame of this wine spread largely by example—most of it bad. Champagne, the foaming, star-bright wine that is known today, came into currency only at the beginning of the 1700's, and some of its earliest converts were celebrated tosspots. In his *History of Champagne* the celebrated André Simon once wrote: "We may be quite certain that during the course of his long, celibate life, Benedictine Dom Perignon never for a moment imagined, as he tried so hard to make wine that would be sparkling but would not burst its bottles, that it would be so acclaimed and abused by women of high rank and low morals." Neither could he imagine, no doubt, that behind every one of those *grandes horizontales* taking to champagne like so many doxies to fire-water, there would be a boob buying it.

In the United States, the popularity of champagne was swelled by the patronage of people who, according to Lucius Beebe's description in *The Big Spenders*, were "largely vulgarians of the first chop, often barbarians with the manner and attire of Texas and Oklahoma and the accents of Ohio well upholstered in diamonds and claw-hammer coats. . . . " Champagne salesmen attended the hangouts of the Diamond Jim Bradys and the Bet-a-Million Gates, and sent bottles to their tables so that they would drink, and be *seen* drinking, the right brands. What the *habitués* of the lobster palaces were seen to do—vulgarians or not—the throng could be sure at least to aspire to imitate.

But that was the taste in the New World. If it was still necessary to cultivate the parvenu element in New York, that stage was long since past in Europe. Bad example already had succeeded there. If the champagne houses in Reims and Epernay needed reassuring as to the nobility of their mission, they had only to look to Victorian Britain where the very pillars of respectability—again, the Forsytes and their kind—were given to breaking out magnums of fizz on every triumphal and sub-triumphal occasion. (If the Forsytes drank anything but champagne, and a little port, they did it when Galsworthy was looking the other way.)

Nor has champagne been promoted simply as the accompaniment to weddings, wakes and balls. The champagne makers have not been above insisting, along with the Guinness people, that their product is not only good, but good *for* you. The visitor to any of the champagne houses—all of which welcome tourists and are worth visiting—may find literature thrust on him which assures him that champagne is recommended for invalids and for persons of all ages, and that a small splash may do wonders even for a peaked child.

I would not argue that this is not so; in fact, I cannot think of anything likely to do an invalid more good, even if he were gasping his last, than a glass of wine. Nevertheless, it is at least debatable whether a glass of champagne would do him more good than a glass of something else. Still, it is a tribute to the assiduity of the champagne makers that the idea has achieved some acceptance.

In *Old Men Forget*, Duff Cooper, the British politician whose name will be familiar to anyone who remembers the nineteen thirties and the approach of the Second World War, wrote, here and there, about wine, of which he was a devotee. And in that memoir, he recalled, among other things, a comment which his father, a physician, was in the habit of making if he saw the young Duff Cooper being dosed with tonic: "What the boy really needs is a pint of champagne and a mutton chop." Champagne and a mutton chop is not my idea of the utterly felicitous union; I would prefer, if you don't mind, a pint of just about anything respectable and red with the chop. But there are numerous adherents to the notion that champagne is the perfect all-the-time, any-time, before-after-or-during meals, with-anything, wine. According to this school, the one champagne will do all the way through, beginning with it as an *apéritif* and continuing with it, presumably, until the arrival of the dawn. (Champagne for breakfast has an undeniable touch of elegance.) Or you could begin with a champagne brut and proceed to a demi-sec by dessert, presumably returning to a sec or brut for the long haul.

Perhaps. But given the splendid variety of wines that exists and the fact that there are so few occasions—leaving aside breakfasts, for which I have already nominated champagne as the indisputable choice, there cannot be more than 35,000 adult lunches and dinners in a seventy-year span—it would be a pity to develop so narrow a preoccupation, much as it might be applauded in Reims and Epernay. In any case, champagne does not, so far as I am concerned, accord with everything as well as its greatest enthusiasts insist.

In Champagne, Champagne the geographical entity, the diligent wine-student can do more research in matching the particular wines of the country with its food than he can elsewhere because, on the spot, he has at hand wines of Champagne which simply are not to be had elsewhere. We have already mentioned the excellent Bouzy. There is also a red still wine, a wine of Champagne nevertheless, produced at a small place called Cumières. There also are a number of still white wines of Champagne which are sold under the name of the place where they are produced—Mesnil, Cramant, Avize among them. These come from the so-called Côte des Blancs, below Epernay, one of the three sections into which Champagne is divided, the other two being the Vallée de la Marne on the north side of the River, the name of which still sounds a sombre note so long after the First World War, and the Montagne de Reims, the hook of slopes already mentioned running up from Epernay to Reims.

The Champagne country is pleasant country, without having the charm of, say, the Beaujolais or St. Emilion or Alsace. It is also, as might be expected, good country for food, as most wine areas are. A renowned restaurant is La Chaumière, just outside Reims on the way to Epernay. South of Epernay in the town of Sézanne, a town which seems to exist mainly to give company to its old square-towered cathedral, there is a lovely spot, the hotel-restaurant

France, which has more wine in its cellars than there is in the whole of Saskatchewan.

The France has the sort of wine-list that the enthusiast reads like a novel. For a start, there are pages of the still wines of Champagne, more pages headed the Grands Marcs de Champagne (a bottle of Moet & Chandon, 1911, at twelve dollars, perhaps, or should we blow the works and have the same firm's Cuvée Elysabeth, 1953, at seventeen dollars?); no fewer than sixty-nine wines of Bordeaux, some of them decidedly pricey by any standard, and a magnificent procession of the greatest *magnificoes* of Burgundy. The France is a place for serious eating and drinking, and since it is just as well to stay overnight, it is convenient that there are thirty-odd comfortable rooms.

I have already expressed my reservations about the champagne-goes-with-everything doctrine that is expounded by its great enthusiasts. Still, faced with champagne with each course, one does not stalk out; one makes do. Among the world's great hardships, this one comes very far down the list. However, there *are* some things champagne goes better with than others and one of them is the light and lovely fish dish that follows. (If the cellar is low in champagne, any other white wine that suits your fancy will do.)

Quenelles de Brochet

1¼ lbs. boneless fish fillets—
   pike, halibut, sole or cod
pinch of nutmeg
½ tsp. salt
¼ tsp. white pepper

1 cup water
1 tsp. salt
4 tbsp. butter
1 cup sifted flour
2 eggs
2 egg whites
2-6 tbsp. *chilled* whipping cream

PATE A CHOUX

In a saucepan bring to a boil the water, butter and salt. When the butter has melted, remove the pan from heat and add, all at once, the flour, beating with a wooden spoon. Continue beating over moderate heat until the mixture rolls away from the side of the pan and forms a mass. Remove from heat and beat in the whole eggs, 1 at a time, then the egg whites. Turn mixture into a mixing bowl.

Put the fish through a food or meat grinder twice, using the finest blade. Beat the fish into the *pâté à choux* along with the nutmeg, salt and pepper. *Chill thoroughly.* Just before cooking, using a wooden spoon, vigorously beat chilled cream into the paste by half-tablespoons. Continue adding cream, slowly, until the paste is just firm enough to shape into *quenelles.* (Note that the paste must not be too soft.) Shape each *quenelle* between 2 tablespoons as follows: Dip the spoons in 1 cup of cold water. Heap some of the paste in one and round it off with the bowl of the second spoon. Then slip the second spoon under the *quenelle* and slide it into a buttered skillet. Form the rest of the paste into *quenelles* and carefully add enough hot salted water to float the *quenelles*—about 3 to 4 inches. Bring the liquid to simmering point and poach uncovered for 15 to 20 minutes, or until firm. Never allow the water to come beyond a simmer. Remove carefully and dry on paper towel.

SAUCE

5 tbsp. butter
7 tbsp. flour
1½ cups milk
1½ cups white-wine
    fish-stock (a recipe can be
    found in any standard
    cooking reference)

½ tsp. salt
dash of white pepper
¾ cup whipping cream
lemon juice
grated Swiss cheese

Melt butter in saucepan, add flour and cook for 2 minutes. Remove from heat. Bring the milk and fish stock to the boil and slowly stir into the butter/flour mixture. Add salt and pepper and boil, stirring, for 1 minute. Reduce to simmer and gradually add the cream. Check the seasoning, adding more if necessary; add a few drops of lemon juice. Butter baking dish and pour ¼" sauce into the bottom. Arrange *quenelles* on top and spoon the rest of the sauce over them. Sprinkle with 3 tbsp. grated Swiss cheese and dot with butter. Reheat in a 350° oven for 10 minutes. Then brown lightly under broiler.

You are not going to find a bottle of Bouzy (pronounced Boozy) in Canada, or in most other places outside the Champagne region itself, because Bouzy always has been said not to travel (a fact which might lead anyone to ask what it was doing in late 1972 in the catalogue of Sherry Lehmann, the New York merchants; ah, well, wine facts are like that). Notwithstanding its reputation as a non-traveller, we'll include here the recipe for *le coq au vin rouge de Bouzy* as prepared by P. Charles of the splendid Hotel de France in Sézanne. If another light red wine was used in the recipe, it would no longer be *de Bouzy*—it wouldn't be boozy either because cooking with wine isn't; the alcohol goes up the flue—but it would still be *coq au vin*, and a second recipe for that (especially from so distinguished a source) won't do anyone any harm.

Le Coq au Vin Rouge de Bouzy

Take a chicken of about 6 pounds* and cut it into pieces. Make a marinade of thyme, bay leaf, chopped onions and carrots, two cloves of garlic crushed, parsley and enough red wine to cover chicken. Marinate for 1 day.

Drain the chicken (dry each piece well on paper towels; it will not brown if damp) and brown in butter until very crisp, along with diced bacon and fresh mushrooms. Add the marinade, salt, and freshly ground pepper, and simmer until completely cooked.

Remove each piece of chicken, the diced bacon and the mushrooms from the pot and strain the sauce through a piece of cheesecloth. Thicken it with a *beurre manie* (flour and butter blended together into a smooth paste) or a little chicken blood, and pour it on the chicken, diced bacon and mushrooms. Serve very hot garnished with small, flaky pastry cut-outs.

*The *coq au vin rouge de Bouzy* could be made equally well with two three-pound chickens.

Well, not
all *Alsatians*
have wet noses

GRAPES HAVE BEEN grown and wine has been made in Alsace almost forever, but this quiet, charming, and in some ways, unreal, corner of France, caught between the Vosges Mountains and the Rhine River, nevertheless is one of the newer of the fine-wine districts of the world.

No less an authority than the association of producers and merchants of Alsatian wines says that grape-seeds—Alsatian grape-seeds, obviously, otherwise why mention them?—have been found in the remains of Stone Age Man (who, in that case, and assuming the old wives' tale to have been well-founded, no doubt died of a ruptured appendix). The Romans cultivated vineyards in Alsace; they did almost everywhere. But what Rome could give, Rome could also take away—and did. Alsace suffered the fate of other vineyards elsewhere at the hands of the Emperor Domitian. In AD 81, he ordered the vines rooted out because foreign wines were making unacceptable inroads into the home market for Roman wines (the complaint has been heard since, in other contexts), and because he preferred to see the Gauls, if not hewers of wood and drawers of water, at least producers of grain and other foodstuffs for the imperial centre. (As Domitian was to the ancient Gauls, so was John Connally to the Canadians of 1972, and vice versa.)

Alsace is, not surprisingly, heavily Germanic. The towns—towns with names like Riquewihr, and Ammerschwihr, and Hunnawihr—look German, and, indeed, like the caricature German of Bavarian operettas. The people, very many of them, speak German. Go into what ought to be called a *weinstube* for a glass or two of *marc de Gewürztraminer* to sleep on—more than two, and you may begin your sleeping right there—and the wedding party that is going

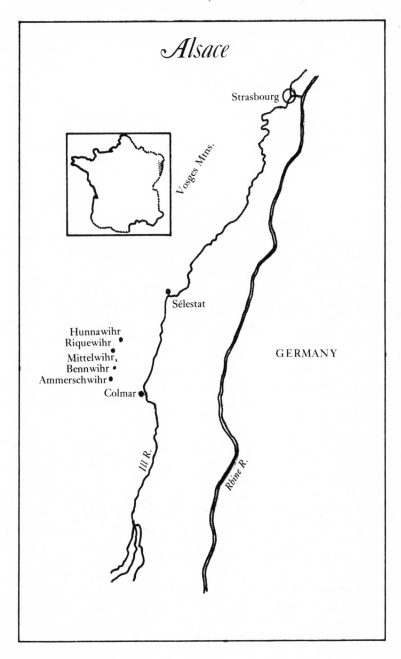

full blast at the next eight tables is singing German songs lustily in German. Unfortunately, the wines are often thought to be poor relations of those of the Rhine and Moselle. That is a great mistake.

It is because the Germans chose to treat Alsace as a viticultural colony in the years of the occupation, 1870 to 1918, that the wines of Alsace even now are so little known. This situation—if you have a taste for prediction, here is one—is going to change greatly in the next few years. They are extremely good value, and worth trying. When Alsace was ceded to Germany, the victors enacted laws which had the effect of ensuring that Alsatian wines would not compete with the German, at home or abroad. Alsatian *vignerons* were to make only ordinary table wines, or wines suitable for blending or for making into sekt, that bad German imitation of champagne. The fine wines of Germany that went by the generic name of hock would still be made where they always had been made, in the Rheingau, Rheinpfalz and Rheinhessen, and in the picturesque towns of the Moselle, and nowhere else.

Even though this policy was somewhat modified before the First World War ever began, and of course ceased to exist at all after it ended, the Alsatian growers in 1918 faced disastrous circumstances. The Germans agreed to take Alsatian wines in the same quantity as before, duty-free, for five years. But after that? Even selling second-rate wines had been better than selling no wine at all. Now the growers were to be left with no foreign markets; in any case, they had not for forty-seven years been encouraged to produce wines of the quality that would interest foreign buyers. At home, they were again part of a land that had no need of more *vins ordinaires* or blend wines of the sort the Germans had taken.

The modern history of Alsace as a fine wine producer, then, begins scarcely fifty years ago. In practical terms, it is shorter than that. After the First World War it was necessary to begin again by grubbing out the inferior, quantity-producing vines and replanting with better varieties—primarily the Riesling, Traminer, Tokay d'Alsace and Muscat, and, secondarily, Sylvaner and Chasselas—a long process. It was mainly to draw attention to the fact that quality vines now were being used in the making of the wines of Alsace that the decision was taken, in the 1920's, to market the wines under the name of the grape type rather than of place of origin.

The place to see the Alsatian wine region in one grand sweep is from the Château Haut-Kœnigsbourg, a hulking red stone castle that is reached by climbing up (and up and up) a winding road behind the town of Sélestat. Here, the whole region is laid out as on a display table. Behind, the Vosges Mountains go on rising, wooded, laced with cold streams from which trout turn up, marvellously transformed, on the tables in the towns below. Alsace, in addition to being wine country, is wonderful country for the knife-and-fork artist, but in that we are getting a little ahead of ourselves.

Before us, the Rhine is off at the horizon to the east. Then comes a broad, flat plain which grows, among other things, the fruits that go into the making of the celebrated (unjustly, to my mind, but that's an idiosyncrasy) *eau-de-vie* of Alsace, and the plebian cabbage which is the foundation of Alsace's even more celebrated *choucroute garnie*, sauerkraut laden with miscellaneous delicatessen. And then, as the ground begins to rise, the vineyards commence, fitting in tight to all the small communities. All of the latter seem to have begun as fortified towns and even now seem to occupy little more than their original walled space. They have filled in, become more tightly packed, so that each is a small clump of houses and shops with narrow streets between them; a church steeple rises over all, the next—and perhaps the only other—building of consequence being the Hôtel de Ville. Viewed from the level of the Castle these villages have the appearance of somehow having been stuck on the landscape, like cut-outs superimposed on the cross-hatched background of vines.

But you drink no wine and eat no *choucroute* viewing the country from the ramparts of the Castle; the way the thing is to be done is by car, poking around, preferably aimlessly. At almost any time—almost—this is ideal country for doing that: it is off the tourist routes, the towns are small, the traffic negligible. Nevertheless, it has been my singular misfortune to have been trapped twice while so wandering, by the Tour de France bicycle race, that national manifestation of the French delusion that a lot of men in their underwear, rumps up, heads down, pedalling like hell across the countryside, is something worth getting excited about. (If ever a list of the world's great dull sports events were wanted, I would be happy to nominate the Tour de France for Number One.)

The second such entrapment was in Alsace. Fully two hours before the first cyclist was to appear, red-faced under the apparently obligatory beany with the peak pointed straight up, the cops closed off all the roads. There we were, with nothing to sustain us but food and drink. First (after a leaden hour), the sound trucks, whipping up interest. Then, in seemingly endless procession, the advertising vans propagandizing the indestructibility of Bic pens, the re-energizing qualities of Perrier table water, the utter unfailingness of Michelin tires, not to mention the assorted merits of various brands of children's toys, soft drinks, athletic supports, television sets, running shoes, bicycles, newspapers, headache tablets and furniture. Finally, whirrp-whirrp (the sound of bicycle tires on pavement), and a clutch of bicyclists, bicycling. Cars filled with excited journalists (it is a condition of employment for all French journalists that they be excitable on the least occasion). Whirrp-whirrp; another clutch of cyclists. More cars, filled this time with officials. More cyclists. More advertising. Whirrp-whirrp.

Short of erecting a hand-carved monument, I can think of no greater tribute to pay to an outdoor café, an attentive waiter, and several *pichets* of the wine of Alsace—and quite ordinary wine it was, at that—than to say they made the whole thing bearable. In fact, after the waiter's fourth trip (or was it the fifth?), there were even the faint stirrings of what may have been a glow of affection for the Tour de France.

Alsace, the countryside, produces its own glow. Here are wine towns that are different from all others. The Second World War cut swathes through Alsace. In the last days of the War, the Germans launched a determined offensive to secure this enclave on the west bank of the Rhine; they succeeded in forming what was called the Colmar pocket, in the wine country, between Strasbourg, the capital of Alsace, in the north, and Colmar, the centre of the wine-trade, in the south. A result of the War in Alsace has been a curious juxtaposition of towns which have been almost entirely rebuilt (Ammerschwihr is the pre-eminent example) just a few miles from others which look as if no stone has been added, no facade altered, since the sixteenth century (of these, Riquewihr is the most notable).

The old town of the city of Colmar is worth anyone's time. In Bennwihr, one of the first of the small wine-towns, there is a modern church, an entire wall of which is done in stained glass—but stained glass of a different sort. Customarily, the various-coloured glass shapes which make up the design of a piece of stained glass are bound together with lead; here, much larger, and perhaps an inch thick, the glass pieces have been cast in concrete to form panels, and these have been put together, row by row, to make the wall.

Mittelwihr, next door, is a tiny and incredibly neat community with roses and geraniums in pots on sills, window-boxes filled with more geraniums, and tubs of petunias by front doors, all very picture postcard-ish, *gemutlicheit*, and cutesy—and yet warmly attractive. But it is at Riquewihr that the wine tourist leaves the automobile age behind, almost literally, and steps back 300 years.

Riquewihr is as if it had been built as a stage set, a planned tourist attraction, a corner of Disneyland. The illusion is assisted by the visitor's being asked to leave his car in the parking lot at the gates, by the Hôtel de Ville. On any street in Riquewihr, two cars would constitute a traffic jam; on most, one would be enough. In any case, the place—all of it, stopping even for a glass of wine—is small enough to be covered comfortably on foot in an hour or so. The streets are cobbled. The buildings have tall, steep-pitched roofs, and here and there on a peak, the bottom of a barrel can be seen to have been put to use as a platform for a stork's nest. Facades are plastered, with dark timbers running across them, windows are leaded, and somehow the whole place leaves one feeling that it cannot have been much different in 1644, the date on the sketch posted outside the Château de Riquewihr, the offices and cellars of the wine firm of Dopff & Irion. Part of the town wall as shown in the sketch is unmistakably still there.

But no one should be fooled by Riquewihr's air of being an outdoor museum. Winemaking—and this is an important centre of it in Alsace—tends to cling at the same time to the very old and the very new, and while the owners of the Château de Riquewihr may point with some pride to the barrel going back to the 1500's that is still used for storing fine wines, they point with as great pride to the modern presses that can press (more gently than human foot ever contrived) four tons of grapes at one time.

In Alsace, all the big wine-shippers own properties of their own, but they also buy grapes from independent producers. A Riesling wine of Alsace is made only of Riesling grapes; a Traminer wine, only of Traminer grapes. Similarly, with the Tokay d'Alsace, Muscat and Sylvaner wines, each is made of its own variety of grape. Wines bearing no date may be a blend of different years, but they will always be wines of the same, single-grape variety.

This practice of marketing wines under the name of the grape type rather than under the name of the place, or better still, the single-vineyard, is virtually unique to Alsace in France. It is not immutable. For instance, the firm of Dopff & Irion makes wines from individual properties which the firm itself owns. These are labelled Les Murailles (Riesling), Les Maquisards (Traminer), Les Sorcières (Gewürztraminer), Les Amandiers (Muscat). Only one of these—Les Maquisards—is to be found in Canada, and that in Ontario only. The Dopff & Irion practice is of course only a variation of the rule, rather than a refutation of it, since the grape type still figures prominently on the label, although below the vineyard name. At the other end of the scale, at the end of it where wines of the more ordinary qualities are to be found, Alsatian producers also make wines under various brand names of their own devising; of these, Clos Ste. Odile (Manitoba, Québec, Saskatchewan and Ontario) is the prime example to be found in Canada.

As a final note on nomenclature, it might be added that where the terms *zwicker* and *edelzwicker* are encountered, they denote, in the first instance, the use of several grape varieties, noble and ordinary, in a blended wine, and in the second, the use of only *noble* varieties in a blended wine. The principal noble varieties are Riesling, Traminer, Tokay and Muscat, and a half-step below, Sylvaner. The ordinary varieties are Chasselas and Knipperlé. Most of the wines that shippers ship under names of their own devising are *zwicker*.

In Alsace, the vines are grown high, as high as six feet, trained along four strands of wire about a foot apart which run between tall wooden stakes. Picking is done late, usually well into October and sometimes beyond, and most of the grapes, within a few hours of being picked, are in tubs in the forecourts of the shippers' establishments. Contrary to all notions of juice being wrung from grapes under great weight in presses operated by gigantic screws, the pressing is done delicately. The newest method of pressing is to place the grapes in a perforated drum through which runs an inflatable sausage. The sausage expands, the cylinder rotates, and the juice flowing out through the perforations parts company with pulp, pits and skins in circumstances of utmost gentility. (A grape seed, as anyone knows who has ever bitten on one, is bitter; if crushed, the pits would impart the bitterness to the wine. The skins contain quantities of tannin which, up to a point, and mainly in red wines, is desirable for the contribution it makes to the wine's keeping qualities—but the essential words are "up to a point".)

The juice for the fine wines of Alsace is always fermented in huge, oval casks, and preferably in old, old casks in which the new wine is supposed to get the idea of how it is done by rubbing shoulders with great vintages past. The casks may be several hundred years old. All wine casks, everywhere, must be kept scrupulously clean, but the juices do have minerals in them, and over a period of time certain inert deposits form. (In Alsace, I was shown a chunk as big as anyone's head of what might have been lava rock, or the corner of a meteorite which had been salvaged.) Consequently, the casks are disassembled at regular, though generously-spaced, intervals to permit their being de-barnacled. When the fermentation is complete—it takes about a month—the cask is filled and tightly closed, and the wine is left to mature for from seven months to a year. It is then ready for bottling. Most Alsatian wine is drunk as it comes on the market, but most bottles which have a vintage indicated on the label at all should be good for ten years.

In very many wine lists where the two are to be found together, the Gewürztraminer will be at a higher price than the Riesling from the same shipper, and therefore—one would be entitled to assume—will be the better wine. This seems to reflect demand rather than anything else, for the Alsatian winegrowers themselves consider the Riesling the king of their wines. In any case, these two are by all odds the most important Alsatian wines—which is not to say of course that a particularly fine Muscat or Tokay automatically will fall in line behind *any* Riesling or Gewürztraminer in the price-order.

The Riesling is the same grape from which all the great German wines are made. The Sylvaner is the same vine from which the *quantity* wines of Germany are made. Although in Germany the Riesling produces wines which, in very long, bright and warm summers, are always at least slightly sweet, this is rarely the case in Alsace. The Alsatian Riesling can be counted upon to be a clean-tasting, dry wine, in some years more fruity than others, and with a not very pronounced, but elegant, bouquet.

Alsatians suggest their Riesling—and drink it with every indication of lusty enjoyment—as an accompaniment to that most Alsatian of dishes, *choucroute*, as it comes with all the gorgeous, fat-making trimmings. Who am I to say them no? However, vast quantities of very good beer are also made in Alsace, and I suspect that a rather larger quantity of *that* gets drunk with sauerkraut than does Riesling. However, in case a platter of *choucroute garnie* with a tall, bedewed bottle of Riesling sounds just the thing you are looking for, here's how they do the *choucroute* in Alsace—at the Aux Armes de France restaurant in Ammerschwihr:

Alsatian Sauerkraut and Sausages

4 lbs. sauerkraut	8 liver dumplings
4 ham knuckles	2 blood sausages
2 lbs. salted pork loin or smoked pork-shoulder	salt, pepper, bay leaf, 3 cloves
1 lb. smoked bacon	8 juniper berries
1 lb. salted bacon	2 onions
½ lb. white sausage	3 cloves garlic
4 Montbéliard sausages (or pieces of Polish sausage, or anything else that strikes your fancy)	16 oz. Sylvaner or Riesling wine
	1 cup water or stock
	1 cup lard
8 wieners	

Wash the sauerkraut in cold running water and drain. Put the lard in an ovenproof pan and gently brown the chopped onions. Add Alsatian wine, and water or stock, and the ham knuckles, pork, smoked and salted bacon. Then add the sauerkraut. Salt and pepper; add the garlic, cloves, juniper berries and bay leaf.

Cook gently for 1½ hours. Heat the wieners, sausages and dumplings in water. Broil the white sausage and blood sausages.

Check seasoning and arrange the sauerkraut with the sausages around and on top it. Serve boiled potatoes on the side.

More to the point though, to my way of thinking, for, say, a Sunday brunch, would be an Alsatian onion pie, a sort of Quiche Lorraine with bells on. This one is from a collection of Alsatian gastronomic specialties.

Onion Pie

CRUST
2 cups flour
½ cup butter or margarine
1 tsp. salt
½ cup water

ONION MIXTURE
½ lb. onions
⅓ cup lard
4 oz. lean bacon

BECHAMEL SAUCE
1 pint milk
½ cup flour
¼ cup butter
salt, pepper, nutmeg
2 egg yolks

Prepare crust without handling it too much.

Slice onions and cook them gently in the lard; they should be slightly browned.

To prepare the *Béchamel* sauce, melt butter, add flour (do not let it brown), then milk (mix well to avoid lumps). Season, let cook, remove from heat, and incorporate the egg yolks. Then add onions and check seasoning.

Cut bacon into small strips and cook lightly.

Put crust in pie tin and half fill with the onion/sauce mixture. (The filling puffs up while cooking and will fill the crust.) Arrange the bacon on top. Bake in hot oven for 20 to 25 minutes.

Serve very hot: accompany with a Sylvaner. Serves 4 to 6.

Gewürztraminer—Gewurz simply means spicy, so that Gewürztraminer and Traminer are not greatly different—is a more noticeable wine than the Riesling, with more taste, more body, more bouquet. (The *Comité Interprofessionnel du Vin d'Alsace*, in what may be either a commendation or a warning, says: "It has a powerful, subtle and heady bouquet which invades the senses.") In any case, its place in the Alsatian scheme of things is to go with more spicy dishes, and even, in its more luscious manifestations, with desserts.

So, again from a collection of Alsatian gastronomic specialties, a dessert:

Kugelhopf

1 lb. flour (2½ cups)	¾ cup milk
scant tbsp. salt	1 oz. yeast
5 tbsp. sugar	2½ oz. raisins
1 cup butter	12 almonds
2 eggs	

LEAVENING

In a bowl, soften 1 oz. yeast with 7 tbsp. *lukewarm* milk, taken out of the amount indicated. Add to this yeast mixture the flour necessary to make a consistent dough. Set in a warm place to rise (above a radiator for instance) until it has doubled in volume.

DOUGH

Put into a large bowl, in this order: flour, salt, sugar, eggs and the remaining lukewarm milk. Mix well, and beat for about 10 minutes, raising it with your hands and hitting it against the side of the bowl—it must be aired as much as possible. Add the softened creamed butter and continue to knead until the dough no longer sticks to the hands.

Now incorporate the leavening, which should have doubled in volume. Beat again for a few minutes and then form into a ball in the bowl. Cover with a cloth and set in a warm place to rise; this may require a half-hour or more. The time depends on several factors (heat, strength of the yeast, summer or winter).

When sufficiently raised, pat the dough down to its initial volume (in technical terms, *break* the dough). Mix in the washed raisins. Better yet, soak them for a few hours in lukewarm water; it makes them mellower.

Butter well a Kugelhopf mold and line it with a few almonds. Turn the dough into the mold. Let it rise again. This time it should slightly over-top the mold.

Bake in a moderate oven at about 350°. If the top browns too much, cover with a paper. Baking time depends on the volume; about 45 minutes. Cool to lukewarm; remove from mold and serve sprinkled generously with powdered sugar. Serves 5.

Muscat almost always connotes a sweet wine. Not so in Alsace.

It is a dry wine, with the taste of the concentrated fruit. Again, the name Tokay summons up visions of a sweet wine, as in the Tokay Aszu of Hungary. And again, not so. The Tokay of Alsace is a rich, full-bodied wine, but not at all sweet. In fact, while it might be preferable to choose the Riesling of Alsace to accompany delicate fish dishes, and not to choose it to accompany things either spicy or sweet, it would be no great solecism to put *any* of the Alsatian wines with any dish that would suit any of the others—seafood, chicken dishes with sauces, *quiches* and the like, or, if you like, sauerkraut and sausages.

How to go happily into hock, a glass at a time

$\mathcal{T}$HERE ARE SEVERAL ways in which we could approach the wines of Germany, one of them by looking into what is called, with admirable clarity and brevity, the New German Wine Law, which came into effect in July 1971. The new law establishes a series of controls over all German vineyards and their products, from womb to tomb, or in this case, from planting to decanting. More than in passing, it also aspires to simplify for the wine buyer the business of reading German wine-labels, which, previously, were models of clarity if one only knew the key, but which could never successfully be accused of brevity. With much moving of the lips as he plodded through Ye Olde German type on the restaurant wine-card, a diner could find that breakfast was upon him by the time he had decided that it was the one listed as 1969er Wehlener Klosterlay, Auslese, Fuder No. 75, Original-Kellerabfullung, Wachstum S.A. Prum, Wehlen, Mosel, that he wanted, after all, and not really the one labelled Rheingau Kabinettwein, 1966er, Steinberger Auslese, Naturrein, (Orig.-Abfg., der Staatsweinguter, Eltville). Or was it?

But on second thought, there are attractions in going about it geographically, and especially by way of the Moselle, beside which all other wine rivers, whatever charm they may have exerted at the time of a visit, become mere prosaic drainage systems. The Moselle is a wine river what is. To drive along it, particularly in springtime, when the fruit trees are in bloom on the shelf of flat ground below the vineyards, is a great joy. Most of the way down to Koblenz, a distance of about sixty-five miles as the crow flies—no sane crow would follow the course of the river—the river bends, doubles back on itself, and while crawling generally northeastward,

200

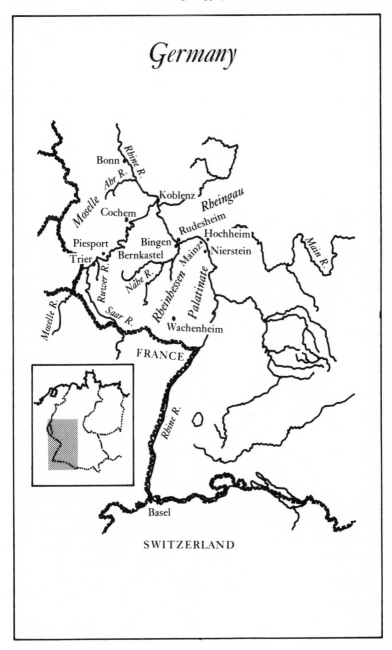

Germany

manages here and there to find itself flowing briefly even southwestward, all of this between looming hills.

The Moselle, of course, rises in France, and it is the French spelling that we have here, but as a wine river of consequence, it is German. We reach it from Alsace by going northwest to Trier, approaching that ancient city, the oldest in Germany, by way of the Saar, which is a tributary of the Moselle and itself an important wine river. (The wines of the Saar and another tributary, the Ruwer, usually are lumped together with those of the Moselle, and the labels on the bottles—Moselle bottles are green; Rhine bottles brown —usually show all three names.) The Saar joins the Moselle above Trier and the Ruwer below it, both from the southeast.

Trier is not particularly noted as a wine town. Most of the wine is grown downriver, beginning at about the point where the Ruwer River enters, and the flow of wine is the same way as that of the Moselle. But the city has undeniable associations. For a start, various charitable and other public institutions in Trier, including Karl Marx's old school, own sizable vineyard properties on the Moselle. Also, Trier abounds in reminders that it was the northern outpost of the Roman Empire and luxuriated for a time in the name of the second Rome—and of course it was the Romans who brought the wine grape to the Moselle, as to everywhere else. The question, to which no answer is to be found here, unfortunately, is whether the Romans knew something, or were merely taking a shot in the dark, for the German vineyards, the most northerly in Europe, ought not in all logic to do better than produce bunches of little green pellets as hard as bullets, and even those, only in good years.

However, several things combine to make the impossible feasible, although never easy. The Valley is so deeply cut as to provide shelter from the northern winds, and it is possible that the River's loops and bends preclude any funnelling effect. Then, walled in on either side as it is, the River acts as a sort of warming humidifier in the enclosed space. Finally, there is the slate, the most important factor of all. The slopes of the Moselle are *slate*, still in slabs, or decomposing and decomposed, and this provides both the soil in which the vines grow and a crude form of heat storage.

Since the slopes of the Moselle in very many places are so steep as to defeat any but foot-power, if slate has to be moved, to recover what may have slipped down the slope or to bring in new, it can only be moved on baskets on men's backs. Also, here the vines are trained high because it has been found that that is the way the grapes ripen best. Humping bundles of eight- and ten-foot-long stakes up a curved slope like the inside of a soup bowl must surely diminish the appreciation of the view from the top—assuming the carrier is not so stooped by the time he gets there as to be able to see nothing but his shoes. Still, change is coming. The basic topography cannot be altered, but there has been some consolidation of vineyards in recent years, and with larger units it has been possible to spare more ground on which to build terraced walls to support lateral tractor paths.

The bowl-like aspect of the river bank in extensive places is something else which accounts for its being possible to produce great wines at so northerly a location. The river bends, and the ground on the inside of the bend is low, the enclosing hills on that side being a little farther off. The play of the sun on the ground that rises sharply from the River around the outside of the bend is unobstructed. The vines catch it from very nearly first light to last, and when the sun sinks low, towards evening, they catch it still reflected off the water. A sun-trap, as the London real-estate agents, usually lying in their teeth, are wont to say of postage-stamp gardens caught between buildings.

In spite of this bonus of sunshine, it frequently happens (as it also does in northern France) that the grapes in the Moselle Valley, and along the Rhine, do not produce enough sugar on their own. It is necessary in those years, in order to make wines that will achieve an essential minimum level of alcohol, to add cane or beet sugar to the must. The wines of the Moselle, even in the sunniest, warmest of years, are anything but high in alcohol; their essential characteristics are that they are light and flowery, delicate in both taste and bouquet. They rarely exceed eleven degrees of alcohol, the *minimum* as established by law for some French wines, and they often do well to reach nine. Without the addition of sugar to the unfermented juice, the wines of poor years would be thin and excessively acid. It used to be the case that German wine-labels made explicit statements about the use of sugar—*naturrein*, for instance, or *naturwein*, meant that the wine relied solely on the natural sugar in the grapes—but this now will be left to be inferred from the category to which the wine has been assigned. And perhaps here, before we set off to look at some of the wine towns along the Moselle on the way down to its meeting with the Rhine at

Koblenz, is the time to take up the dreary matter of that New
Wine Law.

First it might be useful to dispose of something which is covered
by that law but not essentially changed by it, and that is what
is to be made of those two sturdy pillars of the German wine community, Moselblumchen on the Moselle and its even more ubiquitous
friend in the brown bottle, Liebfraumilch. These are, and will continue to be, generic terms for what should be middling-to-good
blended wines of the Moselle and the Rhine. The names represent
no town or vineyard, no variety of grape, nor anything else, really,
except the presumable best effort of the firms making these wines
to produce something which will be fairly well standard from bottle
to bottle and year to year, and which will sell at a certain price.
Since the ideas of any two firms on what will sell are likely to
differ quite as much with wine as with any other product, it is
as meaningless to conceive a liking for Liebfraumilch in general
as it would be to express an indiscriminate high regard for toothpaste.
Somebody's Liebfraumilch, perhaps, but not everybody's.

As with all proprietary brands, they do have the great merit (if
that is what it is) of being safe; pick the one you like and stick
with it and you will never go wrong. But that is the very opposite
of what the wine enthusiast is about. It is precisely because there
is a tremendous variety, and because anyone may drink his way
up or down a river without ever leaving his own table, making
notes town by town along the way if desired, that the enterprise
brings with it something more than the mere slaking of thirst. And
in any case, if I might just mutter it behind my hand, there are
still some town wines around which are not only more interesting,
but cheaper, than the well-advertised Liebfraumilchs and Moselblumchens. The name, Liebfraumilch, incidentally, was lifted from
a small vineyard at the Liebfrauenkirche, the Church of Our Lady,
at Worms; Moselblumchen was invented, for all I know, around
a boardroom table.

The New Wine Law (to come, at long last, to that) does three
main things so far as the wine drinker is concerned. First, for labelling
purposes it knocks out a tremendous number of names by making
what may have been four or five properties into one—we are not
speaking now of ownership, but of locality. This has only a limited
relevance so far as the Canadian wine-drinker is concerned because
the commissions have not burdened him with the luxury of choosing

between, say, Bernkasteler Doktor, Bernkasteler Badstube, Bernkasteler Lay and Bernkasteler Schlossberg, as they might have done. Second, the New Law removes some of the reading matter from German wine-labels by striking out certain terms, such as *naturrein*, already referred to, and *original-abfullung*, meaning, of the grower's own bottling, and *feine* and *feinste*, meaning fine and finest, and others. Third, and most important, it creates three categories of wines; which of these the wine in the bottle falls into will be stated on the label. The categories are

Tafelwein (table wine). This, as the name implies, will be a good ordinary wine for everyday drinking, with not much implied about pedigree except that it was grown at an approved location or locations and of varieties not actually proscribed. Since it is only in exceptional years that a large proportion of German wine does not have to be sugared—and because a wine very likely would claim a higher designation if it were not—it is assumable that most *tafelwein* will have benefitted from *chaptalisation*.

Qualitaetswein bestimmter anbaugebiete (quality wine of designated regions). Quality wine, for a start, must originate from within one region, such as the Moselle, the Rheingau or Rheinhessen. It must be produced only of designated vines. It must achieve a stated alcoholic strength through natural sugar. And analysis and professional tastings must affirm that it *is* a quality wine. Such wines likely will carry village and vineyard names.

Qualitaetswein mit praedikat (quality wine with special attributes). Special attributes have always abounded on German wine labels, whether or not they have done so equally in what has been under the labels. Now, however, government inspection and not grower enthusiasm will rule, and while the terms *kabinet*, *spätlese*, *auslese*, *beerenauslese* and *trockenbeerenauslese* will continue to appear, perhaps they will do so less often.

Kabinett is a term which has been used to indicate superior quality, but up until now it has been the producer who had decided what was superior. *Spätlese* means wine made from a late picking, and *auslese* wine made from selected grapes from that late picking. *Beerenauslese* means a wine made of grapes which have been shrivelled by the *pourriture noble*, or noble rot, called *edelfaule* in Germany, the same phenomenon which gives us the Sauternes in France. *Trockenbeerenauslese* is the very end of the line, the wine of grapes picked one by one from those disastrous-looking berries containing the highly-concentrated sugar. A bottle of *trockenbeerenauslese* costs the earth—but then how many near-raisins do you have to snip off with a pair of scissors to get enough juice to make even a glassful of wine?

It will be seen from this that *trockenbeerenauslese* is a description derived from the way in which the grapes were picked; it has nothing to do with place, nor with the variety of grape. A wine described as *trockenbeerenauslese* may be made in any of the wine regions of Germany when the right conditions are present. If we were talking about automobiles, this would be the top of the line, the one with all the extras. So it is not a name, but a style, and the style is a wine which is richly sweet, designed to be drunk with dessert, if with food at all, but most appropriately, alone. Similarly, what the terms *beerenauslese*, *auslese* and *spätlese* on the label tell the buyer, is something about the lateness of the picking of the grapes and hence about the probable degree of sweetness of the wine. (In saying that, I am conscious of the danger of misleading. Insofar at least as *spätlese* and *auslese* are concerned, a degree of sweetness means only that they will be not quite dry, with a reminder of sun-ripened fruit about them.)

And that will do for the New Wine Law, although there is much more to it, including the advice that twenty-eight g/l (three and a half degrees alcohol) represents the maximum improvement that may be made in a *qualitaetswein* in Zone A, excepting red wine made from the *blauer portugieser* in the district of (among others) Darmstadt. With that, and having said earlier that it is possible to drink one's way up or down a river, it is appropriate to steal quickly out and do just that—in this case, down, towards Koblenz.

The mere mention of the names of the first few towns that sit with their backs to the slopes, spreading fantails of vineyards behind them, is hardly likely to cause wine lovers everywhere to spring to their feet. The condescending way to put it is to say that they make good but minor wines; but on the spot . . . ah, well. Far down-river at Cochem, where the wines by reputation are even more minor than they are here, I once had as good a meal as I have ever eaten—an omelet, boiled new potatoes with parsley, and a bottle of the hotel man's own local wine; this on a terrace in the sunshine. Take your Bernkasteler Doktors and your Wehlener Sonnenuhrs; perfection is the right wine in the right place.

But leaving those little-known towns behind—Mehring, Detzem,

Thornich and Clusserath—we come to the Middle Moselle proper, the prime wine-growing section of the River. This middle portion can be said to begin at a mighty loop that carries it around a full 180 degrees. Here, their vine-areas touching around the bend, are Leiwen, which cannot in truth be said to be much more renowned than those towns which have preceded it, and Trittenheim, which makes wines that are fresh and delicate and most often as pale as ice. They are not only good to drink, but have the additional great merit of not being terribly expensive.

After this, the pretty little towns that the Moselle's fame rests on—and most of them *are* pretty little towns—come along like hiccups: Piesport, on a sweeping big bend, Brauneberg, Bernkastel (just what a movie director would order if he were casting a German wine-town), Graach, Zeltingen, Traben-Trarbach (a name that appeals to me), Enkirch. But before rushing off from Leiwen and Trittenheim it is worth mentioning that the Ontario commission from time to time has had in stock a wine of each—Leiwener Klostergarten and Trittenheimer Altarchen. (The *-er* in German after the name simply attaches the thing to the place, as in the case of the hamburger and the frankfurter—with either of which, incidentally, both of these wines would be too good.) These two are gossamer wines, as lightly engaging as a reminiscence. Altarchen is one of the better properties of Trittenheim, and its wines have been a relative bargain.

Piesport is the first really famous name we come to—no slight to Trittenheim implied—and a good place to pause again to look at the New German Wine Law. Piesport's 120-odd acres are divided into numerous parcels, of which unquestionably the most famous is Goldtropfchen, so much the most famous, in fact, that there has been more than the suspicion at times that more Piesporter Goldtropfchen was to be found on the market than the ground was capable of producing. Now, the one name Goldtropfchen is to be given to the wines from most of those 120 acres behind the town. The effect will be to legitimize what has been suspected of happening, but of course in the process a certain downgrading of what was legitimately Goldtropfchen must take place.

Bernkastel is a delightful town. At one time or another, ten thousand pictures have been published of Bernkastel—I have seen that many myself—all of them essentially the same. They are taken from high up in the vineyards behind the town; a couple of sturdy husbandmen appear in the foreground wearing those Wermacht-style caps and earnestly applying their hoes around the celebrated roots, while the pointy roofs and assorted other schmaltz of the town snuggle between the base of the hills and the River below. How much Bernkastel owes its reputation to its ineffable charm and how much to its wines is a matter of debate. There is no argument about the quality of the best of its wines, but whether they warrant the town's pre-eminence—especially in the United States market—is the question. Graach, Wehlen and Zeltingen all have their champions who insist that Bernkastel on its best day did not produce better wines than theirs, and they are probably right, but Bernkastel has the fame. These, anyway, with the addition of Traben-Trarbach, Enkirch, Drohn, Wintrich and Brauneberg, and Erden are the principal ones to look for on Moselle labels and, with luck, to find.

After Zell (famous for Zeller Schwarze Katz, of which there is a suspicious lot) and Bullay and Alf (a German town named Alf?) the Moselle Valley becomes less dramatic, more amenable, and as might be suspected, given the well-known perversity of the wine grape, the wines go downhill. They are still wonderfully pleasant, light, summer drinking, as I have already testified about the wine of Cochem, but they are more ordinary. And shortly after Cochem, the Moselle straightens out, and but for a few minor bends, runs on sedately down to Koblenz in country fit only for fruit trees and moo-cows. We are now at the Rhine.

That English magazine fiction to which I developed a fortunately short-lived addiction in my middle teens, the same fiction that impressed Pommard and Alfa-Romeos barking in the driveway on my youthful mind, also dwelt inordinately, it seems to me now, on clean-cut young men in flannels with picnic baskets and bottles of hock. And punts. (The Pommard men were older and darker.) If one were going for a day on the river, one naturally took, not necessarily in this order, Elspeth, a hamper, a rather nice bottle, and an old mac. The hamper and the hock out of the way, came the turn of Elspeth and the old mac—or so I have always assumed, although that aspect of things was never very satisfactorily developed.

Having disclosed that I had then a dreadful taste in fiction and have now a dreadful power of recall over the inconsequential, we can pass on to the matter that is supposed to be engaging us—namely the wines of the Rhine, which the English persist in calling hock. Hock is a cosy diminutive for Hochheim and in the beginning, undoubtedly was reserved for the wines of that one place. Later, however, the meaning was expanded to embrace all wines of the Rheingau district of the Rhine, and finally came to include *all* Rhine wines; the term was not very appropriate in either case, since Hochheim is not really in the Rheingau and not at all on the Rhine. It overlooks the Main.

So much for nit-picking; a good bottle of Rheingau wine and a picnic hamper could make anyone's day on the river an occasion of absolute bliss. (As for Elspeth, I am unable to say.)

There are vineyards north along the Rhine, certainly as far north as Bonn, as there are along the little Ahr River, which flows into the Rhine between Bonn and Koblenz, but all those of real consequence are to be found in the other direction. Consequently, if one is coming from the Moselle it is necessary to follow the Rhine *up* river, which means travelling in a southeasterly direction. The first of the three divisions into which the whole wine region of the Rhine falls is the Rheingau. Here are to be found such world-renowned names as Schloss Johannisberg, Marcobrunner and Schloss Vollrads. The towns which effectively locate the two ends of the Rheingau are Bingen, which in addition to large tracts of vineyards of its own, is notable for the rush of water in the River in front of it, and Mainz. The latter is a centre of the wine trade and has even a vineyard or two of its own, but it is notable more for its cathedral and for its Gutenberg museum, where Johann Gutenberg's original hand press is to be found in the basement.

At Bingen, the Rhine is in process of taking a sharp right-hand bend, as German rivers have a way of doing, and there, and thereafter for a while, the River sluices merrily through a defile in a way which has given rise to dozens of happy legends about shipwrecks, drownings and like inconveniences. But the happiest story of all is the one about the Mauseturm, or Mouse Tower, that stands guard, from a little island in the River, over the celebrated Bingen Hole—celebrated mainly as a hazard to shipping. It seems that one Bishop Hatto of Mainz, tired of the snivelling complaints of his parishioners, who were starving at the end of a particularly nasty winter, had the pack of them corralled in a barn, which was then set on fire. When he gloated over the sound of his mice squeaking, a horde of actual mice streamed out of the barn, chased him to Bingen tower and ate him (no doubt washing him down, gaiters and all, with a cool bottle of Rudesheimer Berg Rottland Spätlese, 1408.

Rudesheim, which to me is the beginning of the Rheingau, is a strip of pleasant town stuck on what amounts to a ledge, its back dug into the base of a great swathe of vine-covered hills, its feet in the River. Undiscovered, Rudesheim is not; every bus and boat tour along the Rhine seems to stop in. Still, in all sorts of narrow streets there are large and small *weinstubes* and restaurants which, touristy or not, can still be great fun, especially with a pitcher of wine on the scoured-wood table top. There is also a wine museum in town. The best way to see the vineyards themselves, and all the countryside for miles around, is to take a cable car directly up over the vines—if you are up over anything around Rudesheim, it necessarily will be either vines or the River—to the Niederwald Park. I have a vivid recollection from 1959 of a six-year-old kid spitting on the vines far below and saying, "That'll make them grow." And finally, tiring of that (and already preparing to fit action to the word) he announced, "Hey, Dad, if I peed on them, they'd *really* have a great crop." (It was, in fact, an extraordinarily good vintage.)

In the Niederwald, there is a great lumpy piece of statuary called the Germania monument, which was built in 1871 in the full flush of the national fervour of the Franco-Prussian War. Unfortunately, it looks like it: there is something essentially tasteless about winners' monuments. Still, the foot of the Germania lump is as good a place as there is from which to see the area in one swoop, from the Nahe flowing into the Rhine from the far side, over there to the right, to the vineyards of the great Johannisberg off there to the left.

Johannisberg itself, the place, is nothing much, just a village; but the Schloss, or castle, is something else again. The vineyards in front of it unquestionably are the most important in the Rheingau, so highly regarded, in fact, that the Riesling grape in some parts of the world is called the Johannisberg, although it is the grape of *all* the great German vineyards and not just of Schloss Johannisberg. It is true of Schloss Johannisberg and it is true of Schloss Vollrads a little farther on, at Winkel, that their wines are marketed with a bewildering variety of labels and capsules (the colour of the capsule, the lead-foil wrapping that goes over the cork and around the neck of the bottle, is a common way of indicating graduations in quality in Germany), but any label bearing the signature Furst Paul von Metternich in the one case, and Graf Matuschka in the other, will signify a wine of excellent credentials.

(It is worth at least a parenthetical note here that the wine of Schloss Vollrads is not all of Winkel, nor is Schloss Johannisberg all of Johannisberg. The Canadian wine-buyer here and there will find himself looking at something described simply as Johannisberg Riesling; in French terms, this would be called a commune wine of Johannisberg. It will have been grown within the confines of the area entitled to call itself Johannisberg, and as the label says, will have been grown of the Riesling grape. It can be said, then, to be related in two ways to greatness.)

It is true to say that the really fine German wines have been badly represented in Canada, less well, even, than the French. The standard-brand canned soups of the wine world, the Liebfraumilchs and Moselblumchens, if anything, have been over-represented, but the wines of individual vineyards have been hard to find. The best list of the wines of the Rheingau that could be compiled would encompass a Marcobrunner Spätlese and Hattenheimer Pfaffenberg Spätlese, in Ontario; and the same Marcobrunner (at very nearly $2 less) in Alberta, plus the excellent Raunthaler Wulfen. And allowing for one or two of what, in French terms again, would be called commune wines—such as Winkeler Riesling and Mittelheimer Riesling, both in Ontario—that would about exhaust the list of the senior Rheingaus.

Other, lesser names to look for in wines of the Rheingau include Hallgarten (there is a Hallgarten family which ships wines from Hallgarten, among other places, so it can be confusing), Hattenheim, Erbach, Raunthal, Eltville, and of course Hochheim, where the Koningen-Viktoria-Berg vineyard commemorates none other than Victoria Regina herself, who liked her sup of Hochheimer, which may account for the English adoption of the abbreviation, hock, to cover all the Rheingau, and eventually all of the Rhine.

The next of the three main wine regions of the Rhine, as we continue travelling up river in the direction of Switzerland, is Rheinhessen. Anyone who has even seen the name Nierstein—and almost everyone who has ever studied a wine list has—can claim at least a tenuous acquaintanceship with the wines of Rheinhessen. Nierstein is the area's main centre. There, smack on the River, on the west bank, is a great swatch of ground, every inch of it planted in vines, and so perfectly graded as to resemble the side of a football stadium. Without being at all beautiful, the slope at Nierstein is attractive for its well-ordered sweep.

So far as the wine is concerned, there is Nierstein and there is Nierstein. There is, for instance, quite a lot of the Sylvaner grape grown here, and the Sylvaner is acknowledged to be inferior to perhaps very few others, but inferior to the Riesling. Next door to Nierstein is a pretty town called Oppenheim, and although Nierstein is the better-known name, if I had to choose blind between the two, a bottle of Oppenheimer Krotenbrunnen (available in Ontario) would appeal to me far more than, say, a Niersteiner Domtal, a name that has come to be loosely used.

Nierstein, which is a very large, continuous wine-slope—nearly 1500 acres—dominats Rheinhessen as no single name does either the Rheingau or the Palatinate, the third of our Rhine wine-regions. In the Palatinate, the greatest name perhaps is Forst—but it could be Wachenheim, or Deidesheim, or Ruppertsberg. These are all great names, and if the lucky wine-drinker stumbles on one of them, he can be sure that he is batting better than .300 that day. Still, it *is* the case that none of the individual properties, or *lagen*, in any of these others, quite have the fame of Forster Jesuitengarten, or Kirchenstuck, or Freundstuck. The list of wines of the German Palatinate to be found in Canada is fairly well exhausted with Gimmeldinger Meerspinne, a good vineyard of a minor town in the district, and Hambacher Feuer Riesling, from an even more minor town. (Both of these are to be found in Ontario.)

As a final note to this survey of German wines which are or have been available in Canada, it is worth mentioning a piece of relative exotica in the list of the Newfoundland liquor commission—Winzenheimer Rosenheck Auslese. Winzenheim is a small town on the Nahe River, which parallels the Moselle and enters the Rhine south of it at Bingen. Rosenheck is one of the several best vineyards of Winzenheim, but neither town nor vineyard is at the tip of every wine-drinker's tongue.

What sorts of dishes do German wines go well with? Anyone who has had his eyes open around him in a German restaurant knows the answer to that: any sort. Although the Germans are great beer-drinkers, and although such things as ham hocks and sauerkraut do not really cry out for wine, they do drink their own wines, too—with seafood, pork, ham, beef, goose, chicken and whatever happens to be going.

But obviously their wines go better with some things than with others, and it seems to me, although it may reflect only an ingrained prejudice against a white wine with red meat, that they are best with fish, poultry of any kind, hot or cold, and pork. What, for instance, could be better with a plate of cold shrimps, say, or a fresh-caught trout, than a bottle of pale, crisp Moselle with that quality of producing a faintly prickling feeling on the tip of the tongue which the Germans call *spritzig*?

It is worth remembering that while all German wines should have some acidity—without it, they are not right, for they are then flabby and blah—they have always a bit of the ripe grape sweetness, and a trace of the fresh fruit smell as well. And of course they go on, from that bit of sweetness, through the designations *spätlese*, *auslese*, *beerenauslese* and *trockenbeerenauslese*, to richly, lusciously sweet. So that too has some bearing on what they accompany well.

A way that German wine-lovers sometimes drink the very greatest of their own wines—eccentric though it may appear to be—is alone; just a glass or two of wine for its own sake. That is worth trying, too.

But let us say that there you are, with a goose suddenly in your hand, and a bottle of, let us say, Oppenheimer Krotenbrunnen, or for that matter anything else up to perhaps an *auslese* quality. What to do with it? You could try this, which is the answer provided by the wife of a German diplomat:

Roasted Goose

7-8 lb. goose	thyme
salt, pepper	small red apples
water	flour
1 onion	

Rub goose, inside and out, with salt and pepper. Place in large pan and cover with 1½ quarts water. Add salt, onion and thyme and boil, covered, for 1 hour. Drain. Stuff with whole small red apples; then place in a roasting pan and bake in a 350° oven for 3 hours, turning every 20 minutes to brown evenly. When goose is cooked, remove pan juices to a small saucepan and set aside to cool. Sprinkle the goose with water and return to a hot oven, 400° for 10 minutes or until the skin becomes crisp.

Degrease the pan juices carefully; add stock made with the goose giblets and thicken with a little flour.

Serve with dumplings, red cabbage and cranberry compote.

Or this:

Rouladen
(Flank-Steak Wrap-Arounds)

1 large flank steak	¼ cup flour
3 slices bacon, cut in half	2 tbsp. oil
2 dill pickles, cut in	½ cup water
lengthwise slices	¼ cup ketchup
½ tsp. salt	1 tsp. Worcestershire sauce
dash pepper	¼ tsp. thyme

Cut steak in 4 or 6 rectangular pieces. Lay half slice of bacon and a pickle slice on each. Roll up; fasten with toothpick. Add salt and pepper to flour; roll meat in mixture. Brown in hot oil. Place in 1½-qt. casserole. Combine water, ketchup and Worcestershire sauce; pour over meat and sprinkle with thyme. Cover and bake in moderate oven (350°) till tender, about 3 hours. Serves 4 to 6.

WITH SAUERKRAUT
Sometimes the dill pickle is omitted, and instead, sauerkraut is piled inside each roulade. About 1 cup of sauerkraut will be needed.

Every wine-region has its fraternity which allows boosters to dress up, eat largely, drink correspondingly, and—perhaps not least—promote the local product.

The gentle look of the slope in the foreground is misleading. The delicate, flowery wines of the Moselle are grown on slopes that are leg-wearying to look at.

The look is faintly Chinese, but these painstakingly terraced fields are on the Rhine, at St. Goarhausen. That is Castle Katz brooding over it all.

Deutsche Wein—Information

Two steps backwards and ... splash, into the Rhine. The steep slopes ensure that in a northern climate—this is near Rudesheim—the vines get all the sun that is going.

Deutsche Wein—Information

Not every wine-cellar in Germany runs to chandeliers, but for that intimate little wine-and-cheese party, what better atmosphere than to be surrounded by ancient casks?

Can a fine wine be happy with a meatball?

*T*HAT CHIANTI BOTTLE with the round bottom in the grass skirt, of which there is an empty in every basement recreation room and summer cottage in the English-speaking world, is on the way to joining the amphora as an artifact of the Italian wine-industry. The reasons are two, both economic, one at the in-going end and the other at the out-going. In part, it is disappearing because the little old lady in Poggibonsi, or wherever, who used to knit up the raffia baskets with her nimble fingers, has hitched up her skirt and gone off to work for more money on the assembly line at Fiat.

But there is more than a suspicion—which brings us to the second part—that the progressive elements in the Italian wine-industry are taking her desertion less badly than might be expected, given all that the raffia basket has done for them and their ancestors. In fact, it may have done almost *too* much. Italy is now generally the world's largest wine producer, overtaken only in occasional years (such as 1970) when France has an extraordinary crop. It has also been taking mighty steps to improve quality. What is needed now is to break the image of Italian wines as the little wines that are called for in certain, narrowly-defined circumstances—an image that is enhanced by the distinctive raffia baskets—and to replace it with an image of fine wines that will stand up against all others in any circumstances.

Say that you are in Mamma Faciano's Neapolitan restaurant, a checked cloth on the table, the Parmesan cheese-shaker beside the ash-tray, the mirror behind the bar artfully hung with ropes of onions and green peppers, the Italian flag on the cash-register, and the waiters running around being ineffably Italian,

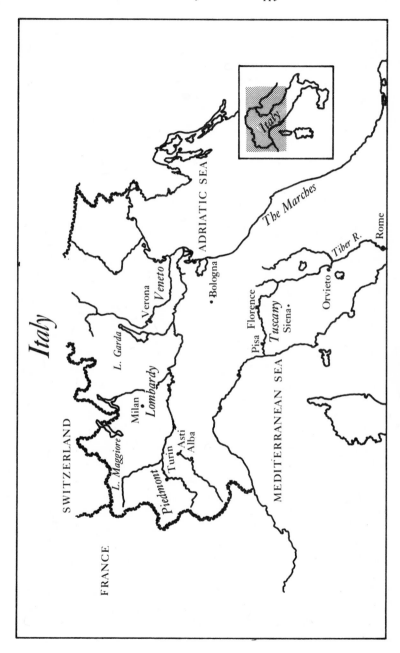

as what else. What to order? Obviously, one of those nice raffia-
covered bottles of Chianti with the red-white-and-green border
around the label; with the *cotolette alla calabrese* and stuffed
eggplant, it would be contrary to some obscure convention of the
United Nations not to. That is conditioning.

And of course up to a point, that is okay (circle of thumb and
middle finger).

But the next night you are in Leon's Chuck Wagon (Where Steak
is King) scanning the wine list—Leon's offers a choice of three—to
see what would be just the right thing to go with your New York
cut, medium rare. Does the thought of an Italian wine flit through
your mind, assuming it has flitted through Leon's beforehand?
Never. And there you have the essence of the problem—an excess
of identification with checked tablecloths and stuffed eggplant. Man
does not live by stuffed eggplant alone; nor does the Italian wine-
industry if it can help it.

Consequently, anyone watching the ads placed by the principal
Italian wine-houses the past year or so in magazines devoted to
the promotion of gracious living, would have observed that raffia
is very much at a discount these days, and that emphasis on the
Denominazione di Origine Controllatta ("Denominazione on the label,
means a finer wine on your table") and other assertions of quality,
are in. It must be added, although it is hardly charitable to do
so, that in addition to expanding and improving, the Italian wine-
industry is working its way out of a little valley of humiliation
that it found itself in a few years ago. That occurred when stories
began to get into the papers about people who had been caught
fabricating wines—not just teasing ten good gallons into fifteen by
mixing in a quantity of plonk, as in the bad old (and, one hopes,
dead old) French tradition, but making them up out of whole cloth.
(In fact, whole cloth would have been wholesome compared with
some of the ingredients they were reported to be using.)

What all this amounts to is a very long way of saying that anyone
who is interested in wines should take a hard look at what the
Italians are doing. Right now, some of the best values on the market,
to my mind, are in the Italian wines; if quality continues to improve,
and if French prices continue to soar up, up and away, they will
become even better values. In the circumstances, it is worth exploring
the variety of Italian wines that exist—white as well as red—beyond
the familiar, and frequently much underrated, Chianti.

The structure of the Italian wine-industry can be compared with that of Champagne, in that a relatively small number of large firms dominate the export field. They have large properties of their own, but they have even larger wineries, which they feed by buying grapes from small growers around them. However, unlike the Champagne firms which make one wine (although usually in several styles differing in sweetness), the large Italian firms usually make several entirely different wines, red and white, and even, in some cases, different grades of the same wine, as for example, a Chianti Classico and a Chianti Classico Riserva. The names of the firms that are likely to be encountered in Canada are fairly well exhausted with these few—Antinori, Bertolli, Bolla, Folonari, Fontanafredda, Frescobaldi, Lamberti, Melini, Negrar, Ricasoli and Ruffino.

Since we have got this far in our wine travels by having gone most recently down the Moselle and up the Rhine (south), the logical way in which to approach the Italian wine areas is from north to south. (A drive over the Simplon Pass from Switzerland, preferably in fog, can clear the brain and sharpen the perceptions like few things in this world. But then, there are tunnels.) Still, logic or no logic, Chianti is the Italian wine that is on every wine-list where there *is* an Italian wine, and in recognition of its pre-eminence, a leap ahead to Tuscany—no bad thing in itself—is in order. To find where Chianti comes from, find Florence, for the Chianti region lies around it: to the north, to the west towards Pisa, and most particularly to the south, from a short distance below Florence almost to Siena.

It is a large area, and before the promulgation of the *Denominazione di Origine Controllata* decrees in 1963, Chianti very often was any red wine grown for miles around which the grower *said* was Chianti. The Italian National Committee for the Protection of the Denomination of Origin of Wines, backed by the new laws, has put an end to such free-and-easy practices. However, long before 1963, producers in some areas of Italy had banded together in what were called *consorzios* to press for the enactment of particular laws to define their own areas, somewhat in the manner that a private bill might be sought from the Parliament in Ottawa. One such area, so delimited as long ago as the early 1930's, was what was called Chianti Classico, the heart of the whole region. It lies roughly between San Casciano in Val di Pesa, below Florence, and Castelnuevo, above Siena; authentic wine of that hilly country has been entitled since the 1930's to carry a seal at the neck of the bottle showing a black cockerel on a gold ground.

To qualify under the *Denominazione di Origine Controllata* for the right to be called Chianti Classico, a wine must have been grown within the specified area of specified grape varieties which have yielded not more than a specified number of tons (four and a half) per acre, and it must have achieved a level of at least twelve degrees of alcohol. In the case of a wine called simply Chianti, the permitted yield per acre is higher and the finished wine can make do with half a degree less of alcohol.

If a Chianti Classico is aged in barrel for two years before being bottled and has not less than twelve and a half degrees of alcoholic strength, it may be designated as *vecchio*, which means old. Another year in barrel and the same alcoholic strength, and it may be called *riserva*. These, however, are minimums and some firms improve on them. The Chianti Classico Riserva of Castel Brolio, made by the Barone Bettino Ricasoli, is kept in barrel for five years before being bottled. In 1972, the wine of Brolio still on the market in Canada was the 1964, whereas most of the French wines were at least 1967's and some were 1969's and even 1970's. Brolio, incidentally, has been one of the homes of the Ricasolis and a place for making wine since at least the tenth century.

Chianti of this quality will keep and is worth keeping, and anyone on the point of starting a cellar could do worse—especially with good clarets beginning at twice the price—than to invest in a few bottles. Some others similar in quality to the Brolio Riserva are Villa Antinori, Frescobaldi Nipozzano and the Riserva Ducale of the firm of Ruffino. (There is, incidentally, a good sub-district of Chianti called Rufina, so that there could be on the market a Ruffino Chianti Rufina, althought I do not know that there is.)

Undoubtedly, it is a pointless exercise to compare wines made in places far apart, in different soils, of different grapes and by different methods. Each has its own merits. But a good Chianti, it seems to me, is equipped to play the same role at the table as a claret; these are wines which might be said to be of the same weight. Chianti, like claret, although less so, tends to be tannic when young, and to soften and become velvety with age. Certainly, a Chianti Riserva of some age deserves a better fate than to be assigned to accompany dishes with highly spiced sauces, a role which often falls to it because of Chianti's old spaghetti-parlour image.

The trouble with too many other Italian wines, from a marketing point of view, is that they have no image at all. Italian authorities estimate that there are some 1500 different wines produced in the country, but very many of those, obviously, are known only to the people who make, and probably drink, them. Even so, there are still something over 400 which are recognized as being wines of some quality and which enter the market-place. It is doubtful if the names of ten of them are household words in Canada, even in households which take in a lot of wine in a year. In large part, the reason for this is that the Italians until recently have taken a matter-of-fact attitude towards the business of wine-drinking, for themselves and everyone else. Wine is wine. They have been content to consume much of their own vast production themselves, without developing any great mystique either about the consumption or the thing consumed, and they have exported the rest in the same spirit. Consequently, there has not been—not until now, in any event—any great push to impress foreigners with names, districts and dates.

Italy produces very great quantities of wine in the south, but most of its *best* wine is produced north of Rome, and most of that, Chianti notably excepted, in the far north of the country, particularly in Piedmont in the west and Veneto in the east. So let us go back to where we crossed the Simplon Pass, come into Italy by way of Domodossola and the side of Lake Maggiore, and turn southwest in the direction of Turin (although we will not go that far).

The three most famous wines of Piedmont—to which a fourth, Asti Spumante, may be added, if you insist upon it—are Barolo, Barbaresco and Barbera, in that order of precedence, each of them red. In my exposures to Barolo I have not been moved to throw my hat in the air (although I have found it enjoyable), but this may be that I have not yet had the luck to lay hands on a bottle of the right age, for this wine is widely regarded as the best of the red wines of Italy. It has a deep red colour, which seems to me to belie the official description of it as being pomegranate red; the last pomegranate I looked square in the eye was not so deep a red as that.

Barolo has the reputation of being a wine which benefits, first, from a good few years in the bottle, and second, from being opened for an hour or so before being served. That exposure to the air helps to release its bouquet and its flavour. There is supposed to be a saying in Piedmont that the best wine, the wine for the guest of honour, is the wine that was opened the previous day. The trouble with *that* is that the wine which usually benefits most from very early opening, although all will benefit from being opened at least a little while before, is the harsh, young bottle. Somehow it implies that Piedmont wines need all the help they can get. That is not so at all of Barolo. But it is worth remembering that it is not a wine designed to be drunk young and it will repay being given a decent opportunity to breathe.

The wine called Barbaresco, which is less frequently encountered, is produced in the same locality, around the town of Alba; it is made of the same grape, the Nebbiolo, which is a noble grape of Italy, and not surprisingly, perhaps, it has many of the same characteristics as Barolo, such as the strong colour and full flavour. However, it matures earlier.

The third of these three B's of Piedmont, Barbera, is grown nearer the town of Asti, almost due east of Turin. Asti, of course, has fame enough of its own as the home and namesake of Asti Spumante—the name simply means sparkling wine of Asti—but it is also the metropolis of a considerable red table-wine area. Most of this red wine is made of the Barbera grape. It is a lesser grape than the Nebbiolo, on which Barolo and Barbaresco depend, and the wine, when young, tends to grip the back of the throat. But with maturity it attains more grace, and provided the price is right (as usually it is laughable to suggest), it can be right-on for barbecues and similar free-and-easy occasions.

It is necessary to say a word about the sparkling wine of Asti, if only to admit my own blind, unreasoning prejudice. I am not, for a start, particularly a fan of sparkling wines, most of which strike me as sparkling mainly for the purpose of masking their fundamental inadequacies. I admit that this is an insupportable, unreasonable and illogical position to take, but there you have it. The sparkling white wine of Asti, on top of it all, is a faintly sweet wine, and fervently though I may have proclaimed my admiration elsewhere for sweet wines, this feeling cannot be stretched to include sweet sparkling wines. However, if the Asti Spumante is not needed for anything more important than a wake or a christening—in other words, if it is not meant to be taken seriously—then by all means, Asti Spumante.

On that note, and hastening, we leave Piedmont. It is necessary here to cross to the other side of the country, perhaps by the autostrada, stopping off in Milan if only to stand in the Piazza di Duomo and watch the pigeons wheel about the 200 white marble statues on the roof of the ancient church. There are very many wines made in Lombardy, the department to which Milan belongs, but none of them enters seriously into export trade, and they therefore may be passed over in favour of those of Veneto, which do. Many fine wines come from the area which revolves around Verona, including notably, Bardolino and Valpolicella, and what is to me Italy's most enjoyable white wine, Soave.

Bardolino, Valpolicella and Valpantena, the latter actually a Valpolicella made at a place called Valpantena, are all made of the same varieties of grapes, are all light wines—ten and a half to eleven degrees of alcohol—and are all of good colour. Valpolicella is a deeper ruby red than Bardolino. Bardolino is grown along the eastern shores of Lake Garda, the largest of the Italian lakes. If it comes from the heartland of the delimited area, it may be labelled as *classico*, and if the alcoholic strength reaches eleven and a half degrees it may be called *superiore*. Since it is delicate in both taste and bouquet, it is not the wine for very strongly flavoured dishes. The Italians themselves say that it does well with fish, but the idea of any red wine with fish takes some getting used to—a psychological quirk, really, since there is no reason why Bardolino's dry, distantly bitter taste should *not* accompany a fish dish very well.

The Ontario Liquor Control Board, hewing to Oscar Wilde's rule that nothing succeeds like excess, lists no fewer than six bottlings of Bardolino and as many of Valpolicella. Discounting the possibility that considerations of politics enter into this—a possibility that I would not want to discount absolutely to zero—this can be taken to reflect something of the popularity of these two wines. Valpolicella, after Chianti and perhaps Asti Spumante, is Italy's best-known wine. It comes from an area north of the city of Verona, is light in alcohol—eleven degrees—is sometimes faintly sweet, and is made to be drunk young.

There is a scent that is common to a number of Italian white wines, although it is evident in them in different degrees, that I associate with that of a green twig. Break a piece of willow and sniff it, and there it is. Whether or not this satisfies anyone else's sense of what is apt, it does mine. It is not a scent that repels me, but neither does it really attract; therefore, my feelings for these Italian white wines tend to be equivocal. However, Soave is something else again—a pale, gentle wine, with just a taste of the fruit and an underlying trace of sweetness. It makes a good wine to go with fish dishes, and a good summer wine to go with anything. A bottle labelled Soave Classico will have been made of grapes grown in the original heart of the district.

Due south from Verona and closer to Bologna is the district that is the source of a wine on which I have seen heaped kind words, but for which I cannot marshal a great deal of enthusiasm. That is Lambrusco. It is said to be tonic for the kidneys, which if true is something in its favour, but a faintly sweet, mildly prickling red wine is not really to my taste. My kidneys will have to make out the best they can. Bologna is noted for its rich dishes, and Lambrusco with its mild *pétillance* is advertised as just the thing to wash them down. Perhaps, but it remains Bologna to me.

Farther south yet, we encounter Verdicchio, or Verdicchio dei Castelli di Jesi, to give it its full name—it's not only a wine, but a language lesson; Verdicchio comes from the Marche, on the Adriatic coast. As might be expected in the circumstances, it is a wine to go with fish. It is also a strong wine, with a minimum alcoholic strength of twelve degrees, and a slightly bitter after-taste.

Beyond question the wine with the world's oddest name is the wine grown around the town of Montefiascone, by Lake Bolsena, sixty miles north of Rome. The name, which it is customary to sprinkle to taste with exclamation marks is Est! Est! Est! The story behind the odd name is that a Dutch or a German bishop—accounts differ—one Johann Fugger, a fussy man, was making a tour, and sent a servant ahead to find the inns with the good wine and to mark the doors, "Is," or "Is Not". So carried away was the servant with what he found at the inn in Montefiascone that he chalked on the door, "Est! Est! Est!", exclamation marks and all. In fact, he and the Bishop, when the latter arrived, stayed on and quietly (it is only charitable to assume) drank themselves into the grave. Not everyone since has been so kind to the wines of Montefiascone, and I have seen it suggested that the servant was not so much discerning as drunk when he scrawled his message. The wine, in any case, is a pale straw yellow in colour, may be either dry or slightly sweet, and must have a minimum alcoholic content of eleven degrees.

From just north of Rome as well, comes the popular Italian white wine, Orvieto, and from just south of the city, the most popular of the Castelli Romani wines, especially in Rome itself, Frascati.

I have already acknowledged my mixed feelings toward the Italian white wines, excepting Soave, and they extend to these two, and more particularly to the Frascati. However, one million Romans can't be wrong and I am prepared to bow to their judgement.

Frascati is a wine which is drunk by itself, simply for refreshment, but it is also strongly recommended by its numerous admirers to accompany fish dishes, particularly such things as heaping platters of miscellaneous seafood fried in a batter. But all Italian wine is made to go with food. Perhaps what helps to explain the matter-of-fact way that Italians treat their wine—they do not pay it reverence as the French do—is that they look upon it first simply as something to make the food go better.

Italian wines, as already noted, need not be confined to accompanying Italian dishes, but if Italian dishes are going, why not? Here are a couple of examples of what the Italian national wine committee thinks make happy company, the first for a white wine, the second for a red.

(I have also a recipe for Arancini, which is described as porcupine balls, but I have withheld it since it seems to me the principal ingredients could be obtained only at unacceptable risk. In any event, they are dipped in beaten egg and fried with breadcrumbs. A white wine is called for—especially, no doubt, by the porcupine.)

Scampi alla Peoceta
(Shrimp Peoceta)

1 lb. shrimp	4 tbsp. butter
½ tsp. capers	1 tbsp. brandy
1 cup steamed, shelled mussels	1 large fresh tomato
salt and pepper	2 tsp. tomato paste
	¾ cup cream

Shell and de-vein the shrimp and cook them in hot butter for 3 minutes, then add the capers and brandy. Stir, and add salt and pepper and cream. The fresh tomato, which will previously have been peeled and seeded, is then added. Let it all cook for 5 minutes more. Now add mussels and the tomato paste, and blend. Turn heat to maximum for a second just before serving. Serves 4.

Pollo alla Fiorentina
(Chicken Florentine)

2 frying chickens, cut in pieces	6 slices lean bacon, chopped
2 oz. dried mushrooms	1 onion, chopped
5 tbsp. olive oil	¾ cup dry white wine
2 tbsp. chopped parsley	7 pear-shaped canned tomatoes

Put mushrooms in hot water for 1 hour. Drain them and cut in thin strips. Brown chicken in oil with bacon and onion. Add wine, mushrooms, tomatoes and parsley. Salt and pepper to taste and cook slowly until chicken is tender.

Prepare a steaming plate of pasta and drench it with the sauce and chicken. A liberal sprinkling of cheese adds zest. Serves 6.

You mean
I should drink
(yuk) Schluck?

*E*ARLY IN 1972, the *Manchester Guardian* carried
a long article, the heading of which proclaimed the bleak news that

IT WILL SOON BE IMPOSSIBLE FOR ALL BUT
THE WEALTHY TO DRINK FINE CLARET

The *Guardian* was late on two counts. First, it is hardly likely
that even its least perceptive reader—if the *Guardian* can be said
to have any but acutely perceptive readers—could have failed to
receive some earlier inkling of the direction in which events were
heading. Second, if the newspaper had taken a more global view,
it would have recognized that the future it was predicting had arrived,
long since, in some benighted regions of the world, among which,
in this respect, Canada has the dubious distinction to belong.

However, leaving aside the parochialism which caused the
Guardian to overlook our unaccustomed pre-eminence, what it had
to say was unchallengeably, irrefutably, unarguably—and dismally—right. The price of fine claret has been going up like a scalded
Apollo since 1959, so that a wine lover, if he *had* two or three bottles
of Château Lafite put aside to brighten his declining years, would
be sorely perplexed to know whether to keep them by him in the
cool of the cellar or to sock them into his safety deposit box. And
of course there was no need to stop at claret; the prices of the
wines from the great, but mostly miniscule, vineyards of Burgundy
have soared equally majestically, and what is more, the wines have
become hard to find at any price.

It would be unwise in any consideration of price rises not to
make a generous allowance for simple greed—greed on the part
of growers, middlemen and sellers (retail mark-ups in excess of 100

per cent *are* greedy)—but there have been other factors as well, the principal one being a tremendous increase of demand, both from the enlargement of existing markets and the coming into being of new ones.

Consider Canada, which has no great wine-drinking tradition and which may be considered, really, a new market. Twenty-five years ago the greatest number of Canadian wine-drinkers did their wine drinking in doorways and culverts. In some considerable circles, to admit to consuming wine on occasions other than communion Sunday was to acknowledge being a sot, very probably of the kind who dispenses with the grace-note of taking the bottle out of the paper bag before starting on it. Lately, the domestic wine industry, greatly benefiting from the solicitude of friendly liquor control boards in most provinces, has been enjoying its palmiest days. It has become one of the veriest of growth industries. In the decade between 1961 and 1971, it managed to increase sales by within a hair's breadth (incidentally, would a hare's breath be known as rabbit-breathing?) of 100 per cent. Even so, and with every discouragement from the politicians who control the policies of the People's Dispensaries, sales of *imported* wines increased in the same period by nearly half as much again (although, obviously, the volume remained leagues behind that of the cheaper domestic product).

But Canada has been only a very small factor in the growing world demand for fine wines. The same phenomenon observed in this country has occurred in the United States, and given not only the population and the wealth of that country, but the taste for what has been decreed to be The Best, there has been a great run on chateau-bottled clarets of the classified chateaux, and of those, especially the First Growths (Lafite, Latour, Margaux and Haut-Brion) and Mouton-Rothschild, the misplaced first of the Seconds. These, of course, have passed beyond being the preserve of the merely wealthy; nowadays, to be caught consuming a bottle of any of them in a public place—*especially* in a public place, given the standard 100 per cent restaurant mark-up on top of the liquor board mark-up—should constitute a *prima facie* case of fiddling the tax-collector. How matters got that way was a concern of Steven J. Schneider, writing in *Vintage* magazine (New York) early in 1971:

> . . .it is mostly America which created the 'super-demand' for these Premier Crus. America was waking up to fine wine in the 1960's; the Premier

Crus were, after all, the famous wines, and everyone wanted to try them. They tried them, and found out what everyone by now realizes. The Premier Crus frequently make wonderful wines, but so do the rest of the fine wine-producing Chateaux of Bordeaux. There is, at best, marginal difference. . . . When they come through, in fine vintages, they are worth a premium of maybe 25 percent or 35 percent at most over other fine wines . . . But they do not always come through and by no stretch of the imagination could they ever deserve a premium of 200 percent on the basic fine wines, no less the stupid premium of 400 percent which the Chateaux are demanding now. Indeed, it is a rare vintage when one cannot point to a score of classed growths whose wine that year is not superior to most or all of the (Firsts). And as the American market gets more sophisticated it will be more confident of its judgment . . .*

Of course (as Mr. Schneider did not go on to say), much the same observation could be made about the so-called classed growths as a whole. *Because* they are classified, they too command premiums which are not always justified by any discernible superior merit over some others which are not. But buyers, and especially buyers who are not confident of their own judgement, like classifications: the wine property which bears the designation of a Great Growth bears a mark of the esteem of experts, and therefore is OK, a safe buy. Thus, the demand for wines of good credentials, and therefore the prices, have gone up and up. But they have merely led the way for a general sharp rise in French wine prices. Because France traditionally has been the prime supplier of fine wines, the fact of a wine's being French has been a sort of credential in itself for the buyer venturing for the first time into imported wines.

The best of the German wines have always been expensive because they are hard to raise and because there is never enough of them to satisfy the numbers who want them, but German prices have not risen in the same degree as the French. It would not be safe to assume that they are not on the point of doing so. Italy has never had quite the reputation of those other two for *really* fine wines, but we have already seen something of what is going on there, and Italy is the likeliest candidate to fill the gap, which seems increasingly to be opening in the French picture, between pig-rinse at one end and over-priced great names at the other.

*From "Is It Enough? The Commercial Outlook for Fine Bordeaux Wines" by Steven J. Schneider in *Vintage* Magazine (New York, Philip Seldon, April, 1971), p. 33.

Meanwhile, the beginning wine enthusiast who wants to adventure further afield than the domestic wines (although God knows some of the so-called fun wines ought to be adventure enough for anyone) has a considerable world to dabble in, if his liquor board will only give him a modicum of access to it. So let us, beginning in western Europe and going to the east, do a brief run-through of some other wine-regions—where they are and what they produce, with here and there perhaps, a dab at their backgrounds. (Even so, we will be setting aside some very considerable parts of the wine world, such as Australia and South Africa, both of which send large quantities of wine to Canada; the United States, where, particularly in California, very great improvement in quality has been brought about in recent years; and the several wine-producing countries in South America, including Chile, which makes some excellent red wines and almost equally good white wines, of which we see far too little in Canada.)

Portugal

In 1703 the English were not only out of sorts with the French, as happened from time to time, but were on the look-out for new markets for their woollen cloth, as happened all the time. The Methuen Treaty resulted. In part, it pledged that His Sacred Royal Majesty of Portugal, in his own name and that of his successors, forever and ever, would see to it that "the woollen cloths and the rest of the woollen manufactures of the Britons" were admitted freely into his country, and in return Her Sacred Royal Majesty of Great Britain (Queen Anne, it was) promised that "whether there shall be Peace or War between the Kingdoms of Britain and France" the wines of Portugal would enjoy a one-third preference in the British market. (The Portuguese evidently wanted to be sure that they were not simply a passing fancy.)

The results of John Methuen's treaty were not altogether foreseen. For a start, Englishmen were not readily turned off claret by the coarse, heavy wines that were shipped from the Douro valley in Portugal. Scarcely did they find any merit in them at all until the shippers discovered the trick of stopping the fermentation in full flight by the addition of a dollop of brandy. With that, port was born. Also, in the passion to do down the French, the British laws on distilling were relaxed so as to ensure the production of a cheap home-based substitute for French brandy. It was only a step from that to the setting off of the great gin binge, memorialized by Hogarth and reflected at the time in pub-window signs saying "Drunk for 1d. Dead drunk 2d. Straw free."

Tastes established in a dominant market—and Britain was that in the eighteenth century—have a way of becoming universal and lasting. (Think about those Coke signs in every corner of the world.) Portugal became known for port, and the idea clung that Portuguese tables wines were not very good. (The same is very largely true of Spain and sherry.) The supremacy of France as a producer of fine red wines was reaffirmed. (It has always had to share the honour with Germany as to whites.)

Whether the Portuguese developed as abiding an affection for worsteds and cheviots as their treaty partners did for port, I cannot say. In any case, what the one-third preference in the Methuen Treaty was not able to do for Portuguese tables wines in Britain, the soaring prices for French and German wines may do for them, and others, world-wide. But now it is necessary to say a word or two about port, which, at its best, is a truly great drink and one which does not deserve to be out of fashion to the extent that it is (although there are indications that it may be coming back).

It is the case with all wines that fermentation goes on until one of three things happens: one, all of the sugar that was in the grapes is fermented out, which is to say, is converted into alcohol; two, the alcohol reaches a strength, at about sixteen degrees, at which the yeasts are knocked out and the fermentation process stops, leaving some sugar unconverted (this is the case with the sweet white wines of Sauternes in France and of the Rhine in Germany); or, three, fermentation is stopped by the alcoholic strength being raised *artificially* by the addition of brandy.

When table wines were still made along the Douro in Portugal, they were made from grapes rich in sugar; these, when allowed to ferment out naturally, produced wines that were high in alcohol, but rough and heavy. When fermentation was stopped by the addition of brandy, the resulting wine was not only stronger in alcohol, in other words, fortified; it also retained a good deal of its natural sugar, so that given time, it attained a velvety texture and a resinous sweetness—it had enough of a spirity taste not to be sweet, and enough sweetness not to be edged like any spirit.

Various designations appear on bottles of port. Vintage Port, so-labelled, with the year and a daub of white paint at the shoulder of the bottle (so that you will know which side is up after the bottle has lain for forty years and the label has disintegrated), is *the* Port. It is bottled after two years in cask, and thereafter should be left to mature in bottle for at least ten years, but preferably for twenty-five. It is made only in very good years, perhaps four or five times a decade. (Vintage Port is to be found in Newfoundland, and whether regularly or not, at least occasionally, in Alberta and Ontario.)

One of the penalties that have to be paid for the enjoyment of Vintage Port—and the same is true of Crusted Port, the second category that we will come to—is that it develops a very heavy sediment in the bottle. Given the fact that a heavy, hard-wax seal is used over the cork, and that the cork is of unusual length (in both cases because of the length of time it is intended the wine should remain in bottle), decanting without muddying the wine is a delicate task. Vintage Port and Crusted Port are always decanted. The essential difference between Vintage and Crusted is that whereas the first is made from the wine of one exceptional year, Crusted is made from a blend of years, including, obviously, some which are less excellent.

Late-bottled Vintage Port, usually marked LBV on the label, is wine of one year which has been aged in the wood so that, first, it leaves its sediment behind before being bottled, and, second, it is ready to drink right away. It does not come up to the high standards of those just mentioned, but it can be very good. Tawny Port is a blend of several years which has been kept long enough in cask to have lost much of its early deep redness and to have assumed a more mellow shade, and of course Ruby is a younger version of the same. There are also white ports and dry ports, but these are for the sort of people who pose on the arms of chairs and talk determinedly brightly.

The great libel that has been committed against port is the old claim that the drinking of it leads inescapably to gout. The portrait of the red-faced Blimp sitting in some dreary men's club with a bandaged foot up on a stool is a great cliché. It is, I suspect, a fabrication put about in the great days of port by women who did not like port themselves (or perhaps were not invited to try it), and did not like being shoved off into a form of after-dinner *purdah* while the men lingered for an hour or two over the decanters. But the case against port is altogether unproved. For one thing, of course, gout is traceable to a time centuries before there *was* any port to blame it on. Hippocrates, the patron saint of all television's men in white coats, made the observation that eunuchs did not suffer from gout. There was no port in Hippocrates' day. In any case, it would have to be acknowledged that as preventive medicine, the implied prescription in Hippocrate's finding leaves a little something, or perhaps even two little somethings, to be desired.

But none of this gets us very far with the table wines of Portugal—which port is not; it is a drink for the end of the meal, or even to be had by itself in the late afternoon of a cold day, before a fire.

In northern Portugal, from the region between the Douro and Minho rivers, come enjoyable summer wines which go by the name of Vinho Verde. These may be white, rosé or red, but they are usually seen as white or rosé. The white wine is almost without colour, and the rosé is a pale pink. In all cases, these wines are *pétillant*, strung with pinpoint bubbles which do not last long but which produce a fresh, prickly feeling on the tongue. The Vinho Verde wines achieve this sort of zestiness—they are not strong in alcohol—by being bottled within weeks of being made, so that a secondary fermentation takes place in the bottle. There are Vinho Verde wines to be found in Canada, some called just that. What is probably the best-known Portuguese wine after port—it is sold world-wide—is the pink Mateus, a Vinho Verde wine.

More substantial are the white and red wines (mostly red) which bear the name Dao, a region in central Portugal for which some professionals see a promising future if the producers do not content themselves with producing as much as they can of good, but unremarkable, wines and shoot for real quality. These wines remain inexpensive so that everyone can afford to judge the potentialities for himself.

Spain

After Italy and France (although well behind both of them), Spain is the largest wine-producer in Europe. As in Portugal, the wine with the most prestige is not a table wine, but a fortified wine, sherry, a name that comes from the effort to wrap the English tongue around the Spanish words, Jerez, for Jerez de la Frontera, the sherry capital, in the southwest of the country. Find Gibraltar on the map, follow the coast along about one third of the way to the border with Portugal, and there, a little bit inland, is Jerez. It was wine from here, although probably not the wine that we now know as sherry, that Falstaff meant when he went on about sack. One reason for thinking it was not the same is that the practice of fortifying wine with brandy seems to have come along later than Shakespeare's time—certainly the *solera* system, which is fundamental to making sherry nowadays, did. Another, is that the thought of drinking any one of the various types of sherry by the pint measure is more than the mind can bear.

Two characteristics of the making of sherry are the use of *soleras*, and the growth of the *flor*, a white, fungus-like substance which appears on the top of the new wine after it has been a few months in the butt. Not very much is known about how the *flor* comes and goes, or what, scientifically, it does before eventually it sinks and the wine becomes clear. But it is agreed that sherry would not be sherry without it. As for the *solera* system, it can only be described briefly by saying that it is a method of constantly refreshing banks of older barrels from newer barrels: some wine is taken from the oldest and is replaced by an equal amount of the same type from the second oldest; it, in turn, is replaced by wine from the next oldest, and so on down the line. Sherry is in two ways a blended wine: it is a blend of different wines of the same year, and it is also a blend of wines of sometimes quite different ages, the blending being done by the shippers, each hewing to his own standard in each type.

In type, sherries run from wines so dry as to make your ears crackle to others of syrupy sweetness. A *fino* is pale with only the slightest touch of gold to it, and always quite dry. *Manzanilla* is a *fino* which possesses whatever mysterious benefits may have been conferred on it by having been exposed to the sea breezes at Sanlucar de Barrameda, at the mouth of the Guadalquivir River. I have seen a faintly salty taste attributed to it and have convinced myself at times, after deep concentration, that I have detected just that, but I would not want to swear on it. *Amontillado* should be a *fino* which has been left only long enough to have taken on more colour and a nutty flavor, presumably from the wood, but that would not account for the fact that most *amontillados* are also sweeter than a straight *fino*, so presumably in commercial circumstances they owe something to blending. And then there are *olorosos*, which a purist would say are also dry, but which rarely are, having had blended into them quantities of wine made from the Pedro Ximenez grape, which on its own produces an excessively sweet wine.

Most sherries are marketed under brand names, and it is not always safe to assume that what the shipper has chosen to call dry, you will consider dry. But most dry sherries are *finos* or *amontillados*. Cream sherries are *olorosos* of varying degrees of sweetness. Sometimes the actual term *fino, manzanilla, amontillado* or *oloroso* is to be found on the label, which is a help.

Wines in the full range of types and colours are made in all parts of Spain, from Malaga in the far south, where a sweet dessert wine is produced (which a limited experience and innate charity do not permit me to comment on); to the Rioja district in the north, where very good red and white table wines are made and west to east, from Portugal to the Mediterranean. One of the largest wine-growing areas, from which some good wines come carrying the name of Valdepenas, is in central Spain, due south of Madrid. But the area which generally is held to be the best is the Rioja, beginning roughly seventy-five miles southwest of the French-Spanish frontier at the point where the Spanish coast begins its long run out to the Atlantic. Here, in high country, are produced wines which are lighter and finer than most of those of Spain, which, as is characteristic of southern wines, tend to be rough and heavy. The Rioja district lies between the towns of Haro and Logrono and either of these names may be looked for as a means of identifying Rioja wines. Bodegas Bilbainas (a *bodega* is a wine-storage, but the term is also synonymous with winery) are the largest wine-makers in the district. Bodegas Rioja Santiago produces red and white wines which it puts up in square bottles under the trade-name Yago, one a semi-sweet white wine with an aroma which it would be best to let go at calling strange.

Switzerland

Switzerland, as is well known, is a country which would cover a larger area than the Soviet Union if only someone had thought to put an iron to it while it was still damp. As it is, a large part of its surface runs in the vertical plane rather than in the more conventional horizontal. This is the sort of thought that is bound to occur to anyone driving east along the Rhône River through such places as Sion and Sierre and looking at the vineyards growing up the wall that rises into the mists to his left. (Although the French prefer not to let on, the Rhône is first of all a Swiss River.) These vineyards, in the canton of Valais, are the highest in Europe, and very probably the highest anywhere, for that matter.

The Swiss, composed of French, German and Italian strains—wine-drinkers all—consume large quantities of wine, including most of their own, and a good deal of their neighbours'. There is a well-developed taste, for instance, for the wines of Beaujolais. Consequently, there is not a lot of Swiss wine left to export, and only a little of that comes our way.

Not all Swiss wines are white wines, but most of them, and the best of them, are. For the most part, the white wines can be compared with those of Germany and Alsace, for the very good reason that some of the grape varieties used are the same. But one cannot be dogmatic about that either, for the Swiss also employ varieties which originate in Burgundy and on the (French) Rhône. In Switzerland, the Riesling that does so well along the German Rhine and Moselle, and in Alsace, in France, is called the Johannisberger, no doubt after the great Schloss Johannisberger in the Rheingau. A bottle of Swiss wine identified as Johannisberger will provide a good example of what Swiss wines are about. But the popular and cheaper wine in Switzerland is Fendant, which is a refreshing light wine to drink under an umbrella on a hot day. I once knew a correspondent who became so enamoured of it while assigned to Geneva to cover an important international conference of some weeks' duration that his newspaper heard nothing much from him after the first week except cabled requests for more money. Considering that Fendant is light in alcohol, this represented a prodigy of application. But then Swiss wines are easy to drink, especially in Switzerland. Elsewhere, for which may be read, Canada, they tend to be a little pricey when compared to some others of equal quality. Wines of other cantons than Valais which may be found in export markets are those of Vaud and Neuchâtel.

Austria

A good management-consultant no doubt would advise the Austrians that for the English-language market they could devise a more euphonious name for a wine than Schluck. Somehow, to be asked if you would care for a glass of Schluck is not instantly appealing. Wine-drinkers in Ontario, at least, can test for themselves whether it is, for a Kremser Schluck—the addition of Kremser does not seem to help anything either—is one of a relatively long list of Austrian wines which that commission offers.

Austrian practices in wine marketing are very much the same as those in Germany, no doubt for the very good reason that German is the common language. In any case, Kremser means a wine from Krems, as Niersteiner is the wine of Nierstein or Rudesheimer is the wine of Rudesheim. Krems is a town west of Vienna on the Danube, and the home-base of the large wine firm of Lenz Moser. Schluck, to get back to that, is a light, heigh-ho sort of wine, made of the Sylvaner grape, and meant to be drunk without a thought either for the morrow or for the price, which is supposed to be low. The Austrians have been making wine since shortly after the dawn of time, and usually they have drunk most of it themselves, and most of that straight from the barrel at little country inns. However, the fact that there is a big, thirsty world out there looking for new sources is no longer being overlooked, and more wine is being produced so that more can be sent abroad. Except for Ontario, which almost eccentrically lists three times as many Austrian wines as does Army & Navy Stores Ltd., Victoria Street, London, S.W.1.—and there are not many nationalities of wine about which *that* can be said—the collected People's Dispensaries of Canada have managed to keep a cool head. Of those which Ontario offers, those of Durnstein and Stein come from near Krems; Grinzing is in the very suburbs of Vienna itself, and Gumpoldskirchn is due south of it. Gumpoldskirchner wines are to be found as well in Quebec, Manitoba and British Columbia, and Ontario wine-drinkers can rest happy in the knowledge that they pay more for theirs than do any of their compatriots.

The Austrian wines sound like German wines, the bottles and labels look like German bottles and labels, and if the wines *taste* like German wines—which they do, if usually a little more dry and a little less fine—it is because the main grape varieties used, notably the Riesling and Sylvaner, are the same.

Hungary

Back in the days when Russian aristocrats were still around to practice the most exquisite taste in everything except human relationships, their imports of consumer durables ran to caseload lots of Rembrandts (now to be found chock-a-block in the Winter Palace in Leningrad), to small oceans of sweet champagne, and what quantities they could get of a wine the colour of old gold and the consistency of maple syrup, called Tokay. The wine reached its highest expression in the form called Tokay Essence.

The most extravagant attributes have been credited to the great Tokay, including the power of restoring life. However, nowadays one has to take it all on faith because if any of the renowned essence passes into circulation at all, it does not do so via ordinary commercial channels. The Hungarians may have their version of Fort Knox filled with the precious liquid. The juice of Tokay Essence is not pressed; nothing so gross as that. For a start, the grapes are picked one by one from among those which have been attacked by *botrytis cinerea*, the same beneficial mould that is essential to the making of the sweet wines of Sauternes and the *trockenbeerenauslese* wines of Germany, so that what juice is left in them is a sugary concentrate. Collected, they simply are permitted to exude as much of it as they will under their own weight. It runs off through a grating. In the circumstances, it will be appreciated that the resulting wine was never, even at the Russian court, the sort of thing to be tossed back, over a cigarette, after fried liver and onions.

In any case, the problem of finding the right occasion on which to broach the bottle is not one that any of us need worry his head over. But it is possible to get some idea of what all the shouting was about; there is still Tokay Aszu to be had. Tokay Aszu is made by adding the juice of some overripe, or *azu*, grapes—the sort from which the Essence was made—to the juice of grapes gathered in the regular picking. The container by which the measurement is made is a *puttonyo*. If five *puttonyos* go into the thirty-five gallon cask, the wine will be virtually pure aszu. Labels on the bottles state how many *puttonyos* of the overripe grapes went into the wines, the more, of course, the richer. The Tokay which is to be found in Canada is three *puttonyos*.

Tokay Aszu is a dessert wine, or a wine to be drunk by itself. But it is far from the only wine Hungary produces. Egri Bikaver is a dark red, strongly flavoured wine which comes from around the town of Eger, eighty or ninety miles northeast of Budapest. It has been reputed to sustain warriors, and it just might. What is more important is that it is a good wine to accompany steaks and the like at a still-reasonable price. Another red wine which is exported to Canada is Szekszardi Voros, from Szeksard, due south of Budapest—and exported, moreover, in full litre bottles, which makes it a bargain as a wine for no special occasion. (It is only fair to note, however, that the quality seems to vary from one bottle to another even when the labels proclaim the same vintage.)

Of the Hungarian white wines that may be encountered, the most common in Canada are Badacsonyi Szurkebarat, which at times may be faintly sweet; Jaszberenyi Rizling (Riesling), dry; and Debroi Harslevelu, characteristically sweet. There is one shipper in Hungary, Monimpex, the state wine monopoly, and whether or not Hungarian wines are what they once were may be a matter for argument; certainly it is not one to which I have anything to contribute. But they remain inexpensive and generally give good value for money.

Yugoslavia

Yugoslavia makes and exports both red and white wines, but the whites are the better known. The best of these come from around Ljutomer, which is in the topmost, northeastern corner of the country, near the borders with both Hungary and Italy. The town name itself does not tell much because half a dozen different varieties of grapes are grown in the district, producing as many varieties of wine. However, the wine that is most exported is the Ljutomer Riesling. The names of two Yugoslavian red wines which come to Canada, Prokupac and Plavac, are not the names of places but of grape varieties. My experience has been to find them a little rough around the edges.

There are other wine-growing countries in Europe than these, including Luxembourg, where some pleasant light wines, somewhat like those of the Moselle, are made; Greece, which is not so obsessed with the aberrant notion that resin improves the taste of wine that it is not capable of making table wines without it; Bulgaria, which produces large quantities of mainly red wines, and Rumania, which runs mainly to sweet or sweetish whites. Some of these do not come our way at all, or do not in sufficient quantities to be worth worrying about; others may be put aside simply on their merits.

OK,
pour the wine,
you've talked
long enough

*I*T IS IN the very forefront of the consciousness
of most Canadians, I suspect, that if they indulge in so pagan a
pleasure as drinking wine, they surely must expect to pay for it,
for pleasure is sin and sin must be paid for, preferably (this being
essentially a Presbyterian doctrine) in hard cash. In the remainder
of our countrymen, this sense of wine-as-sin lurks merely in the
subconscious, but lurk it does. They are aware that they are being
under-served and over-charged but...

But what? Just "but". They really would stand up and say something about it, write their member of the legislature and complain,
or do something, except that, well, supposing he replied and said,
"What are you trying to do—take the bread out of the mouths
of orphans, and the bed-pan out from under the hospital patient?
Are you proposing that essential revenues should be sacrificed so
that you can save a few pennies while satisfying your craving for
drink?" What, in the circumstances, would there be to say? That,
Goddamnit, an average mark-up of 105 per cent, plus provincial
sales tax (as in Ontario), is price-gouging—and of a sort that would
cause the Department of Consumer and Corporate Affairs to seek
to disperse to the winds any private monopoly engaging in similar
practices. That if supporting meritorious works is the purpose of
it all, why should the drinker of the native product be denied his
full opportunity to do good? (It may be the case that drinking the
domestic product is less a sin than drinking wines that come from
abroad because it is less a pleasure, but I have not been aware
that the domestic producers have been making a point of saying
so.)

But, no; no barricades are raised, or stormed, and the Canadian wine-enthusiast goes on pushing his inordinate sums through the wicket, quietly taking his brown paper bag, all the while silently mouthing his thanks for the fact that, given his general state of rottenness, he is not deprived of the opportunity altogether. Ah, Canadians, thy national bird should be a cross between the mourning dove and the chicken.

However, since this habit of extreme docility in the face of manifest boondoggling seems to a character defect, and ineradicable, presumably nothing is to be done except to make the best of it. The price of fine wines everywhere is high, and very probably going higher. In Canada the price of fine wines is extortionate—not everywhere equally, but not, on the other hand, so unequally as to invalidate the statement. It is essential, therefore, to get the most out of them.

Somebody once said that there were two subjects which no man would admit he knew nothing about—wine and sex. Presumably the remark was confined to men because at the time no woman—no lady, at least—would admit that she knew *anything* at all about either. But at least ten million printed words have been expended in the past few years in satisfying the evidently bi-sexual and world-wide thirst for self-improvement in the second of these, and the notion underlying what follows is that male pride and female reticence have diminished concerning the other as well, and that we may talk about it, well, man-to-man. (Women's Lib may say what it likes, but things *have* inched forward since Cato the Elder said that "the husband is the judge and censor of his wife; there is no appeal from his decision; if she has acted wrongfully, he punishes her; if she has drunk wine or if she has committed adultery, he kills her." None of this holds good today—although no well-informed jury would be likely to convict of murder if He could show that She, knowingly, had given his life's only bottle of Chambertin to the postman for Christmas.)

Let us suppose—laughable though it may be—that you have decided to start a cellar. I might say that the best way to begin would be by going out and robbing a bank, but counselling to commit a crime is itself an offence, and we assume that you have been touched by the good fairy or have otherwise managed to acquire two or three notes to rub together, preferably notes of coarse denominations.

Canadians would not be the people they are (whatever that is) if life had been made easy for them; in their small way, the liquor commissions do their bit to see that it is not. For instance, while in other, more civilized jurisdictions there is a bonus in the case-price of wine—as there very well might be, since handling costs are reduced—it is all one to the liquor commissions in Canada whether you buy one bottle or sixty; the price is by the bottle. The one main effect of this is to make it hardly worth while wasting much thought on stocking up on white wines. It is not that I do not think they will keep for as long as you may want to keep them—to my mind, talk about the short lives of white wines is much over-done—but rather that in most cases they will not be a lot better for the keeping, and if there is no saving to be gained by buying more than one or two bottles at a time, why bother? Of course, if you find something you thoroughly enjoy, there may be some incentive to stock up against the danger that the next lot to come in will please you less and cost you more, a very real danger given the almost invariable practice in Canada of never having more than one vintage on hand at one time.

There is more reason to lay down (as the phrase goes) red wines. Red wines are cellared because with the several exceptions already abundantly noted, they improve with time. In most places, the customer is given a price incentive to buy wines young, since when he does, it is *his* money that thereafter is tied up and not the wine merchant's. In Canada, the liquor commissions operate essentially as discount merchants do in some of the large US cities, not really cellaring any wines themselves, but, in effect, taking it in the warehouse door and pushing it straightaway out the retail door. The essential difference is that the discounter passes on the saving—or some of it—to the customer; not so here. Stilll, saving or no saving, the wine lover who can afford it will want to put some bottles aside so that he will have them when no more are available of that year. (A small supply of 1961 clarets would be a nice thing to have now.)

Even if one is not contemplating a cellar, it is always a good idea to buy wine a *little* in advance of when it is to be used, to allow it to settle. But it will not undergo any profound change of character sitting on the sideboard over the weekend, or in six months, or a year, perhaps, or in some cases, in anything less than several years. A cellar is a long-time proposition, but then so is building a stamp collection.

Bottles should always be stored on their sides. The purpose in this is to keep the wine inside in contact with the cork. A dried out cork may become loose, with the result that some air is admitted and the wine spoils (perish the thought). It is not a bad idea when you buy a bottle to check on whether the neighbourhood liquor store has heeded the prescribed observances; give the cork a press with the thumb through the lead capsule that encases the neck of the bottle; if the cork gives readily, send the bottle back and ask for another; at the prices prevailing, you are entitled.

Any place for storing wine should be cool. Short of freezing, wine will stand a lot of cold and damp; heat is what is bad for it. The supposed ideal temperature—about fifty degrees—is almost impossible to obtain without air-conditioning, but a basement corner far from the furnace will usually stay at about sixty degrees winter and summer, and sixty is fine.

Bottles should be stored label side up. That is not really so that you will be able to read the label without moving the bottle, although that is reason enough in itself, but so that when a bottle has been brought up and allowed to warm to room temperature, and is ready to be poured, you will know which side not to pour it from, out of. To put that another way, as seems desirable, what you are after is to avoid sloshing the contents around and muddying the wine with the, oh, twenty-five years of sediment that has built up while the wine has been in your keeping. If the bottle has been stored on its side, label to the top, the sediment will be on the other (or bottom) side. (Clever.) When it is stood up, some of the sediment will slide harmlessly down the side into the punt, which is that peculiar dimple in the bottom of the bottle that you have always thought was put there in order to cheat you out of some wine. The rest of the sediment will stay on the side and if the bottle is decanted with a steady hand, again label side up, you should be able to pour a wine that is as star-bright as when it was made. Always stop pouring when the first trace of sediment begins to appear in the neck of the bottle. That last murky ounce may be poured over the turkey as it cooks. (The sediment can be drunk without ill-effect—it is a perfectly normal by-product of the wine's aging—but since we are talking here about getting the most out of a bottle of wine, why not have it look its best?)

Among wine enthusiasts there are decanterers and there are non-decanterers; I belong with the first lot. One reason for decanting is that it is the one way to be sure that the wine will be free of sediment—and incidentally, wine-baskets are a joke if that is what you are after; tipping the bottle back and forth to fill glasses must ensure that the deposit will be thoroughly infused in the wine, whether the bottle is in the hand or in a cradle. Decanting, on the other hand (your steady one, remember), can be done in one continuous motion. But the even better reason for decanting is that a pair of graceful decanters filled with rich red wine—somehow, the same does not seem so true of white—just plain *look* good on the table.

White wines should be chilled, but not so as to make the teeth ache—unless, of course, it is your devious purpose to kill the taste. (Chill it enough and you could pass Listerine off as Chablis.) The customary advice is to serve red wines at room temperature, which is all very well so long as you are not addicted to cold rooms. What needs to be remembered, in any case, is that a bottle of wine brought in from somewhere cool will not attain the temperature of the room in an hour or two, or even in six if it started from very cool, and that to serve good red wine chilled should be a crime punishable by having to subsist through the rest of your life on the wine-list of Prince Edward Island. An exception can be made in the case of Beaujolais, which in summer goes down wonderfully well just a little bit cool. Of course, with *any* wine, as indicated, if it is disguise you are after, by all means chill away, according to a rule of the cheaper, the longer.

There is something about suggesting that a bottle of wine be left to breathe before being served that brings out the beast in the kind of guy who says that the best wine in the world is the Dago Red he drank in the army, and that anyone who disagrees with him is a wine snob. And off he goes, mincing across the room with one hand on his hip, saying, "Ooo-h, he says it has to bree-eathe." To hell with the Philistine. The fact is, as anyone can prove for himself, there *is* something to be said for letting a wine breathe, which is to say, letting it stand, opened, for some time before it is served. How long that should be will depend on the wine. A young wine that may be expected to be just a little rough around the edges will be much better for an hour or more breathing. The older the wine, the less time is necessary, but almost any wine, red or white, but most certainly red, will benefit from being allowed to, ah, breathe. And again, at the price, why not get all that is going?

But here we have the wine almost drunk and have not opened it yet. One way and another, I have received an impressive amount of advice on getting the cork out of a bottle of wine, most of it misleading. I have read earnest accounts of how the only proper corkscrew is the old-fashioned t-formation corkscrew, with the squiggly bit down below and the pulling bit straight across at right angles up above. Not for me. My doubts about the old-fashioned corkscrew that Father placed his faith in began a long time ago when I first noticed that no one who was professionally in the business of drawing corks was still going through the contortions of screwing the screw into the cork, placing the bottle between his knees, and with great effort, getting the cork out intact—occasionally (and on the occasions when the cork broke, doing himself an excruciating injury).

From the traditional (or brute-force) model, I travelled to the other extreme, to the kind of cork remover which consists of a hollow needle attached to a pump mechanism; the pump allows air to be pumped through the needle to the underside of the cork, thus slowly and inexorably lifting it. Ingenious, but in my experience, unreliable.

The ideal sort is the one with a good, sturdy screw-mechanism and a pair of lever handles. Insert the point of the screw bit into the very centre of the cork, give it a good push to get it started, turn steadily and firmly thereafter, and when the thing has gone as far as it will go, press down the two levers and up she comes as neatly as can be. It is true that the screw on this sort of corkscrew is not always long enough to go the length of the cork in some bottles of wine. Corks in bottles of wine that are intended to last for a very long time are unusually long, and those in bottles of port are longest of all. But when you run into that sort of cork in that sort of bottle of wine—lucky you—it is always possible to bring the cork out as far as it will go, reverse direction for a moment and screw the corkscrew in farther, as you will now be able to do, and carry on as before.

There is no reason, really, why the business of drawing a cork should ever be bungled, except for the very rare occasion when the cork itself may have a flaw in its make-up. And that, of course, brings us to the case of the bad cork, celebrated in song and story. What about the ritual of smelling the cork? At any hour of the day or night, somewhere around the globe, there is a wine waiter—very probably hundreds of wine waiters—frowning slightly, and with an air of great attention, solemnly smelling a wine cork. Is he doing this because he gets some mild erotic stimulation from it? Never. He is doing it because the *maître d'hôtel*, when he was hired, said, "Look, when you take the cork out of the bottle of wine, smell it. Not the bottle, dummy, the cork. Don't ask me why you should smell it, okay? Just do like I tell you."

I know—and could produce, if required by the authorities to do so—a guy who claimed to have established at a select club the practice of flaming the cork, by the simple device of asking if they didn't. "Flame the cork?" said the headwaiter, blankly. "Of course," said the guest, bringing out his cigarette lighter and proceeding to do so, "flame the cork." Whereupon he scorched the end of it, stubbed it out in the ash-tray, sniffed, and said, "Ahhh, yes. That will be fine." And another tradition was born.

If it happens that sniffing corks turns you on, there is no harm in it—your psychotherapist will have heard stranger cases—but for your own sake, you should know why you are doing it. You will find it set down solemnly in all sort of places that if the cork is right, what you should smell is wine, and nothing but wine. After a long career as a diligent cork-sniffer, I have concluded that there is one other thing that a cork will smell of quite as often as it will of wine, and that is cork. In fact, an entirely undue amount of worry is wasted on bad corks; they occur very rarely, and are readily identifiable in the taste and smell of the wine, in any case. If it tastes and smells all right, it *is* all right; if it does not, send it back.

That disposed of, there is nothing left to do—and not before time—but to pour it. That necessitates glasses.

To say that there is a right shape for a wine glass is not to suggest that there is some fashion that anyone must get right with, but simply to say that there is a shape which has been found best for getting the most out of a wine. That is the tulip shape, or if you prefer, the shape of an egg with the top cut off. The glass should be stemmed of course. There is no need to take this advice about the egg-shaped glass on faith; make the experiment using, say, a straight-sided tumbler as the other glass, and see.

Good wine, great wine, is something for the eye and the nose as well as the palate. The taste, of course, you could get as well drinking (wine) from the dog's dish, but the colour and bouquet are something else. To see the colour, it is preferable to have a plain glass—not a coloured one. As for the bouquet, that will be concentrated in a glass of which the opening is smaller than its maximum girth; a straight-sided glass, and particularly one of a conical section, like a Martini glass, does the opposite and disperses the bouquet. (The same principle, but applied primarily to a different facet of the wine, applies in the case of the champagne glass. What is better by far than the traditional saucer for champagne, is the flute glass, which can only be likened to a smaller and narrower lager glass. It does not provide so large a surface from which the bubbles may escape—and since the bubbles are so much a part of what you are paying for, why throw them away?)

The management of some restaurants and hotels has concluded that the ultimate chic is the balloon glass, especially for burgundy. Never mind how narrow the wine list and how inflated the prices; all will be made right with that. If your taste in table *décor* runs to plastic flowers and lacquered place-mats with pictures of Anne Hathaway's cottage or Audubon's birds on them, there is something to be said for the balloon glass. It may be filled one-third full of water and a rosebud floated in it. But for wine, no; not, at least, for me. This type of glass, usually called a brandy snifter, is so big-bellied and the opening so relatively small, that it can be drunk from only at the risk of pouring some of the contents down your bib. Moreover, since it usually has a short stem, it is awkward in the hand.

It usually turns up with a burgundy because the conventional thing is to say that burgundy, being the bigger wine, should be served in a bigger glass than, say, claret. This strikes me as a piece of pretentious nonsense; the one wine-glass of the proper shape will do for all—red burgundy, claret, white burgundy, Rhône, Rhine or anything else, red, white or rosé.

The bottles opened, the glasses in place, and the guests by now making pitiful little whimpering noises, the question is how much—how much in the glass, and how much (in due course) in the guests? The glass should be filled no more than two-thirds full because otherwise the bouquet will be lost. Guests may be filled more than two-thirds full unless they begin to sing smutty songs or otherwise behave indiscreetly.

But, no. If there is going to be one wine, not much less than half a bottle each should be allowed, unless one of the guests is Uncle Ed, who tends to become tiddly at the sight of the label. It there is going to be a white before the red, four persons to the bottle for the first, and three to the bottle for the second, should see everyone into an expansive frame of mind. However, if you are going to do the thing up properly, useful instruction may be taken from the lists of wines served at some little affairs given by Berry Brothers and Rudd in the 1930's as related by H. Warner Allen in *Number Three St. James's Street* (which happens to be the address, in London, of Berry Bros.).

At a dinner in February 1933—to which, incidentally, ten sat down—there was an Amontillado sherry to start, followed by a 1904 Montrachet, a magnum of Château Lafite, 1862, a jeroboam of Château Lafite 1865, a magnum of Château Lafite 1868, a magnum of Château Lafite 1864, and finally, to round things off, an 1858 cognac. Allowing that a magnum is the equivalent of two bottles and a jeroboam the equivalent of six, that made twelve bottles of claret, and since ten persons hardly can have been served from the one bottle of 1904 Montrachet, there were presumable at least two of those—plus, of course, the sherry before and the cognac after. If the gentlemen did not all leave singing—and of course it was an all-male dinner—it can only have been because they were so wrapped in beatific smiles as to be unable to shape the notes.

Just in passing, there are one or two more points to be drawn from that list. Consider, for instance, the vintage of the Montrachet. In 1933, that wine was twenty-nine years old, a fact which ought to say something about the supposed perishability of white wines, at least the finest of them. The other point which will have been observed is that only Château Lafite of different vintages—the youngest sixty-five years old, the oldest, seventy-five, was served. That is a stunt in a way, although a glorious one. The more practical point is that while hardly anyone ever is going to be able to come up with four vintages of Château Lafite, it is usual to stay in the one wine region if several wines are being offered—bordeaux or burgundy, but not both—and only common sense to proceed in order from the least to the best. We can assume then that the

1864 Château Lafite was considered the better wine than the 1862 Château Lafite, a point worth bearing in mind in case the choice ever presents itself.

Let us look at one more dinner held at number three St. James's—a dinner given in March 1934, at which two of the nine around the table were Captain R. Anthony Eden and Captain A. Duff Cooper. These were the wines, after the Amontillado sherry to start: 1929 Chablis Valmur, 1928 Puilly-Fuissé—the second white wine, 1924 Romanée-Conti, 1923 Hospices de Beaune (Rollin), 1923 Clos de Vougeot (a magnum of that), 1915 Clos de Vougeot, 1918 Richebourg (a magnum of that, too), and a 1904 Chambolle-Musigny. After that, there was cognac. All of these, whites as well as reds, were burgundies, but the interesting point—apart from the fact that nine men put away ten bottles of some of the finest wines on earth—was that the place of honour at the end, after the Romanée-Conti, two vintages of Clos de Vougeot and the rest, was reserved for the *commune* wine of Chambolle-Musigny. Old charts show that 1904 among vintages was a great among greats; nevertheless, this placement should put at rest any notion that a mere commune wine can never be more than a poor relation of a bottle from one of the great *climats*.

Passing reference has already been made, in the chapter on Champagne, to the encomium on wine contained in the book of memoirs of one of the guests at that dinner, *Old Men Forget*, by Duff Cooper. There he wrote of having dined alone in a club with an imperial pint of Veuve Cliquot (champagne) and, from the club library, *Through the Looking Glass*, and after dinner, a cloud of depression had gone:

> *Whether it was the humour of Lewis Carroll or the sparkle of the widow Cliquot that had restored my spirits would be hard to say. I think it was the mating of the two. I have already made mention of the happiness I have derived throughout my life from literature, and I should here, perhaps, acknowledge the consolation I have never failed to find in the fermented juice of the grape. Writing in my sixty-fourth year, I can truthfully say that since I reached the age of discretion I have consistently drunk more than most people would say was good for me. Nor do I regret it. Wine has been to me a firm friend and a wise counsellor. Often, as on the occasion just related, wine has shown me matters in their true perspective, and has, as though by the touch of a magic wand, reduced great disasters to small inconveniences. Wine has lit up for me*

the pages of literature, and revealed in life romance lurking in the common-place. Wine has made me bold but not foolish; has induced me to say silly things but not to do them. Under its influence words have often come too easily which had better not been spoken, and letters have been written which had better not been sent. But if such small indiscretions standing in the debit column of wine's account were added up, they would amount to nothing in comparison with the vast accumulation on the credit side*.

That, as hardly need be added, is saying it very well. As an interest not confined to the sniffing and sipping end of things, wine can lead into some corners of reading that might otherwise have gone unexplored, and into travel in places to which otherwise there would have been no excuse to go. And very nice, most of them, too, as I hope I have been able to suggest. Of course, in totting up his little list of things that belong in the debit column of wine's account, Duff Cooper might also have added what *usually* goes into debit columns, namely, figures. But then there are also those if your particular kink happens to incline you towards rose culture or raising Afghan hounds. In fact, now that I mention those, I realize that it also belongs in the credit side of the ledger that wine has no thorns, and a bottle does not need to be taken out to the corner on wet nights. All in all, the balance is all in its favour.

*From *Old Men Forget* by Alfred Duff Cooper (London, Hart-Davis, 1953) pp. 64-5, by permission of Granada Publishing Limited.

Appendix

VINTAGE CHART

Red Wines

	Médoc Graves	St. Emilion Pomerol	Burgundy	Beaujolais	Rhône
1971	Good	Good	Very good	Very good	Very good
1970	Excellent	Excellent	Excellent	Very good	Very good
1969	Good	Good	Excellent	Excellent	Very good
1968	Poor	Poor	Poor	Fair	Good
1967	Good	Excellent	Good	Good	Very good
1966	Excellent	Excellent	Very good	Very good	Excellent
1965	Poor	Poor	Poor	Poor	Good
1964	Good	Excellent	Good	Very good	Good
1963	Poor	Poor	Poor	Fair	Fair
1962	Very good	Good	Good	Good	Good
1961	Excellent	Excellent	Excellent	Excellent	Excellent
1960	Good	Very good	Fair	Fair	Good
1959	Excellent	Very good	Excellent	Good	Good

VINTAGE CHART

White Wines

	Sauternes Barsac	Graves	Burgundy	Alsace	Champagne	Rhine	Moselle
1971	Good	Very good	Very good	Very good	Very good	Excellent	Excellent
1970	Excellent	Excellent	Very good	Good	Good	Very good	Very good
1969	Good	Good	Excellent	Very good	Very good	Very good	Very good
1968	Poor	Poor	Fair	Fair	N.V.	Poor	Poor
1967	Excellent	Good	Very good	Very good	N.V.	Very good	Excellent
1966	Fair	Excellent	Excellent	Very good	Very good	Excellent	Excellent
1965	Poor	Poor	Poor	Fair	N.V.	Fair	Poor
1964	Poor	Good	Good	Very good	Very good	Very good	Excellent
1963	Poor	Fair	Fair	Good	N.V.	Fair	Fair
1962	Very good	Very good	Excellent	Good	Very good	Good	Good
1961	Excellent	Excellent	Excellent	Good	Very good	Good	Good
1960	Poor	Good	Good	Fair	N.V.	Fair	Fair
1959	Excellent	Excellent	Very good	Very good	Very good	Excellent	Excellent

Médoc Classification

First Growths

Château Lafite	Pauillac
Ch. Margaux	Margaux
Ch. Latour	Pauillac
Ch. Haut-Brion	Pessac (Graves)

Second Growths

Ch. Mouton-Rothschild	Pauillac
Ch. Rausan-Ségla	Margaux
Ch. Rausan-Gassies	Margaux
Ch. Léoville-Las-Cases	St. Julien
Ch. Léoville-Poyferré	St. Julien
Ch. Léoville-Barton	St. Julien
Ch. Durfort-Vivens	Margaux
Ch. Lascombes	Margaux
Ch. Gruaud-Larose	St. Julien
Ch. Brane-Cantenac	Cantenac-Margaux
Ch. Pichon-Longueville	Pauillac
Ch. Pichon-Longueville Comtesse de Lalande	Pauillac
Ch. Ducru-Beaucaillou	St. Julien
Ch. Cos-d'Estournel	St. Estèphe
Ch. Montrose	St. Estèphe

Third Growths

Ch. Giscours	Labarde-Margaux
Ch. Kirwan	Cantenac-Margaux
Ch. d'Issan	Cantenac-Margaux
Ch. Lagrange	St. Julien
Ch. Langoa	St. Julien
Ch. Malescot-Saint-Exupéry	Margaux
Ch. Cantenac-Brown	Cantenac-Margaux
Ch. Palmer	Cantenac-Margaux
Ch. La Lagune	Ludon
Ch. Desmirail	Margaux
Ch. Ferrière	Margaux
Ch. Calon-Ségur	St. Estèphe
Ch. Marquis d'Alesme Becker	Margaux
Ch. Boyd-Cantenac	Margaux

Fourth Growths

Ch. Saint-Pierre-Bontemps	St. Julien
Ch. Saint-Pierre-Sevaistre	St. Julien
Ch. Branaire-Ducru	St. Julien
Ch. Talbot	St. Julien
Ch. Duhart-Milon	Pauillac
Ch. Pouget	Cantenac-Margaux
Ch. La Tour-Carnet	St. Laurent
Ch. Lafon-Rochet	St. Estèphe
Ch. Beychevelle	St. Julien
Ch. Prieuré-Lichine	Cantenac-Margaux
Ch. Marquis-de-Terme	Margaux

Fifth Growths

Ch. Pontet-Canet	Pauillac
Ch. Batailley	Pauillac
Ch. Grand-Puy-Lacoste	Pauillac
Ch. Grand-Puy-Ducasse	Pauillac
Ch. Haut-Batailley	Pauillac
Ch. Lynch-Bages	Pauillac
Ch. Lynch-Moussas	Pauillac
Ch. Dauzac	Labarde-Margaux
Ch. Mouton-d'Armailhacq (now called Mouton-Baron-Philippe)	Pauillac
Ch. Le Tertre	Arsac-Margaux
Ch. Haut-Bages-Libéral	Pauillac
Ch. Pédesclaux	Pauillac
Ch. Belgrave	St. Laurent
Ch. Camensac	St. Laurent
Ch. Cos Labory	St. Estèphe
Ch. Clerc-Milon-Mondon	Pauillac
Ch. Croizet-Bages	Pauillac
Ch. Cantemerle	Macau

Exceptional Growths

Ch. Villegeorge	Avensan
Ch. Angludet	Cantenac-Margaux
Ch. Chasse-Spleen	Moulis
Ch. Poujeaux-Theil	Moulis
Ch. la Couronne	Pauillac
Ch. Moulin-Riche	St. Julien
Ch. Bel-Air-Marquis-d'Aligre	Soussans-Margaux

Some Other Good Growths

Ch. Ségur	Parempuyre
Ch. Terrefort	Macau
Ch. Siran	Labarde
Ch. de Labégorce	Margaux
Ch. d'Avensan	Avensan
Ch. Belair-Marquis d'Aligre	Soussans
Ch. Paveil	Soussans
Ch. Chasse Spleen	Moulis
Ch. Maucaillou	Moulis
Ch. Fourcas-Dupré	Listrac
Ch. Fourcas-Hostein	Listrac
Ch. Lanessan	Cussac
Ch. Gloria	St. Julien
Ch. Bellegrave	Pauillac
Ch. Fonbadet	Pauillac
Ch. Monpelou	Pauillac
Ch. Duroc-Milon	Pauillac
Ch. La Tour-Pibran	Pauillac
Ch. Liversan	St. Sauveur
Ch. Tronquoy-Lalande	St. Estèphe
Ch. Meyney	St. Estèphe
Ch. Le Crock	St. Estèphe
Ch. les Ormes de Pez	St. Estèphe
Ch. Beau Site	St. Estèphe
Ch. Phélan-Ségur	St. Estèphe
Ch. Capbern	St. Estèphe

Classification of Graves

Red Wines:
Ch. Haut-Brion
Ch. Haut-Bailly
Ch. La Mission Haut-Brion
Ch. Latour Haut-Brion
Ch. Carbonnieux
Ch. Malartic-Lagravière
Domaine de Chevalier
Ch. Olivier
Ch. Latour-Martillac
Ch. Smith-Haut-Lafitte
Ch. Bouscaut
Ch. Pape Clément
Ch. Fieuzal

White Wines:
Ch. Haut-Brion
Ch. Carbonnieux
Ch. Bouscaut
Domaine de Chevalier
Ch. Olivier
Ch. Laville Haut-Brion
Ch. Malartic-Lagravière
Ch. Couhins
Ch. Latour-Martillac

Classification of St. Emilion

First Great Growths
Ch. Cheval Blanc
Ch. Ausone
Ch. Beauséjour
Ch. Belair
Ch. Canon
Ch. Figeac
Ch. La Gaffelière-Naudes
Ch. Magdelaine
Ch. Pavie
Ch. Trottevieille
Clos Fourtet

The long list of Great Growths includes the following:
Ch. l'Angélus
Ch. Balestard-la-Tonnelle
Ch. Bellevue
Ch. Grand-Mayne
Ch. La Clotte
Ch. Corbin
Ch. Fonplegade
Ch. Franc-Mayne
Ch. La Tour Figeac
Ch. Le Prieuré
Ch. Grand-Pontet
Ch. Ripeau
Ch. Soutard
Ch. Tertre-Daugay
Ch. Trimoulet
Ch. Troplong-Mondot
Clos de la Madeleine
Ch. Canon-la-Gaffelière
Ch. Curé Bon
Ch. Larcis-Ducasse

A few years ago, Alexis Lichine, who occupies three roles in the field of wine as owner, shipper and author, essayed his own consolidated classification of the red-wine vineyards of the whole of Bordeaux. This is how it went:

Outstanding Growths

Médoc
Ch. Lafite-Rothschild
Ch. Margaux
Ch. Latour
Ch. Mouton-Rothschild

Graves
Ch. Haut-Brion

St. Emilion
Ch. Cheval-Blanc
Ch. Ausone

Pomerol
Ch. Pétrus

Exceptional Growths

Médoc
Ch. Beychevelle
Ch. Brane-Cantenac
Ch. Calon-Ségur
Ch. Cantemerle
Ch. Cos d'Estournel
Ch. Ducru-Beaucaillou
Ch. Gruaud-Larose
Ch. Lascombes
Ch. Léoville-Barton
Ch. Léoville-Las-Cases
Ch. Léoville-Poyferré
Ch. Lynch-Bages
Ch. Montrose
Ch. Palmer
Ch. Pichon-Longueville (Baron)
Ch. Pichon-Longueville (Comtesse de Lalande)
Ch. Rausan-Ségla

Graves
Domaine de Chevalier
Ch. La Mission-Haut-Brion

St. Emilion
Ch. Belair
Ch. Canon
Ch. Figeac
Ch. la Gaffelière

Pomerol
Ch. la Conseillante
Ch. l'Evangile
Ch. Vieux-Château-Certan

Great Growths

Médoc
Ch. Branaire-Ducru
Ch. Cantenac-Brown
Ch. Duhart-Milon
Ch. Durfort
Ch. Giscours
Ch. Grand-Puy-Lacoste
Ch. d'Issan
Ch. la Lagune
Ch. Malescot-Saint-Exupéry
Ch. Mouton-Baron-Philippe
Ch. Pontet-Canet
Ch. Prieuré-Lichine
Ch. Rausan-Gassies
Ch. Talbot

Graves
Ch. Haut-Bailly
Ch. Pape-Clément

St. Emilion
Ch. Fourtet
Ch. Magdelaine
Ch. Pavie

Pomerol
Ch. Certan de May
Ch. Gazin
Ch. Lafleur
Ch. Lafleur-Pétrus
Ch. Petit-Village
Ch. Trotanoy

Superior Growths

Médoc
Ch. Batailley
Ch. Chasse-Spleen
Ch. Ferrière
Ch. Gloria
Ch. Grand-Puy-Ducasse
Ch. Haut-Batailley
Ch. Kirwan
Ch. Langoa-Barton
Ch. La Tour-de-Mons
Ch. Marquis-d'Alesme Becker
Ch. Marquis-de-Terme

Graves
Ch. Carbonnieux
Ch. Malartic-Lagravière
Ch. Smith-Haut-Lafitte
Ch. La Tour-Haut-Brion
Ch. La Tour-Martillac or La Tour-Kressmann

St. Emilion
Ch. l'Angélus
Ch. Beauséjour-Duffau-Lagarosse
Ch. Beauséjour-Fagouet
Ch. Canon-la-Gaffelière
Ch. Croque-Michotte
Ch. Curé-Bon-la-Madeleine
Ch. Larcis-Ducasse
Ch. Ripeau
Ch. Trottevieille
Ch. Villemaurine

Pomerol
Ch. Beauregard
Ch. Certan-Giraud
Clos de l'Eglise-Clinet
Clos l'Eglise
Ch. Lagrange
Ch. Latour-Pomerol
Ch. Nenin
Ch. La Pointe

Good Growths

Médoc
Ch. Angludet
Ch. Bel-Air-Marquis-d'Aligre
Ch. Belgrave
Ch. Boyd-Cantenac
Ch. Capbern
Ch. Clerc-Milon-Mondon
Ch. Cos-Labory
Ch. Croizet-Bages
Ch. Dutruch-Lambert
Ch. Fourcas-Dupré
Ch. Fourcas-Hostein
Cru Gressier-Grand-Poujeaux
Ch. Haut-Bages-Libéral
Ch. Lagrange
Ch. Lanessan
Ch. Lynch-Moussas
Ch. Les Ormes-de-Pez
Ch. Paveil
Ch. de Pez
Ch. Phélan-Ségur
Ch. Poujeaux-Theil
Ch. St. Pierre
Ch. Siran
Ch. La Tour-Carnet

Graves
Ch. Bouscaut
Ch. Fieuzal

St. Emilion
Ch. Baleau
Ch. Balestard-la-Tonnelle
Ch. Cap-de-Mourlin
Ch. Le Châtelet
Ch. La Clotte
Ch. Corbin
Ch. Corbin-Michotte
Ch. Coutet
Ch. La Dominique
Ch. Fonroque
Ch. Grand-Barrail-Lamarzelle-Figeac
Ch. Grand-Corbin
Ch. Grand-Corbin-Despagne
Ch. Les Grandes-Murailles
Clos des Jacobins
Ch. Saint-Georges-Côte-Pavie
Ch. Soutard
Ch. La Tour-du-Pin-Figeac
Ch. Troplong-Mondot

Pomerol
Ch. La Croix
Ch. La Croix-de-Gay
Ch. Feytit-Clinet
Ch. Gombaude-Guillot
Ch. la Fleur-Pourret
Ch. Mazeyres
Ch. Rouget
Ch. de Sales*

Classification of Sauternes and Barsac

First Great Growth
Ch. d'Yquem

First Growths
Ch. Guiraud
Ch. La Tour-Blanche
Ch. Lafaurie-Peyraguey
Ch. Rayne-Vigneau
Ch. Rabaud-Promis
Ch. Suduiraut
Clos Haut-Peyraguey
Ch. Coutet
Ch. Climens
Ch. Rieussec
Ch. Rabaud-Sigalas

Second Growths
Ch. Doisy Daëne
Ch. Dubroca
Ch. Doisy Védrines
Ch. Filhot
Ch. Myrat
Ch. d'Arche
Ch. Broustet
Ch. Caillou
Ch. Suau
Ch. de Malle
Ch. Romer Lafon
Ch. Romer de la Miremory
Ch. Lamothe
Ch. d'Arche Lafaurie
Ch. Nairac

Here, for the principal communes, are some—by no means all—of the superior vineyards of the Côte d'Or:

Côte de Nuits

Fixin
Les Hervelets
Clos du Chapitre
Perrière

Gevrey-Chambertin
Chambertin
Chambertin Clos de Bèze
Chapelle-Chambertin
Charmes-(or Mazoyères-) Chambertin
Latricière-Chambertin
Mazis-Chambertin

Morey-St. Denis
Bonnes-Mares
Clos de la Roche
Clos Saint Denis
Clos de Tart
Clos des Lambrays

Chambolle-Musigny
Bonnes-Mares
Clos de Tart
Musigny
Amoureuses
Aux Combottes

Vougeot
Clos de Vougeot

Vosne-Romanée
Romanée-Conti
Richebourg
Echezeaux
Grands Echezeaux
La Romanée
La Tâche
Romanée-St. Vivant
Beaux Monts
Malconsorts
Suchots

Nuits-St. Georges and Prémeaux
Le Saint-Georges
Vaucrains
Boudots
Cailles
Porets
Roncières
Clos des Forêts

Côte de Beaune

Aloxe-Corton
Corton
Corton-Charlemagne (white)
Clos du Roi

Beaune
Bressandes
Clos-des-Mouches (red and white)
Fèves
Grèves
Marconnets
Teurons
Cent-Vignes

Pommard
Clos de la Commaraine
Epenots
Rugiens
Arvelets

Volnay
Caillerets
Champans
Santenots
Fremiets

Meursault
Goutte d'Or
Genevrières Dessous and Genevrières Dessus
Perrières
Charmes

Puligny-Montrachet
Montrachet
Bâtard-Montrachet
Chevalier-Montrachet
Bienvenue-Bâtard-Montrachet
Caillerets
Combettes
Pucelles

Chassagne-Montrachet
Montrachet
Bâtard-Montrachet
Criots-Bâtard-Montrachet
Caillerets
Grands Ruchottes
Morgeot